Batsford Chess Library

Winning With the Fischer-Sozin Attack

Gary Lane

An Owl Book
Henry Holt and Company
New York

Henry Holt and Company, Inc.
Publishers since 1866
115 West 18th Street
New York, New York 10011

Henry Holt® is a registered
trademark of Henry Holt and Company, Inc.

First published in the United States in 1994 by
Henry Holt and Company, Inc.
Originally published in Great Britain in 1994 by
B. T. Batsford Ltd.

Library of Congress Catalog Card Number: 94-76061

ISBN 0-8050-3576-1 (An Owl Book: pbk.)

First American Edition—1994

Printed in the United Kingdom
All first editions are printed on acid-free paper.∞

10 9 8 7 6 5 4 3 2 1

Adviser: R. D. Keene, GM, OBE
Technical Editor: Graham Burgess

Contents

Symbols

+	Check
++	Double check
#	Checkmate
± (∓)	Slight advantage for White (Black)
± (±)	Clear advantage for White (Black)
+− (−+)	Decisive advantage for White (Black)
=	Equal position
∞	Unclear position
!	Good move
?	Bad move
!!	Excellent move
??	Blunder
Ch	Championship
Wch	World Championship
Z	Zonal
IZ	Interzonal
Ct	Candidates
OL	Olympiad
Corr	Postal game
(D)	Diagram follows

Introduction

The Najdorf Variation is one of the sharpest reliable openings at Black's disposal. It is named after the Polish-born grandmaster Miguel Najdorf, who was the most prominent of a group of players who pioneered it in the 1930s and 1940s. It was elevated to general acclaim after an impressive performance in the radio match Spain-Argentina 1949.

The Najdorf's enduring success led Bobby Fischer to devise an aggressive system, based on the move ♗c4, to confront it. Throughout the 1950s and 1960s the 'Fischer Attack' scored a number of victories, with Fischer enriching the system with numerous tactical nuances. Ironically, its appeal was diminished somewhat when Fischer himself defeated it in spectacular fashion as Black at the Sousse Interzonal in 1967. The trend for 6 ♗g5 saw Fischer's variation being only occasionally employed until the 1990s. Then the 1993 Kasparov-Short PCA World Championship match gave the opening a higher profile. The Englishman found some impressive new ideas to revitalize White's aggressive formation. In the wake of this match, the line with 6 ♗c4 has regained its reputation as one of the most dangerous weapons available for White to confront the Najdorf.

The Ideas Behind the Fischer Attack

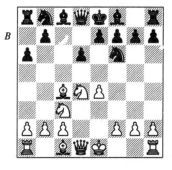

The first point to note is that by developing his king's bishop on c4 White exerts pressure on Black's kingside and makes it difficult for Black to execute the freeing ...d5 break. White can continue by castling short before choosing a method of attack; this often involves a kingside pawn storm. Alternatively

White may choose to defer castling, when the direction play takes depends on Black's response. Black can try to take advantage of the temporarily unguarded bishop on c4 to advance on the queenside, or seek to hunt down the bishop and exchange it for his queen's knight.

If Black follows the standard idea of simply developing, then he risks being demolished by a direct attack.

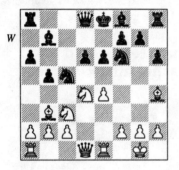

In this case it would appear that Black has fended off any attacking ambitions by taking care to avoid sacrifices on e6. However, Fischer found a way to storm the defences: 12 ♗d5!. This is an important way to open up the position which, if ignored, leaves Black with dire positional weaknesses. After 12...exd5 13 exd5+ ♔d7 14 b4 ♘a4 15 ♘xa4 bxa4 16 c4 ♔c8 17 ♕xa4, in return for his piece White has two pawns rolling towards the vulnerable black king, and so is clearly better. See Game 12.

It is understandable that Black is keen to lessen the influence of the light-squared bishop with ...e6. Naturally White will not then want his 'Fischer' bishop to be left as a mere spectator, so will try to activate it by pushing his e- or f-pawn to undermine e6 or even by sacrificing a piece on this square. If this scheme fails then there will have been little point to White's plan of development; this is why the attack must be handled so carefully. The following position is typical of the sharp nature of the system.

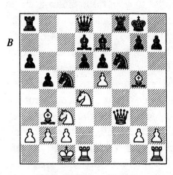

Now Black could have taken advantage of White's reckless opening play with 14...♘d5! 15 ♗xe7 ♘xe7 16 ♕h3 d5 locking the bishop out of the game. However, the multitude of tactics snared even Kasparov, who actually continued 14...♘fe4? 15 ♗xe7 ♕xe7 16 ♘xe4 ♖xf3 17 exd6 ♘xb3+ 18 ♘xb3 ♕f8 19 gxf3 ♕xf3 20 ♘ec5 when White had a clear advantage. Game 6 has further details.

The rapid advance of the e- or f-pawns initiates immediate piece play, in which White will target the sensitive point at f7 and look for sacrificial opportunities on e6. This is a feature of Chapter 1 which is clearly illustrated in Games 1 and 8. The drawback is that if Black can develop without any problems then the over-stretched pawns can become vulnerable targets. Consider this position:

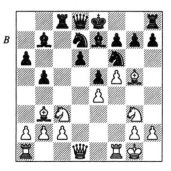

Now Black plays 13...h5! when suddenly the e-pawn has become a liability. See Game 7 for more on this type of position. Naturally, in modern grandmaster practice, White's approach has been refined to the point where such calamities should not take place.

White can also choose to play a slower game without committing his e- and f-pawns, though sharp play is usually assured.

In the following diagram, White can exploit the lack of harmony

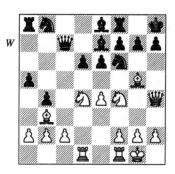

amongst Black's forces with a standard sacrifice: 19 ♘dxe6!, a devastating blow to Black's defences, opening up lines for the attack. In this specific instance, after 19...fxe6 20 ♘xe6 ♕a7 21 e5! dxe5 22 ♘xf8 ♗xf8 23 ♗xf6 gxf6 24 ♖d8 White enjoyed a crushing advantage. See Game 14 for further details.

It is also possible for both sides to deviate earlier in order to avoid the main lines. An early ...♗d7 (examined in Game 23) tends to transpose to other lines or merely lose time.

Game 18 deals with a line that was not favoured by Kasparov in the actual match against Short but is likely to become popular as Black tries to avoid the well-known lines.

A recommended way for White to diverge after 7...♗e7 can be found in Games 20, 21 and 22; this can form the basis of a repertoire.

It is possible for White to go in for the heavily analysed immediate attacking options, or to try a more independent approach.

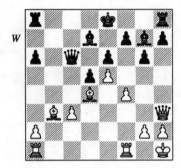

Here Anand has preferred to rely on his space advantage rather than try for a direct attack from the outset. Nevertheless, he was able to drum up attacking chances. He now played 25 f5! gxf5 26 g4 ♛c7 25 ♖ae1 ♝b5 26 gxf5 ♝xf1 27 ♖xf1 with a tremendous game. For more details on this line, Game 19 should be examined.

The Ideas Behind the Sozin Attack

In view of the Fischer Attack's successes against lines with an early ...♘bd7 or ...b5, many players have begun to resort to systems with ...♘c6. In the slightly changed circumstances White is guided by similar principles to those relevant in the Fischer Attack, and so familiarity with common themes will help orientate White. Fischer's original treatment of this variation, which was introduced against Olafsson in

the Stockholm Interzonal of 1962, concentrated on a quick f4. This is still of interest although some of the details have been refined over the years.

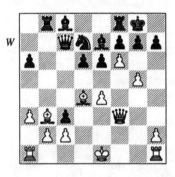

Here we see that Judit Polgar has managed to create a typically sharp attack by flinging forward her f- and g-pawns. Now 17 fxg7! ♘e5 18 gxf8♛+ ♚xf8 19 ♛xc3 ♛xc3+ 20 ♝xc3 ♝xg5 21 ♖d1 gave her a commanding position. For further analysis see Game 27.

In the PCA World Championship match against Short, Kasparov tried a number of new ideas in a bid for equality. These are covered in Games 28 and 29.

An early knight sortie to exchange the light-squared bishop is covered in Game 31. The lines considered there can arise from various move-orders, but cannot be recommended for Black, since the time spent in eliminating the bishop is too high a price.

The Ideas Behind the Velimirović Attack

The Velimirović Attack has its devo-tees amongst those who like to stake everything on a direct attack. It has a reputation for fantastic complica-tions, though the drawback is that it can involve a lot of memory work. The Yugoslav, Dragoljub Velimi-rović, pioneered the plan of ♗e3, ♕e2, 0-0-0 and g4 in the 1960s. One of the ideas behind it is that a pawn on e5 or f5 in the Fischer/Sozin sys-tem can eventually become a liabil-ity; thus here the pawn storm is launched by g4-g5, driving the knight away from f6. This can be followed up by advancing the h-pawn, intending g6 followed by h5 to open up lines. Alternatively, White may play for a mating attack based on ♖hg1-g3-h3 and ♕h5.

Enormous complications are in-herent in such lines and these re-quire precise calculation:

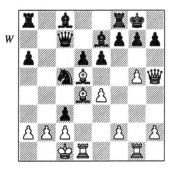

Now White plays 18 ♕h6! f6 19 ♗xa8! gxh6 20 gxf6+ ♔f7 21 ♖g7+ ♔e8 22 ♖xe7+ ♕xe7 23 fxe7 ♔xe7 24 e5 with a winning position. For further details examine Game 33 with reference to the note to White's 19th move.

Naturally, Black can take evasive action by queenside castling, but this is a rather slow manoeuvre. Another scheme is to leave the king in the centre and rely on the traditional queenside counter-attack. This leads to a double-edged game where White can break through with ♘d5 or ♘f5 to gain access to the king. Black's play tends to be based on ...a6, ...♘a5, ...b5 and ...♕c7, with or without kingside castling.

The Ideas Behind ♗c4 against the Scheveningen Variation

This variation is dealt with briefly since most lines transpose to other lines already discussed. However, adherents to the Scheveningen may wish to avoid being lured into un-known territory, so I would like to draw your attention to a little-known line where Black avoids ...a6 in fa-vour of advancing ...a7-a5 without losing a tempo.

Consider the position overleaf:

Now White avoids the positional trap 11 a4 which is well met by

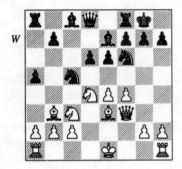

11...e5!. Instead 11 0-0-0 invites dynamic chances which are illustrated using games by the Romanian Istratescu. Games 37 and 38 deal extensively with these double-edged possibilities.

The Ideas Behind the Benko Variation

The Benko Variation is an attractive option for Black since it avoids the brunt of the Sozin and Velimirović Attacks. Black's early queen sortie limits White's aggressive options, although the queen may become a target for White's pieces. White continues with short castling and develops his queen's bishop to e3 or g5; he may then advance his f-pawn. Games 39 and 40 deal with the main lines, from which White should emerge with a small advantage. Game 41 examines a lesser-known line, against which Benko himself fails to cope with a fresh set of problems.

The Ideas Behind ♗c4 against the Dragon and Accelerated Dragon

This system has a number of similarities to the Fischer Attack. As usual ,White's light-squared bishop targets f7. The main practical merit is that in comparison with the main lines of the Dragon there is much less theory for White to absorb. From an objective viewpoint the plan of castling kingside followed by ♗g5 and ♕d2 is perfectly viable and poses interesting problems. The line has various positional points that allow White to press for the advantage with the minimum of risk:

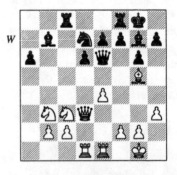

In this position White proceeded smoothly with 18 ♘d5 ♖fe8 19 c3 ♘c5 20 ♘xc5 ♖xc5 21 b4 ♖cc8 22 c4 when White has the initiative on the queenside. For further details see Game 43.

The Ideas Behind ♗c4 against the Pseudo-Dragon

This little-known variation is brought about by 6...♗d7 in response to ♗c4. Black keeps his options open: he may fianchetto, or continue along more standard Sozin lines. However, the concepts already discussed are capable of dealing with it, and none of the possible

transpositions are too troublesome. The main game in the chapter demonstrates how Fischer deals with the problem, although it is possible to seek a quieter line by following the note to White's 8th move in Game 48 and transposing to the lines covered in the Chapter on the Dragon.

In order to obtain an understanding of the typical middlegames that occur, the reader is recommended to play through each illustrative game.

1 Fischer Attack with 7...♘bd7

The Fischer Attack is characterized by 6 ♗c4 which targets the weak point f7. It is one of the most aggressive ways to combat the Najdorf and is in the repertoire of the world's best players. The Short-Kasparov match revealed many new possibilities, and this has resulted in a tremendous surge of interest.

In this and the next two chapters we consider all lines arising from the Najdorf move-order which do not transpose to the Sozin Attack by means of an early ...♘c6 by Black. There are two principal 'Najdorf' systems for Black after 6...e6 7 ♗b3:

a) 7...♘bd7 followed by ...♘c5, by which Black puts pressure on e4, supports the sensitive e6 pawn, and reserves the option of exchanging off White's light-squared bishop at a favourable moment (Games 1 to 6);

b) 7...b5, after which the bishop or queen will come to the long diagonal to attack e4, while ...b4 will be in the air to further undermine this key point (Chapter 2; Games 7 to 19).

The move 7...♗e7 will often transpose to a Sozin, or one of the lines mentioned above, but there are some independent possibilities, notably 8 g4 which is discussed in Chapter 3 (Games 20 to 22).

The somewhat inflexible 7...♗d7 generally leads to Sozin positions (Game 23).

Game 1
Short – Kasparov
London PCA Wch (8) 1993

1	e4	c5
2	♘f3	d6
3	d4	cxd4
4	♘xd4	♘f6
5	♘c3	a6
6	♗c4	e6
7	♗b3	

The move 7 a3 to make room for the bishop merely represents a loss of a tempo. For example: 7...♗e7 8 ♗a2 0-0 9 f4 b5 10 f5 e5 11 ♘de2 ♗b7 12 ♘g3 ♘bd7 13 ♗g5 ♖c8 14 0-0 ♖xc3! (14...♘b6?! 15 ♘h5! ♖xc3 16 bxc3 ♘xh5 17 ♗xe7 ♕xe7 18 ♕xh5 ♗xe4 19 ♕g4! d5 20 f6! ♕c5+ 21 ♔h1 g6 22 ♖ae1 ♖e8 23 ♕h4 h5 24 ♕g5 ♘c4 25 ♗xc4 bxc4 26 ♖e3 +− F.Olafsson-Fischer, Bled Ct 1959) 15 bxc3 ♘xe4 16 ♘xe4

♗xe4 17 ♗xe7 ♕xe7 18 c4 ♖c8! 19
♕e2 ♘f6 20 ♖ac1 (20 ♖ad1!?)
20...h5! 21 cxb5 axb5 22 ♕xb5
♕a7+ 23 ♔h1 h4 24 ♕b3 ♘g4 25
h3 ♘e3 26 ♖g1 ♘xf5 27 ♔h2 d5 28
c4 ♖b8 29 ♕c3 ♕f2 30 ♕xe5 ♖b2
31 cxd5 ♕xg2+ 32 ♖xg2 ♖xg2+ 33
♔h1 ♘g3+ 0-1 Ermenkov-Portisch,
Skara 1980.

7	...	♘bd7
8	f4	♘c5
9	e5 *(D)*	

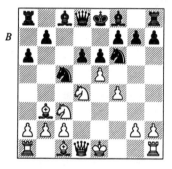

Short employs a hazardous line to
invite complications. The idea is that
White will be able to accelerate his
development and then enjoy greater
activity. The focus of attention will
be the weak point f7 and also e6
where a sacrifice may prove viable.
Black will rely on attacking the
static pawn on e5; if the attack can
be beaten off then the black pieces
will be well placed for a counter-attack. Note that if White wishes to
play e4-e5, it is best not delayed; 9
0-0 ♗e7 10 e5 was less effective in

Sandler-Danailov, Adelaide 1990/1:
10...dxe5 11 fxe5 ♘fd7 12 ♕h5 ♘f6
(12...g6 13 ♕e2 ♕c7 14 ♗h6 ♗f8
15 ♘d5 ♕d8 16 ♕f2 f5 17 exf6
♗xh6 18 ♕h4 ♘e5 19 ♕xh6 ♘f7
20 ♕e3 ♕d6 21 ♖ad1 ♗d7 22
♘xe6! +−) 13 ♕d1 (13 exf6 ♕xd4+
14 ♔h1 gxf6 15 ♗h6 ♖g8 16 ♖ad1
♕e5 ∓ Sandler) 13...♘d7 14 ♕h5
♘f6 15 ♕d1 ½-½.

9 ... dxe5

Kasparov accepts the challenge
and enters the sharpest line. Other
moves come into consideration:

a) 9...♘fe4 10 ♘xe4 ♘xe4 11
0-0 ♗e7 12 c3 0-0 13 ♗c2 ♘c5 14
b4 ♘d7 15 ♕d3 g6 16 exd6 ♗f6 17
♗e3 e5 18 ♘f5 gxf5 19 ♕xf5 e4 20
♗xe4 ♖e8 21 ♕xh7+ ♔f8 22 ♖f3
♖e6 23 ♗d5 ♗g7 24 ♖g3 ♕f6 25
♗d4 1-0 Hraček-Rašik, Czech Ch
1993.

b) 9...♘fd7 10 exd6 (10 ♕e2?
dxe5 11 fxe5 ♕h4+ −+) 10...♘f6 11
♗e3 ♗xd6 12 ♕f3 and now:

b1) 12...0-0 13 0-0-0 ♕c7 (or
13...♘xb3+ 14 ♘xb3 ♕c7 15
♖xd6!? ♕xd6 16 ♗c5 ♕c7 17 ♗xf8
♔xf8 18 ♖d1 ♗d7 19 g3 = Moroze-
vich-Mukhutdinov, Moscow 1992)
14 g4 ♗d7 15 g5 ♘e8 16 ♔b1 ♖c8
17 h4 ♘xb3 18 cxb3 ♗c5 19 ♖hg1
♘d6 20 h5 b5 21 h6 g6 22 ♖c1 ♕b8
23 ♖gd1 ♖fd8 24 ♕e2 b4 25 ♘a4
♗xa4 26 bxa4 ♕b7 27 ♗g1 ♕e4+
28 ♕xe4 ♘xe4 29 ♘c6 ♖xd1 30
♖xd1 ♗f8 ± Tischbierek-Grünberg,
Bundesliga 1991/92.

b2) 12...♗d7 13 0-0-0 ♕c7 14
♔b1 (14 g4 ♘xb3+ 15 axb3 0-0 16
g5!? ♘d5 17 ♘xd5 exd5 = Yanov-
sky-Timoshchenko, Hastings Chal-
lengers 1991/92) 14...0-0-0 15 g4
♘xb3 16 axb3 ♖he8 17 ♖d3 ♗c6 18
♘xc6 ♕xc6 19 ♕xc6+ bxc6 20 h3
½-½ Gi.Hernandez-Vera, Cuba
1993.

10 fxe5   ♘fd7
In Pugachev-Boger, USSR 1991,
White developed a kingside attack
after 10...♘xb3 11 axb3 ♗c5 (or
11...♘d5 12 ♕g4!?) 12 ♗e3 ♘d5?!
13 ♘xe6! ♗xe6 14 ♗xc5 ♕g5 15
♕d4 ♘xc3 (15...♘f4 16 g3 ♘g6 17
♗d6; 15...♕xg2 16 0-0-0 0-0-0 17
♘e4 ±) 16 bxc3 ♖d8 17 ♗d6 f6 18
0-0! fxe5 19 ♕c5 ♖c8 20 ♕f2 ♖xc3
21 ♖ae1 1-0.

11 ♗f4 (D)

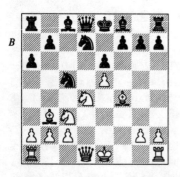

11 ...   b5
An improvement over Mikhalchi-
shin-Stangl, Dortmund 1991, where
Black allowed his opponent to develop quickly: 11...♘xb3 12 axb3

♗c5 13 ♘e4 (13 ♕d3!?) 13...0-0 14
♕d3 ♕h4+ 15 ♗g3 ♕h5 16 ♘xc5
♘xc5 17 ♕e3 f5 18 exf6 ♖xf6 19
♘f3 ♘d7 20 0-0-0 h6 21 ♖he1 a5 22
♖d4 ±.
     Also possible: 11...g5!? 12 ♘xe6
(12 ♗g3 h5 13 h3 ♕c7 14 ♕e2 b5
∞) 12...♘xe6 13 ♗xe6 gxf4 14
♗xf7+ ♔xf7 15 ♕h5+ ♔g7 16
♕g4+ ♔h6 17 h4 ♘xe5 18 ♕xf4+
♔g7 19 ♕xe5+ ♕f6 20 ♕g3+ ♕g6
21 ♕e5+ ♕f6 (21...♔g8 22 0-0-0 ∞)
22 ♕g3+ ♕g6 ½-½ A.Sokolov–
Har-Zvi, Biel 1992.

12 ♕g4
This the most aggressive response. A different square for the
queen has also been tried: 12 ♕e2
♗b7 13 0-0-0 b4 (13...♕a5 14 ♖hf1
♘xb3+ 15 ♘xb3 ♕c7 16 ♘d4 ♘c5
17 a3 ♗e7 18 ♕g4 0-0 = Motwani-
Pigott, British Ch 1989) 14 ♘a4
♘xb3+ 15 axb3 ♕c7 16 ♖hf1 ♘c5
17 ♘f5 exf5 18 e6 ♘xb3+ 19 ♔b1
♕c6 20 ♘b6 ♕xe6 21 ♖fe1 ♘c5 22
♘xa8 ♕xe2 23 ♖xe2+ ♘e4 24
♘c7+ ♔e7 25 g4 g6 26 ♗e5 f6 27
♗d6+ ♔d7 28 ♗f4+ ♔c8 29 ♘e6
♗e7 30 gxf5 gxf5 ± Emms-
A.Petrosian, London 1991.

12 ...   h5
Trying to create counterplay.
Black has two less convincing alternatives:
     a) 12...♘b6?! 13 0-0-0 ♗d7 14
♖hf1 h5?! 15 ♕f3 ♖c8 16 ♔b1 ♘c4
17 ♗xc4 bxc4 18 ♗g5! 1-0 Zapol-
skis-Tataev, Stare Mesto 1992.

b) 12...g5 13 ♗g3 h5 14 ♕e2 h4 15 ♗f2 ♕c7 16 0-0-0 ♕xe5 17 ♕d2 ♞xb3+ 18 axb3 ♞f6 19 ♚b1 ♗d7 ∞ Borkowski-Sulipa, Poland.

13 ♕g3   h4
14 ♕g4   g5

The best try to justify 13...h4 as 14...♞f6 fails to 15 exf6 ♕xd4 16 fxg7 ♗xg7 17 ♖d1 ♕f6 18 0-0 ±.

15 0-0-0! *(D)*

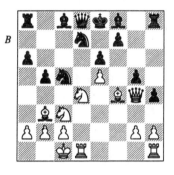

It is not advisable to grab the pawn:

a) 15 ♕xg5 ♕xg5 16 ♗xg5 ♗b7 is good for Black.

b) 15 ♗xg5 ♞xe5! 16 ♕f4 (16 ♗xd8 ♞xg4 −+) 16...♞ed3+ 17 cxd3 ♞xd3+ 18 ♚f1 ♞xf4 19 ♗xd8 ♚xd8 −+.

15 ...   ♕e7?!

In a complex position Black takes steps to avoid the pin on the d-file. Other moves lead to double-edged play:

a) 15...gxf4 16 ♞xe6 and now:

a1) 16...♕a5 (16...♕b6 17 ♞d5 +−) 17 ♞g7+ ♗xg7 18 ♕xg7 ♖f8

19 ♖he1 ♞xb3+ 20 cxb3 ♞c5 21 b4 ♞b3+ 22 axb3 ♕a1+ 23 ♚c2 ♗f5+ 24 ♖e4 ♗xe4+ 25 ♞xe4 ♖c8+ 26 ♞c5 ♕a2 27 e6 +− (Borik).

a2) 16...♞xb3+ 17 axb3 fxe6 18 ♕g6+ ♚e7 19 ♖d6 ♞xe5 20 ♕g5+ ♚d6 21 ♕xd8+ ♚c6 22 ♕f6+ +−.

a3) 16...♞xe6! 17 ♗xe6 ♕e7 18 ♗xd7+ ♗xd7 19 ♕f3 ♖a7 20 ♞d5 ♗c6 21 ♞f6+ ♕xf6 22 exf6 ♗xf3 23 ♖he1+ ♖e7 24 fxe7 ♗xd1 25 exf8♕+ ♚xf8 26 ♖xd1 h3 = (Speelman).

b) 15...♖h6! (Kasparov) and now:

b1) 16 ♕xg5 ♕xg5 17 ♗xg5 ♖h5 18 ♗f4 ♗b7 ∓.

b2) 16 ♗xg5 ♖g6 17 ♗xd8 ♖xg4 18 h3? ♖xd4 −+.

16 ♞c6!

The beginning of a startling combination. The tempting 16 ♗d5?! does not work out well for White, as 16...exd5 17 ♞f5 (17 ♞xd5 ♞b6!) 17...♞b6 18 ♗xg5 ♗xf5 19 ♕xf5 ♕xg5+ 20 ♕xg5 ♗h6 gives Black a clear advantage.

16 ...   ♞xb3+
17 axb3   ♕c5
18 ♞e4   ♕xc6
19 ♗xg5   ♗b7

The only try, since 19...♖g8 20 ♞f6+ ♞xf6 21 ♗xf6 is final.

20 ♖d6!

A wonderful move.

20 ...   ♗xd6

Black is obliged to capture the rook. For example:

a) 20...♕xe4? 21 ♖xe6+ ♗e7 22
♖xe7+ ♔f8 23 ♕xd7 +–.

b) 20...♘xe5? 21 ♘f6+ ♔e7 22
♖xc6 ♘xg4 23 ♘xg4+ ♔d7 24
♘e5+ ♔e8 25 ♖c7 ♗d6 (25...♗xg2
26 ♖e1 ♖h7 27 ♘xf7 +–) 26 ♖xf7
♗xg2 27 ♖e1 ♗xe5 28 ♖e7+ ♔f8
29 ♖xe6 +– (Hübner).

21 ♘xd6+   ♔f8
22 ♖f1   ♘xe5

It is impossible to find a reasonable defence:

a) 22...♕xg2 23 ♖xf7+ ♔g8 24
♕xe6 ♕xg5+ 25 ♖f4 ♔h7 26
♕xd7+ +– (Borik).

b) 22...♖h7 23 ♕xe6 and now:

b1) 23...♔g8 24 ♖xf7 ♖xf7 25
♕xf7+ ♔h8 26 ♘f5 +–.

b2) 23...♕d5 24 ♕xd7 ♗c6 25
♕f5 +–.

b3) 23...♘xe5 24 ♕xe5 ♕xg2 25
♖xf7+ ♔g8 26 ♖f5 +–.

23 ♕xe6   ♕d5 (D)

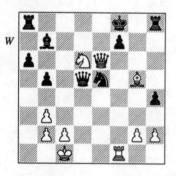

24 ♖xf7+

A stylish way to continue the onslaught while keeping at least a draw

in hand, but a quieter move might
have brought greater dividends:

a) 24 ♗h6+ and now:

a1) 24...♖xh6 25 ♕xh6+ ♔e7 26
♕f6+ ♔f8 27 ♘xb7 +–.

a2) 24...♔g8 25 ♖xf7 ♕xe6 26
♖g7+ ♔f8 27 ♖f7+ =.

b) 24 ♕f6! ♖h7 25 ♖f5 ♕xg2
(25...♘d3+ 26 cxd3; 25...♘g6 26
♕xg6) 26 ♕xe5 ♔g8 27 ♗f6 ♕h1+
28 ♔d2 ♖h6 29 ♖g5+ ♖g6 30 ♕e7
♕xh2+ 31 ♔c3 +– (Hübner).

24 ...   ♘xf7

The game comes to an abrupt finish after 24...♔g8 25 ♖g7+ ♔xg7 26
♘f5+ ♔f8 27 ♕e7+ ♔g8 28 ♕g7#.

25 ♗e7+   ♔g7
26 ♕f6+   ♔h7
27 ♘xf7   ♕h5

This is the only way to avoid 28
♘g5+ and 28 ♕h6+ ♔g8 29 ♕g6#.

28 ♘g5+   ♔g8
29 ♕e6+   ♔g7
30 ♕f6+   ♔g8
31 ♕e6+   ♔g7
32 ♗f6+   ♔h6

Of course, 32...♔g6?? 33 ♗xh8+
♔xg5 34 ♕e5+ mates.

33 ♘f7+   ♔h7
34 ♘g5+

It would appear that White should
have various ways to hunt down the
errant black king but it is a tricky
business:

a) 34 ♕e7 ♖ae8 35 ♘g5+ ♔g6
36 ♕f7+ ♔f5 –+.

b) 34 ♘xh8 ♖xh8 and now:

b1) 35 ♕e7+ ♔g6 36 ♗xh8

♕g5+ 37 ♕xg5+ ♔xg5 38 g3 hxg3
39 hxg3 ♔g4 40 ♗e5 ♗d5 41 ♔d2
♔f3 = (Borik).
  b2) 35 ♕d7+ ♔g6 36 ♗xh8 and
now:
    b21) 36...♗xg2 37 ♕g7+ ♔f5 38
♕xg2 ♕xh8 39 h3 +− (Hübner).
    b22) 36...♕e2 37 ♕g7+ ♔f5 38
♕f6+ ♔g4 39 ♕g6+ ♔f4 40 g3+
hxg3 41 ♕xg3+ ♔f5 42 ♕d3+ +−
(Hübner).
    b23) 36...♕h6+ 37 ♔b1 ♗xg2
38 ♕d3+ ♔f7 39 ♕f5+ ♔e7 40
♗d4 h3 = (Hübner).
  34 ...   ♔h6
  35 ♗xh8+   ♕g6
The only move in view of
35...♔xg5 36 ♕e5+ ♔g4 37 h3#.
  36 ♘f7+   ♔h7
  37 ♕e7   ♕xg2?
In mutual time-trouble Kasparov
plays a daring move which threatens
perpetual check. A calmer approach
is the most accurate defence:
37...♔g8 38 ♕xb7 (38 ♘e5 ♕h7)
38...♖f8 39 ♗d4 ♕xf7 with equality
(Kasparov).
  38 ♗e5?
White is winning after 38 ♗d4!
covering the vital f2 square and allowing the king to evade the checks:
  a) 38...♕f1+ 39 ♔d2 ♕f4+ 40
♗e3 ♕xh2+ 41 ♔d3 +−.
  b) 38...♕h1+ 39 ♔d2 and now:
    b1) 39...♕xh2+ 40 ♔c3 ♖c8+ 41
♔b4 ♕c7 42 ♕f6 +−.
    b2) 39...♕g2+ 40 ♔c3 ♕c6+ 41
♔b4 ♖e8 (41...a5+ 42 ♔a3 ♖e8 43

♕g5 ♕g6 44 ♕xh4+ ♔g8 45 ♘g5
♔f8 46 ♘h7+ ♔f7 47 ♕f4+ ♔e6 48
♕e5+ ♔f7 49 ♘g5+ ♔f8 50 ♕xb5
wins − Hübner) 42 ♕xh4+ ♔g8 43
♘h6+ ♔f8 44 ♗c5+ ♔g7 45 ♘f5+
+− (Kasparov).
  38 ...   ♕f1+
  39 ♔d2   ♕f2+
  40 ♔d3
Not recommended is 40 ♔c3 b4+
41 ♔xb4? ♕b6+ 42 ♔c3 ♖c8+ 43
♔d3 ♕g6+ −+.
  40 ...   ♕f3+
  41 ♔d2   ♕f2+
                ½-½

Game 2

Fischer – Bednarski

Havana OL 1966

1 e4 c5 2 ♘f3 d6 3 d4 cxd4 4 ♘xd4
♘f6 5 ♘c3 a6 6 ♗c4 e6 7 ♗b3
♘bd7 8 f4 ♘c5
  9 f5   ♘fxe4!?
This is a critical test for the whole
line. Since this game, few people
have dared to grab the pawn, so the
main game is an essential example
despite being played in 1966. The
question is whether White's forth-
coming attack is sufficient to com-
pensate for the pawn. Instead
9...♘xb3?! reaches a position which
can arise via the Sozin (the knight
has travelled there via c6 and a5).
We consider this in Game 31.
  The move 9...e5 forces the white
knight to retreat, but at the cost of

losing control of the key square d5. Play might continue 10 ♘de2 ♘xb3 (10...♘cxe4 11 ♘xe4 ♘xe4 12 ♕d5 ♘g5 13 h4 +–; 10...h6 11 ♘g3 ♗d7 12 ♘h5! ♗c6 13 ♘xf6+ ♕xf6 14 ♕e2 ♕h4+ 15 g3 ♕d8 16 ♗d5 ± Ćirić-Bogdanović, Yugoslav Ch 1967) 11 axb3 and now:

a) 11...h6 12 ♘g3 ♗d7 13 ♘h5 ♘xh5 14 ♕xh5 ♗c6 15 ♗e3 b5 16 0-0 ♗e7 (16...b4 17 ♘d5 ♗xd5 18 exd5 ±) 17 ♖fd1 ♕c7 18 ♕g4 ♗f6 19 b4 ♗b7 20 ♖d3 ♔e7 21 ♖ad1 ♖hd8 22 ♕e2 ♖d7 23 ♕d2 ♖ad8 24 ♕f2 ♕b8 25 g4! ♔e8 26 h4 ♗e7 27 f6! ♗xf6 28 ♗xh6 ♖c8 29 g5 ♗d8 30 ♗xg7 ♖xc3 31 ♖xc3 ♗xe4 32 ♔h2 ♗g6 33 ♗f6 ♗h5 34 ♖f1 ♗c7 35 g6! ♗xg6 36 h5 ♗h7 37 ♖g1 1-0 Zapata-Fedorowicz, Philadelphia 1993.

b) 11...d5 12 ♗g5! dxe4 13 ♕xd8+ ♔xd8 14 ♘d5 ♗e7 15 0-0-0 ♘xd5 16 ♖xd5+ ♔e8 17 ♗xe7 ♔xe7 18 ♖xe5+ ± Trapl-Hausner, Trnava 1980.

c) 11...b5 12 ♗g5 ♗b7 13 ♘g3 ♗e7 14 ♗xf6 ♗xf6 15 ♘d5 ± Mikhalchishin.

10   fxe6! *(D)*
10   ...   ♕h4+?!
Black takes up the gauntlet and grabs material. Other paths:

a) 10...♗xe6 11 ♘xe4 ♘xe4 12 ♘xe6 fxe6 (12...♕h4+ 13 g3 ♘xg3 14 ♗g5 ♕e4+ 15 ♔d2 ♘xh1 16 ♘c7+ ♔d7 18 ♘xa8 +–) 13 ♕g4 ♘c5 14 ♗e3! ±.

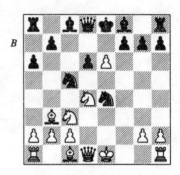

b) 10...fxe6! 11 ♘xe4 ♘xe4 12 0-0 ♕e7 (12...♘c5 13 ♕g4 ♘xb3 14 axb3 e5 15 ♕f3) is better for White according to Fischer.
11   g3   ♘xg3
12   ♘f3!
The move-order is important because 12 exf7+ ♔d8 13 ♘f3 ♕e7+ gives Black the advantage.
12   ...   ♕h5
13   exf7+   ♔d8
14   ♖g1   ♘f5
15   ♘d5!   ♕xf7 *(D)*

For the sake of a pawn Black has paid a heavy price, with his king exposed to attack and his queen loose. For example: 15...♘xb3 (15...h6 16 ♘f4 also wins for White) 16 ♗g5+ ♔d7 (16...♗e7 17 ♘xe7! ♘xe7 18 ♕xd6+ +−) 17 ♘e5+ +−.

| 16 | ♗g5+ | ♔e8 |
| 17 | ♕e2+! | |

In his notes to the game Fischer points out that 17 ♘f6+ gxf6 18 ♗xf7+ wins the queen, but the aim is to achieve the quickest victory.

17	...	♗e6
18	♘f4	♔d7
19	0-0-0 *(D)*	

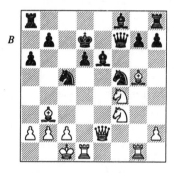

| 19 | ... | ♕e8 |

There is no defence, even after 19...♘xb3+ (19...♗xb3 20 ♘e5+ ♔f7 21 ♘xf7) 20 axb3 ♕e8 21 ♖ge1 ♗g8 22 ♕d3 +−.

| 20 | ♗xe6+ | ♘xe6 |
| 21 | ♕e4! | |

The threats of 22 ♕xf5 and 22 ♘xe6 ♕xe6 23 ♕xb7+ seal Black's fate.

| 21 | ... | g6 |
| 22 | ♘xe6 | 1-0 |

Game 3

Short – Kasparov
London PCA Wch (6) 1993

1 e4 c5 2 ♘f3 d6 3 d4 cxd4 4 ♘xd4 ♘f6 5 ♘c3 a6 6 ♗c4 e6

7	♗b3	♘bd7
8	f4	♘c5
9	f5	♗e7

A safe continuation that normally allows White to extract a small advantage due to his greater freedom.

| 10 | ♕f3 | 0-0 |
| 11 | ♗e3 | |

A less flexible approach is to castle early: 11 0-0 e5 12 ♘de2 ♘xb3 13 axb3 b5 14 g4!? b4 (14...d5!? 15 ♘xd5 ♘xd5 16 exd5 e4 17 ♕xe4 ♖e8 18 ♕d3! ♗b7 19 c4 ♗c5+ 20 ♔g2 ♕h4 21 h3 h5 22 ♕f3 ±; 14...h6! Vera) 15 g5 bxc3 16 gxf6 ♗xf6?! (Black should try 16...cxb2 17 fxe7 bxa1♕ 18 f6 ♕b6+ 19 ♗e3 ♕xf1+ 20 ♔xf1 ♕c6 21 ♕g3 g6 22 ♕h4 h5, with the point that 23 ♕g5 ♕xe4! 24 ♕h6 fails to 24...♗h3+ 25 ♔e1 ♕h4+ followed by 26...♕xf6, and Black wins) 17 ♘xc3 ♗b7 18 ♗e3 ♖c8 19 ♖ad1 ♗e7 (19...♖xc3? 20 bxc3 ♕a8 21 ♖xd6 ♗xe4 22 ♕g4 ±; 19...♕c7 20 ♖f2 intending ♘d5 ±) 20 ♕g4 f6 21 ♖f3 ♕e8! 22 ♖d2 (22 ♖g3 ♕f7 23 ♖h3 ♖xc3 24 bxc3 ♕c6 25 ♕h5 h6 ∞) 22...g5 23 ♖h3 ♖xc3! 24 bxc3 ♕c6 25 ♗xg5 fxg5 26 ♖xh7 ♕c5+ (26...♔xh7 27 ♕h5+ ♔g8 28 ♕g6+ ♔h8 29 ♖d3 +−) 27 ♔f1 ♗xe4 28 ♖h8+ ♔xh8

29 ♕h5+ ♔g8 ½-½ Zapata-Vera, Matanzas 1993.

11 ... e5

The advance of the e-pawn relieves the pressure in the centre. The passive 11...♗d7 is examined in the next game. Other paths:

a) 11...d5 12 exd5 e5 (12...♘xb3 13 ♘xb3 exd5 14 0-0-0 ± Fischer) 13 ♘de2 e4 14 ♕h3 g6 15 0-0 ♘xb3 16 axb3 ♘xd5 17 ♖ad1 ± Matulović-Bogdanović, Yugoslav Ch 1967.

b) 11...♕c7 12 0-0 with a further branch:

b1) 12...b5 13 fxe6 fxe6 14 ♘f5 (or 14 ♕h3 ♘xb3 15 axb3 e5 16 ♘f5 b4 17 ♘a4 ♖b8 ∞ Bogdanović-Bradvarević, Yugoslav Ch 1967) 14...♘xb3 15 ♘xe7+ ♕xe7 16 axb3 ♗b7 17 ♗g5 is equal (Istratescu and Stoica).

b2) 12...♘xb3 13 axb3 ♗d7 14 g4 h6 15 h4 d5 16 g5 dxe4 17 ♕g2 hxg5 18 hxg5 ♘h5 19 ♘xe4 exf5 20 ♘xf5 ♗c6 21 ♕g4 ♗xe4 22 ♕xe4 ♗c5 23 ♗xc5 ♕xc5+ 24 ♖f2 g6 25 ♕g4 ♖ae8 26 ♖f1 ∞ Morozevich-Dragomaretsky, Alushta 1993.

b3) 12...e5 13 ♘de2 ♘xb3 14 axb3 b5 15 g4 b4 16 g5! bxc3 17 gxf6 ♗xf6 18 bxc3 ♗b7 19 c4 d5 20 exd5! ± Fischer-Hamann, Netanya 1968.

12 ♘de2 b5

Kasparov poses White more problems by avoiding the well-known ideas that emerge after 12...♘xb3 13 axb3 b5 and now:

a) 14 ♗g5 b4 15 ♗xf6 bxc3 16 ♗xe7 cxb2 17 ♖b1 ♕xe7 18 0-0 = Fiorito-Sunye, Bogotá 1991.

b) 14 0-0-0 b4 15 ♘a4 ♗b7 16 ♘g3 ♗c6 17 ♘b6 ♖b8 18 ♘d5 ♗xd5 19 exd5 a5 = Schuh-Malishauskas, Debrecen 1992.

c) 14 ♖d1 ♗b7 (14...b4 15 ♘d5 ♘xd5 16 exd5 ∞) 15 0-0!? ♖c8 16 ♖d2 b4 (16...♕a5 17 g4 ♕b4 18 ♘g3 d5 19 ♘xd5 ♗xd5 20 exd5 ♗c5 21 c3 ♕xg4 22 ♔g2 ± Gudmundsson-Gislason, Icelandic Ch 1992) 17 ♘d5 ♘xd5 18 exd5 ♗g5 19 ♘g3 ♗xe3+ 20 ♕xe3 ♕a5 (20...f6 21 ♘e4!) 21 f6 ♕c5 22 ♕xc5 ♖xc5 23 fxg7 ♔xg7 24 ♘f5+ ♔h8 25 ♘e3 ± Golubev-Ginsburg, Simferopol 1992.

d) 14 g4 b4 15 ♘a4 ♗b7 16 ♘g3 d5 17 0-0-0 d4 (17...♘xe4 18 ♘xe4 dxe4 19 ♕h3 ♕c7 20 g5 is unclear; 17...dxe4 18 ♕e2 ♕a5 19 g5 ♘d5 20 f6! ± Winants) 18 ♗d2 ♖c8 19 ♔b1 ♘d7 and now 20 ♖hg1! ♗c6 21 g5 ♗xa4 22 f6 ♗c6 23 ♘f5 ♗c5 (23...♗xf6 24 gxf6 ♘xf6 25 ♖xg7+ ♔h8 26 ♕g3 +−) 24 fxg7 ♖e8 25 ♖g3 would have been winning for White; Winants-Ftačnik, Tilburg 1993.

13 ♗d5 *(D)*

A difficult decision that is intended to put a clamp on the d5 square. The position has not been fully explored since the game Bogdanović-Matulović, Sarajevo 1960, which continued 13 ♘d5 ♘xb3 14

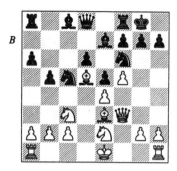

♘xf6+ ♗xf6 15 cxb3 d5 ∞. An old recommendation is 13 ♗xc5 dxc5 14 ♗d5 with claims of a clear advantage, although Speelman notes that 14...♖b8 15 0-0-0 ♕a5 16 g4 b4 17 g5 is a risky strategy.

13 ...   ♖b8
14 b4   ♘cd7

Viktor Korchnoi suggested the line 14...♘a4 15 0-0 (15 ♘xa4 bxa4 ∓) 15...♕c7! (15...♘xd5 16 ♘xd5 ♗b7 17 ♘g3 =) 16 ♗g5 ♕a7+ 17 ♗e3 ♕c7 18 ♗g5 forcing a draw. After the move played, Black should not worry about losing the exchange due to 15 ♗a7 ♘xd5 16 ♘xd5 (16 ♗xb8? ♘xb4) 16...♖a8 17 ♗e3 ♗b7 with reasonable chances for Black.

15 0-0   ♘xd5
16 ♘xd5   ♗b7
17 ♘ec3   ♘f6

Black can also opt to play for control of the c-file: 17...♖c8 18 ♖ad1 ♗xd5 19 ♘xd5 ♖xc2 20 ♖c1 ♖c4 21 ♕e2 (21 ♖xc4 bxc4 22 ♕e2!?) 21...♖xe4? 22 ♖c8! +−.

18 ♖ad1   ♗xd5

White would like to double on the d-file to put pressure on d6, e.g. 18...♖c8 19 ♘xf6+ ♗xf6 20 ♖d3 ±.

19 ♘xd5   ♘xd5
20 ♖xd5   ♖c8 *(D)*

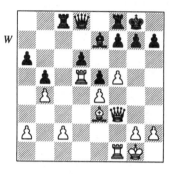

Kasparov suggests 20...♕c7 as a way to exploit White's queenside pawn structure: 21 g4! (21 ♕g4 f6 22 ♖f3 ♕xc2 23 ♖h3 ♖f7 24 ♕h5 h6 25 ♕g6 ♕xe4 26 ♖d1 ♔f8 27 ♗xh6 gxh6 28 ♖xh6 ♔e8 29 ♖h7 ♕c4 ∓) 21...♕xc2 22 g5 f6 23 g6 h6 24 ♕h5 ♕xe4 25 ♗xh6 gxh6 26 ♕xh6 ♕g4+ 27 ♔h1 ♕e4+ =.

21 ♕g4

A direct and natural-looking continuation which aims to start attacking operations on the g- and h-files. Black is obliged to be cautious:

a) 21...♖xc2 22 ♗h6 ♗f6 23 ♗xg7 ♗xf6 24 f6 +−.

b) 21...♔h8 22 ♖f3 ♖xc2 23 ♖h3 (23 ♕h5 g6 24 ♕h6 ♖g8) 23...♕c7 (23...g6 24 ♖h6 ♖g8 25 ♖xd6) 24 ♕h5 h6 25 ♗xh6 +−.

c) 21...g6 22 ♗h6 ♖e8 23 fxg6 hxg6 24 ♖d3 +–.

d) 21...♗f6 22 ♗c5 +–.

21	...	f6
22	♖f3	♖xc2

Black soon gets into a tangle upon 22...♖f7 23 ♖h3 ♗f8 24 ♕h5 h6 25 ♕g6 ±.

23	♖h3	♖f7
24	♕h5	h6

The hopeful 24...g5?! is soon demolished: 25 fxg6 ♖g7 26 gxh7+ ♔h8 27 ♖d2 followed by ♗h6 and White wins.

25	♕g6	♔f8 (D)

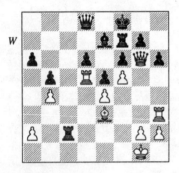

26   ♗xh6

The king can be hunted down by 26 ♕h7! ♔e8 27 ♕g8+, when Black can avoid instant mate, but must suffer an inferior game:

a) 27...♗f8 28 ♗c5 and now:

a1) 28...♕c7 29 ♖hd3! dxc5 30 ♖d8+ ♕xd8 31 ♖xd8+ ♔xd8 32 ♕xf7 +–.

a2) 28...♖c1+ 29 ♔f2 ♖c2+ 30 ♔e1 ♖c1+ 31 ♔e2 ♕c7 32 ♖hd3 ±.

b) 27...♖f8 28 ♕xg7 ♕c7 and now:

b1) 29 ♕xh6 ♕c4 (29...♕c3 30 ♕h5+ ♔d7 ∓) 30 ♕g6+ ♔d7 31 ♕g4 ♖e2!? ∞.

b2) 29 ♖g3?! ♕c4 ∓.

b3) 29 a3! ♖c1+ (29...♕c3 30 ♗d2 ♕a1+ 31 ♔f2 ♕d1 32 ♖hd3 ±; 29...♕c4 30 ♕g4 ♖c3 31 ♗xh6 ♖xh3 32 gxh3 ±) 30 ♗xc1 ♕xc1+ 31 ♔f2 ♕c2+ (31...♕b2+ 32 ♔f3 ♕xa3+ 33 ♔g4 ♕xb4 34 ♖e3 ±) 32 ♔f3 ♔d7 33 ♕xh6 ♖c8 34 ♕d2 ♖c3+ 35 ♔f2 +– Timman.

Tisdall suggests 26 ♗c5!? with the idea that the open d-file allows combinations involving ♕h7 and ♖hd3, but Timman points out that 26...♕c8 27 ♖hd3 dxc5 28 ♕h7 ♔e8 29 ♕g8+ ♖f8 holds Black's position together.

26	...	gxh6
27	♖xh6	♕b6+
28	♖c5	♗d8
29	♖h8+	♔e7
30	♖h7!	

30 ♕g8 fails to 30...dxc5.

30	...	♖xh7
31	♕xh7+	♔f8
	½-½	

Game 4
Winants – Christiansen
Wijk aan Zee 1993

1 e4 c5 2 ♘f3 d6 3 d4 cxd4 4 ♘xd4 ♘f6 5 ♘c3 a6 6 ♗c4 e6 7 ♗b3 ♘bd7 8 f4 ♘c5

9	f5	♗e7
10	♕f3	0-0
11	♗e3	♗d7?!

Black wishes to tailor his development to suit White's plan; in such a sharp line this gives White the initiative.

12 g4

The Belgian embarks on an adventurous plan. White hopes to overcome his opponent by means of a straightforward kingside pawn advance.

12	...	♕a5 *(D)*

The e-pawn, now threatened by 13...♘cxe4, is Black's object of desire. The queen sortie is intended to divert White's attack.

There are other possibilities:

a) 12...♘e8 13 0-0-0 (13 g5!? ♗xg5 14 0-0-0 ∞ Yudasin) 13...♖c8 14 ♖hg1 ± Petelin-Malishauskas, Russia 1991.

b) 12...e5 13 ♘de2 ♘fxe4? 14 ♘xe4 ♘xe4 15 ♕xe4 ♗c6 16 ♗d5 ♕a5+ 17 ♘c3 +-.

c) 12...b5 13 g5 ♘e8 14 ♖g1 b4 15 ♘d5 (15 ♘d1!? d5 16 exd5 e5 ∞; 15 ♘ce2! ♘xb3 16 axb3 d5 17 exd5 ± Winants) 15...exd5 16 ♗xd5 ♘c7! 17 ♗c4 (17 f6 ♘xd5 18 exd5 ∞) 17...d5 18 exd5 ♗d6 (18...♗b5 19 ♗xb5 axb5 20 ♘c6 ♕d7 21 f6 ♗d6 22 fxg7 ♖fe8 ∓; 19 b3!?) 19 0-0-0 ♗b5 20 ♘c6 ♕e8 (20...♕d7 21 ♖g4 ∞) 21 ♖g4 ♘d7 22 ♗xb5 axb5 23 ♖e4 ♕c8 24 ♗f4 ♗xf4+ 25 ♖xf4 ♖e8 26 d6 ∞ Kuksov-Yudasin, USSR 1989.

13	0-0-0	e5
14	♘de2	♘xb3+
15	cxb3	♗c6

The drawback of Black's defensive scheme is its inflexibility; his sole idea is to try to force through ...d5.

16	♘g3	♖fd8 *(D)*

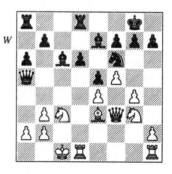

If 16...♘xe4? 17 ♘gxe4 d5 18 ♖xd5 ♗xd5 19 ♘xd5 ♕xd5 20 ♘f6+ and White wins.

17	g5	♘xe4

A sad necessity. 17...♘d7 allows

White to achieve a rapid victory with 18 f6!.

18 ♘gxe4   ♖ac8

The thrust 18...d5 is appealing in the line 19 f6?! ♗b4 (19...dxe4 20 ♕f2 ♗a3! ∞) 20 ♕f2 d4! ∞. The antidote is 19 g6! +−.

19 ♔b1   d5
20 g6   dxe4?!

There are plenty of tactics after the critical 20...d4. Winants' analysis demonstrates that White's attack remains supreme. After 21 ♕h3 h6 22 gxf7+ (22 ♗xh6? dxc3) play might continue:

a) 22...♔xf7 23 ♕h5+ and now:

a1) 23...♔f8 24 f6! ♗xf6 25 ♗xd4 ♗e8 (25...exd4 26 ♕xa5 +−) 26 ♕f5 ♗d7 27 ♗c5+ ♖xc5 28 ♖xd7 +−.

a2) 23...♔g8 24 ♖dg1! dxe3 (White also wins after 24...dxc3 25 ♖xg7+ ♔xg7 26 ♗xh6+) 25 f6 (25 ♕xh6? ♖d1+!) 25...♗f8 26 f7+ ♔h8 27 ♕xh6+! gxh6 28 ♖g8+ ♔h7 29 ♘f6#.

b) 22...♔h7 23 ♖dg1 dxe3 24 ♕g4 ♗f8 25 ♕g6+ ♔h8 26 ♕xh6+ +−.

c) 22...♔f8 23 ♗xh6 dxc3! 24 ♗xg7+ ♔xf7 25 ♕h5+ ♔g8 26 ♘xc3 ♗xh1 and now:

c1) 27 ♖g1 ♕c5 28 ♖g6 (28 ♕g6? ♗e4+ 29 ♔a1 ♗xf5! −+ and 28 ♖g4? ♖d1+ −+ are both bad, while after 28 ♖g3 ♗e4+ White should avoid 29 ♔c1? ♕xc3+! 30 ♖xc3 ♖xc3+ 31 bxc3 ♗a3# and

play instead 29 ♔a1 ♖d3 30 ♖g6 ♖d1+ transposing to the main line) 28...♗e4+ 29 ♔a1 ♖d1+ 30 ♕xd1 ♗xf5 31 ♖g1 ♔f7 32 ♕h5+ ♔e6 33 ♖f1 when White is a pawn up with a dangerous attack.

c2) 27 ♖xh1! ♖d2 (27...♖xc3 28 ♕g6! +−) 28 ♕h8+ (28 ♖g1? ♖xb2+ 29 ♔a1 ♖g2!) 28...♔f7 29 ♕xc8 +−.

21 ♕h3   ♗f6

Faced with the dismal prospect of 21...hxg6 22 fxg6 fxg6 23 ♕e6+ ♔f8 24 ♖hf1+ ♗f6 25 ♖xf6+ gxf6 26 ♗h6#, Black's king must walk the plank.

22 ♕xh7+   ♔f8
23 a3!   ♗d5

Or else b4 followed by ♗c5+

24 ♖xd5   ♖xc3
1-0

Game 5

Istratescu – Ghitescu
Romania 1992

1 e4 c5 2 ♘f3 d6 3 d4 cxd4 4 ♘xd4 ♘f6 5 ♘c3 a6 6 ♗c4 e6 7 ♗b3 ♘bd7 8 f4 ♘c5

9 f5   ♗e7
10 0-0 *(D)*

This is considered one of the quieter continuations as opposite-side castling is more likely to induce a violent attack. This slower strategy, which has attracted the attention of Anand, should be satisfactory for White.

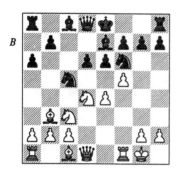

10 ... ♗d7!?

A standard response. Examples of the alternatives:

a) 10...e5 11 ♘de2 h6 12 ♗e3 ♘xb3 13 axb3 0-0 14 ♘g3 b5 15 ♘h5 ♗b7 16 ♘xf6+ ♗xf6 17 ♘d5 and White has created a strong bind; Anand-King, Calcutta 1992.

b) 10...0-0 11 fxe6 fxe6 and now:

b1) 12 ♗g5 ♘xb3 13 axb3 ♗d7 14 ♘f3 ♗c6 15 ♕d3 b5 16 ♘d4 ♗d7 17 b4 ♕b6 18 ♔h1 ♖ac8 19 ♘ce2 ♕b7 20 ♘g3 h6 = Ostojić-King, Germany 1992.

b2) 12 ♕e2 b5 13 ♘c6 ♕c7 14 ♘xe7+ ♕xe7 15 ♗g5 ♗b7 16 e5 dxe5 17 ♕xe5 ♘xb3 18 axb3 ♖ac8 19 ♘e4 ♗xe4 20 ♕xe4 ♕c5+ 21 ♕e3 ♘g4 was unclear in Susnik-Savon, Bled/Rogaška 1992.

b3) 12 ♘f5 ♘xb3 (12...b5 13 ♗g5 b4 14 ♘xe7+ ♕xe7 15 ♘d5 {15 ♗xf6 ♖xf6 16 ♖xf6 ♕xf6 17 ♘d5 ♕d8! ∞ Topalov} 15...exd5 16 ♗xf6 gxf6 17 ♗d5+ ♗e6 18 ♗xa8 ♖xa8 ∓ Nikolov-Topalov, Šumen 1991) 13 ♘xe7+ ♕xe7 14 axb3

♗d7 15 ♗f4! e5 16 ♗g5 ♕e6 (16...♗e6 17 ♘d5 ♗xd5 18 ♗xf6 ♖xf6 19 ♖xf6 gxf6 20 ♕xd5+ ±) 17 ♕d3 ♗c6 18 ♗xf6 ♖xf6 19 ♖xf6 ♕xf6 20 ♕c4+ ♕f7 21 ♖f1 ♕xc4 22 bxc4 ± Istratescu-Gutkin, Biel 1993.

11 ♕f3

White supports e4 while activating his queen for attacking purposes. Alternatives look unlikely to disturb Black:

a) 11 ♕e1 e5 12 ♘f3 ♗c6 13 ♗d5 ♗xd5 14 exd5 ♕d7 = Morozevich-Lazarev, Alushta 1993.

b) 11 ♗g5 and now:

b1) 11...b5 12 ♕f3 ♘xb3 13 axb3 0-0 (13...b4 14 ♘a4 e5 15 ♗xf6 ♗xf6 16 ♘e2 ½-½ Istratescu-Timoschenko, Calimanesti 1992) 14 ♔h1 ♕b6 15 ♘de2 ♕b7 16 ♘g3 ♗c6 17 b4 d5 18 ♗xf6 ♗xf6 19 ♘h5 dxe4 20 ♘xf6+ gxf6 21 ♕g4+ ♔h8 22 ♕h4 ♖g8 23 ♕xf6+ ♖g7 24 ♖f4 exf5 25 ♖xf5 ♔g8 26 ♖g5 ♖g6 27 ♘e2! ± Istratescu-Jaracz, Duisburg 1992.

b2) 11...0-0 12 fxe6 fxe6 13 ♘f5 ♘xb3 14 ♘xe7+ ♕xe7 15 axb3 ♗c6 16 ♕d4 h6 17 ♗xf6 ♖xf6 18 ♖xf6 ♕xf6 19 ♖d1 ♕g6 20 ♖f1 ♖d8 21 ♖f2 ♕g5 22 h3 ♕c5 23 ♖d2 ♕xd4+ 24 ♖xd4 ♔f7 25 ♔f2 ♔e7 26 ♔e3 ½-½ Vujadinović-Kaminski, Vrnjačka Banja 1990.

c) 11 fxe6 fxe6 12 ♗g5 b5 13 ♕f3 ♘xb3 14 axb3 0-0 15 ♔h1 ∞ Hamdouchi-Hellers, Biel IZ 1993.

| 11 | ... | 0-0 |
| 12 | g4!? | |

White reckons that opening the centre with ...d5 would create more problems for Black despite the somewhat exposed white king.

| 12 | ... | ♘xb3 |
| 13 | axb3 | h6 |

It is difficult to find a convincing way for Black halt White's charge, although 13...♘e8 might be considered to slow down the pawn avalanche.

| 14 | g5 | hxg5 |
| 15 | ♗xg5 *(D)* | |

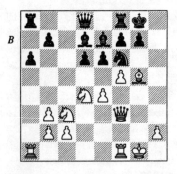

If Black responds passively White can build up a commanding position with ♔h1 followed by doubling rooks on the g-file.

15	...	♘h7
16	♗xe7	♕xe7
17	♔h1	♕h4
18	♖g1	

White targets g7 while Black's only reliable defensive piece is his queen – a sign of serious problems.

18	...	exf5
19	♘xf5	♗xf5
20	exf5	♘f6 *(D)*

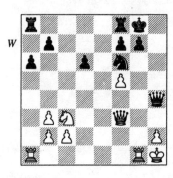

21 ♖a4!

The rook prepares to swing across to the kingside with devastating results. This manoeuvre is a feature of the variation.

21	...	♕h6
22	♕g2	g6
23	fxg6	fxg6
24	♖h4	

The black queen is overloaded, resulting in the collapse of Black's position.

| 24 | ... | ♕g7 |
| 25 | ♘d5 | 1-0 |

Game 6

Short – Kasparov
London PCA Wch (10) 1993

1 e4 c5 2 ♘f3 d6 3 d4 cxd4 4 ♘xd4 ♘f6 5 ♘c3 a6 6 ♗c4 e6 7 ♗b3 ♘bd7 8 f4 ♘c5
    9 ♕f3

This is more flexible then 9 e5 or 9 f5. Now Black must be continuously wary of the advances e5 and f5.

9 ...   b5 *(D)*

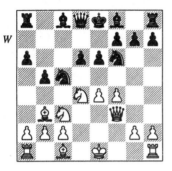

Black can also seek quieter paths:

a) 9...♗e7 and now:

a1) 10 g4 d5 11 e5 ♘fe4 12 0-0 ♕c7 13 ♘ce2 ♗d7 (Filipenko-Akopian, Rostov-on-Don 1993) 14 c4! is unclear.

a2) 10 0-0 0-0 11 ♗e3 ♕c7 12 g4 b5 13 g5 ♘fxe4 14 ♘xe4 ♗b7 15 ♘xc5! dxc5 16 ♘xe6 ♕c8 17 ♗d5 ♗xd5 18 ♕xd5 ♕xe6 19 ♕xe6 fxe6 20 a4 b4 21 ♖ad1 ♖ad8 22 ♖xd8 ♖xd8 23 ♔f2 c4 24 ♔f3 ♔f7 25 ♔e4 ♖d5 26 ♗d4 ♗c5 27 ♗xc5 ♖xc5 28 ♔d4 ♖c6 29 c3 bxc3 30 bxc3 ± Golubev-Mowsziszian, Berlin 1993.

a3) 10 f5 0-0 11 0-0 e5 12 ♘de2 ♘xb3 13 axb3 b5 14 ♗g5 ♗b7 15 ♗xf6 ♗xf6 16 b4 ♖c8 17 ♖fd1 ♕c7 18 ♕g4 ♕b6+ 19 ♔h1 ♖c4 20 b3 ♖c7 21 ♖d3 ♖fc8 22 ♖ad1 ♕f2 23

♖f3 ½-½ Martens-Dam, Amsterdam 1990.

a4) 10 ♗e3 ♕c7 11 f5 ♗d7 12 0-0-0?! ♖c8 13 ♖d2 b5 14 a3 ∓ Schuh-King, Vienna 1991.

b) 9...♕c7 10 f5 e5 11 ♘de2 ♘xb3 12 axb3 ♗d7 13 ♗g5 ♗c6 14 ♘g3 ♗e7 15 h4 0-0-0 16 0-0-0 ♕a5 17 ♗xf6 ♗xf6 18 ♔b1 ♗e7 19 ♘d5 ♗xd5 20 ♖xd5 ♕b4 21 ♘e2 ♔b8 22 ♘c3 ♖c8 23 ♖d3 ♕a5 24 g3 ♖c6 25 b4 ♕d8 26 ♘d5 h6 27 ♖a3 ♖e8 28 ♕e3 b5 29 b3 ♕c8 30 c4 +– Filipenko-Gaponenko, USSR 1991.

c) 9...♕d7 10 0-0 b5 11 e5 ♗b7 12 ♕d1 dxe5 13 fxe5 ♘xb3 14 ♘xb3 ♕xd1 15 ♖xd1 = Ćirić-Bradvarević, Yugoslavia 1965.

10 f5   ♗d7
11 fxe6?!

It is premature to release the tension. If there is instant pressure against e6 then it is commendable; otherwise Black is simply presented with an open f-file.

11 ...   fxe6
12 ♗g5   ♗e7
13 0-0-0   0-0

Black might consider 13...♕c8!? to avoid the pin.

14 e5   ♘fe4? *(D)*

Instead 14...♘d5! 15 ♗xe7 ♘xe7 16 ♕e3 d5 leaves the bishop on b3 a spectator. At the board, Kasparov wrongly focused his attention on the line 15 ♗xe7 ♘xe7 16 ♕e3 ♘xc3 (16...♘f2!?) 17 ♕xc3 ♕g5+ ∓.

15 ♗xe7   ♕xe7

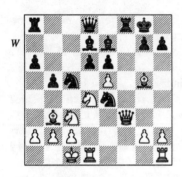

16 ♞xe4!

A forced continuation that had been foreseen by Short.

16 ...	**♖xf3**
17 exd6	**♞xb3+**
18 ♞xb3	**♛f8**
19 gxf3	**♛xf3**

19...♖d8 could be considered, to try to slow down the passed pawn's progress.

20 ♞ec5

The position has clarified: White has an advantage because the passed d-pawn is a real menace which ties down Black's forces.

20 ...	**♗c6**
21 ♖he1	**e5**
22 d7	**♖d8**
23 ♖d6	**a5!?**

Kasparov had initially considered the incredible line 23...♗d5 24 ♖d1 ♗xb3 25 ♞xb3 e4 26 ♞a5 e3 27 ♞c6 e2 28 ♞xd8 ♛f4+ 29 ♔b1 ♛xd6! 30 ♖xd6 e1♛+ 31 ♖d1 ♛xd1#. However, 24 ♞d2! ♛f2 25 ♞d3 spoils the fun. After the move played, Black is objectively lost but

has various resources to prolong the struggle. One way is to time the sacrifice of the bishop for the d-pawn to coincide with taking the h-pawn. Black could then cause problems by pushing the passed e- and h-pawns. The text is a good way to seek confusion by trying to disturb the harmony of White's knights. Now 24 ♞xa5 ♛f4+ 25 ♔b1 ♛b4 26 ♖xe5 ♛xa5 27 ♖xc6 ♛d2 28 a4! is still better for White.

24 a3!	**a4**
25 ♞d2	**♛g2**
26 c3	**♗d5**

The immediate 26...♗xd7 allows White to keep the h-pawn after 27 ♞xd7 ♖e8 28 ♖xe5 ♖xe5 29 ♞xe5.

27 ♞d3	**♗b3**
28 ♞xe5	

Not 28 ♖xe5 h6! 29 ♖e8+ ♔h7 30 ♖xd8?? ♛h1+ −+.

28 ...	**♛xh2**
29 ♞c6	**♛xd6**
30 ♖e8+	**♔f7**
31 ♞xd8+	**♔g6**
32 ♞e6	

In frantic time-trouble Short makes a series of misjudgments. He had seen the line 32 ♖e6+ ♗xe6 33 ♞xe6 ♛xe6 (33...♛xd7 34 ♞f8+) 34 d8♛+− but wanted to find something even clearer. Objectively, the text does no major damage, but it was the first step downhill for Short.

32 ...   **♛h2!**

If 32...♛xd7 then 33 ♞f8+ ♔f7 34 ♞xd7 wins for White.

33 ♘f4+

The appealing 33 d8♕ fails: 33...♕g1+ 34 ♘f1 ♕xf1+ 35 ♔d2 ♕f2+ 36 ♔d3 ♗c2#. Approaching from another angle would prove more successful: 33 ♖f8! ♕h4 34 ♘f3 ♕h1+ 35 ♔d2 ♕d1+ 36 ♔e3 ♕c1+ 37 ♔f2 wins for White.

33	**...**	**♔h6**
34	**♘d3**	**♕g1+**
35	**♖e1**	

35 ♘e1? ♕g4! 36 ♘xb3 ♕xd7 and Black wins.

35 ... ♕g5 *(D)*

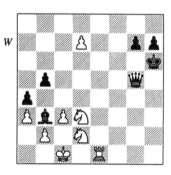

36 ♘e5?

An easy win is possible: 36 ♖h1+ ♔g6 37 ♘e5+ ♔f5 38 ♘c6 +−.

36	**...**	**g6**
37	**♖f1**	

37 ♘c6!? ♕f5 38 ♘e4 ♕f4+ (better than 38...♕xd7? 39 ♖h1+ ♔g7 40 ♖xh7+ ♔xh7 41 ♘f6+ +−) 39 ♔b1 ♗d5! 40 d8♕ (40 ♘c5 ♕d2!) 40...♗xe4+ 41 ♔a1 ♗xc6 keeps an advantage for White.

37	**...**	**♗e6**
38	**♘f7+**	

38 ♖f8!? ♕g1+ 39 ♔c2 ♗xd7 (or 39...♗f5+ 40 ♖xf5) 40 ♘xd7 leaves White much better.

38	**...**	**♗xf7**
39	**♖xf7**	**♕d5**
40	**♖e7?**	

Short misses his last chance to finish the game in style: 40 ♘e4 ♕d3 41 ♖f2 ♕xd7 42 ♖xh2 ♔g7 43 ♖xh7+ ♔xh7 44 ♘f6+ and White wins.

40	**...**	**♕d6**
41	**♖f7**	

The time-control has been reached, and the assessment of the position has altered irrevocably. White's winning chances have vanished due to the threat of perpetual check.

41	**...**	**♕d3**
42	**♘e4**	**♕e3+**
43	**♘d2**	**♕d3**

½-½

2 Fischer Attack with 7...b5

Game 7
Byrne – Fischer
Sousse IZ 1967

1 e4 c5 2 ♘f3 d6 3 d4 cxd4 4 ♘xd4
♘f6 5 ♘c3 a6 6 ♗c4 e6

    7 ♗b3   b5

An active move which aims to put pressure on e4 by threatening ...b4 and preparing to fianchetto.

    8 f4

It can be seen from later games that 8 0-0 is the usual continuation nowadays, but this aggressive and highly committal formation was the fashion in the 1950s and 1960s.

    8 ...   ♗b7 *(D)*

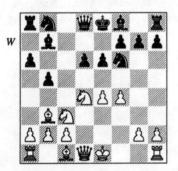

Black enters the critical line of the variation. Others:

a) 8...♗e7 transposes to the next illustrative game.

b) Grabbing the e-pawn is a risky venture: 8...b4?! 9 ♘a4 ♘xe4 10 0-0 g6?! (10...♘f6!?) 11 f5! gxf5 (or 11...exf5 12 ♗d5 ♖a7 13 ♘xf5! gxf5 14 ♕d4 and White wins) 12 ♘xf5 ♖g8 (12...exf5 13 ♕d5 ♖a7 14 ♕d4 +–; 12...d5 13 ♘h6 ♗xh6 14 ♗xh6 ±; 12...♗b7 13 ♘h6!? ♗xh6 14 ♕h5 ♕e7 15 ♗xh6 ♖g8 16 g3 ♘d7 17 ♖ae1 ♘e5 18 ♗f4 ∞ Szeles-Sax, Hungary 1972) 13 ♗d5 ♖a7 (13...exd5 14 ♕xd5 ♗xf5 15 ♖xf5 ♖a7 16 ♕xe4+ ♖e7 17 ♕xb4 ♖e2 18 ♗g5 ♖xg5 19 ♖xg5 ♕xg5 20 ♕xb8+ +– Panov) 14 ♗xe4? (14 ♗e3! ♘c5 15 ♕h5! ♖g6 {15...♘xa4 16 ♗xa7 exd5 17 ♖ae1+} 16 ♖ae1 ± Kevitz) 14...exf5 15 ♗xf5 ♖e7! ∓ Fischer-Tal, Bled Ct 1959.

    9 f5

At this stage it might be best to play 9 ♗e3 transposing to Game 9, especially since the move-order might confuse Black.

For 9 0-0 see Game 11.

White is in no position to bring up sufficient reinforcements to make the tempting sacrifice 9 ♗xe6 worthwhile: 9...fxe6 10 ♘xe6 ♕c8

11 ♘d5 ♗xd5 12 exd5 ♘bd7 (better than 12...♕c4?! 13 b3 ♕e4+ 14 ♔f2 ♔d7 15 c4! bxc4 16 bxc4 ♕xc4 17 ♖b1 ♕xd5 18 ♖b7+!= Gross-Bönsch, Dečin 1976) 13 ♕e2 ♕c4! 14 ♘c7+ ♔d8 15 ♕xc4 bxc4 16 ♘xa8 ♔c8 ∓ Plachetka.

9 ...   e5

It would appear that Black has been forced to make a positional concession. The d-pawn is backward and White has control of d5. However, there is normally insufficient time for White to consolidate and create a bind on d5 because Black can undermine the e4 pawn by advancing his b-pawn – but care is needed, e.g. not 9...b4? 10 fxe6! ±.

10 ♘de2   ♘bd7

Black sensibly continues developing and wisely declines to win the e-pawn at this juncture: 10...♘xe4 (10...b4?! 11 ♘d5 ♘xe4 12 ♗e3 and 0-0 ±) 11 ♗d5!? (11 ♘xe4 ♗xe4 12 0-0 intending ♘g3 ± Nunn) 11...♘c5 12 b4 ♕h4+ 13 g3 ♕xb4 14 ♗xb7 ♘xb7 15 ♕d5 ♖a7 16 ♗e3 ♘c5 17 ♖b1 ♕a3 18 ♖b3! ♕a5 19 ♗xc5 dxc5 20 ♕xe5+ is winning for White.

11 ♗g5

Gobet-Nunn, Biel 1983, continued 11 0-0 ♖c8 12 ♗g5 ♗e7 13 ♔h1! h6 (13...0-0 14 ♘g3! ±) 14 ♗xf6 ♘xf6 15 ♕d3 0-0 16 ♖ad1 ♕c7 17 a3 ♕c5 18 ♘g3 b4 ∞.

11 ...   ♗e7 (D)

12 ♘g3

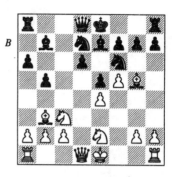

12 ♗xf6 ♘xf6 13 ♕d3 aims to dominate the d5 square, while using the queen to support e4, but this artificial plan is not too convincing:

a) 13...♖c8 14 0-0-0 0-0 15 ♔b1 ♕b6 16 h3 a5 17 g4 a4 18 ♗d5 (Byrne-Popović, Sarajevo 1970) 18...♘xd5 19 exd5 (19 ♘xd5 ♗xd5 20 ♕xd5 ♖c5 21 ♕d3 b4 22 h4 ♖fc8 =) 19...♗a6 20 ♘e4 b4 21 ♕f3 b3 ∞.

b) 13...♕b6!? 14 h3 0-0 15 0-0-0 a5! 16 ♘d5 (16 g4 a4 17 ♗d5 b4! 18 ♗xb7? bxc3 −+) 16...♗xd5 17 ♗xd5 ♖ac8 18 ♔b1 ♖c5! 19 g4 ♖fc8 20 ♘c3? h6 21 ♖d2 a4 ∓ Suetin-Platonov, USSR 1971.

12 ...   ♖c8

Black brings the rook into play and thus the thematic exchange sacrifice ...♖xc3 comes into the reckoning. Castling is rather premature and invites White to launch an attack: 12...0-0 13 ♗xf6 ♘xf6 14 ♘h5 ♘xh5 15 ♕xh5 ♖c8 16 ♕e2 (or 16 ♗d5 ♗xd5 17 ♘xd5 ♖xc2 18 0-0 ♗f6 19 b3 h6 20 ♖fc1 ♖xc1+ 21

♖xc1 with compensation for the pawn; Padevski-Minić, Polanica Zdroj 1963) 16...♕b6 17 0-0-0 ± Hennings-McCurdy, Harrachov 1967.

13   0-0 *(D)*

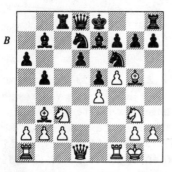

This appears to be a logical move but since this game another route has been examined. Upon 13 ♗xf6 ♘xf6 14 ♘h5 play might continue:

a) 14...♘xh5 15 ♕xh5 0-0 16 ♕e2 =.

b) 14...♖xc3!? 15 bxc3 and now:

b1) 15...♗xe4 16 ♘xg7+ ♔f8 17 ♘h5 ♖g8 (Cosulich-Minić, Bari 1970) 18 ♘xf6 ♗xf6 19 ♕h5 intending 0-0-0 ∞.

b2) 15...♘xe4 16 ♘xg7+ ♔f8 17 ♘h5 (17 ♕h5 ♔xg7!) 17...♕b6! 18 ♕e2 ♗h4+ (18...♘xc3 19 ♕f2) 19 g3 ♘xc3 ∓ King.

13   ...   h5!

A fantastic move that suddenly changes the whole nature of the position. The threat of ...h4 and ...♘xe4 is surprisingly difficult to

contain. This famous game effectively saw Fischer seemingly refute his own system, which caused its popularity to plummet.

14   h4

In Bednarski-Lehmann, Palma 1967, White failed to find an improvement: 14 ♗xf6 ♘xf6 15 ♕f3 ♖xc3 16 ♕xc3 h4 17 ♘e2 ♕b6+ 18 ♔h1 ♘xe4 19 ♕h3 (19 ♕e1 h3!) 19...♘g5 20 ♕g4 h3 21 ♖g1 ♘e4 −+.

14   ...   b4

15   ♗xf6

After 15 ♘d5 ♘xd5 16 ♗xd5 ♗xg5 17 hxg5 ♗xd5 18 ♕xd5 ♕xg5 Black is winning.

15   ...   ♗xf6!

Black reveals his intention of attacking h4 and then the white king. It is far less convincing just to win a pawn: 15...♘xf6 16 ♘d5 ♘xd5 17 exd5 ♗xh4 18 ♘e4 and White has some counterchances.

16   ♘d5   ♗xh4

17   ♘xh5   ♕g5

18   f6

A necessary measure to defend the knight as now 18...♖xh5 19 ♖f5! or 18...♕xh5 19 fxg7 wins.

18   ...   g6

19   ♘g7+   ♔d8

20   ♖f3   ♗g3 *(D)*

White is in dire straits. The open h-file allows Black to create mating threats.

21   ♕d3   ♗h2+

22   ♔f1   ♘c5

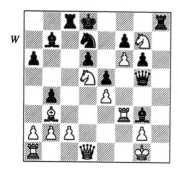

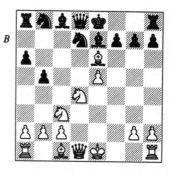

23 Rh3   Rh4!

Fischer has no wish invite complications with 23...Nxd3 24 Rxh8+ Kd7 25 Ba4+, and concentrates on his attack.

24	Qf3	Nxb3
25	axb3	Rxh3
26	Qxh3	Bxd5
27	exd5	Qxf6+
28	Ke1	Qf4

0-1

Game 8
Morozevich – Agrest
St Petersburg Z 1993

1 e4 c5 2 Nf3 e6 3 d4 cxd4 4 Nxd4 a6 5 Nc3 d6 6 Bc4 Nf6 7 Bb3

7	...	Be7
8	f4	b5
9	e5	dxe5
10	fxe5	Nfd7
11	Bxe6!? *(D)*	

A thematic sacrifice. This little-known line has been revived by the ambitious young Russian.

11	...	Nxe5

The only move. Black fights for the initiative, and challenges White to justify his committal play. If 11...fxe6? then White has a crushing attack: 12 Nxe6 Qa5 (12...Qb6 13 Nd5) 13 Nxg7+ Kd8 (13...Kf8 14 0-0+ +−) 14 Ne6+ Ke8 15 Qh5#.

12 Bxc8

The alternatives are not convincing: 12 Bd5 Ra7 13 Bf4 Bd6 intending ...Re7 ∓ or 12 Bf4 fxe6 13 Bxe5 0-0 14 Qg4 (14 Qe2 b4 15 Ne4 Qd5!) 14...Bh4+ 15 g3 Bf6 16 Qe4 Bxe5 17 Qxe5 Bb7 ∓ Nunn.

12	...	Qxc8
13	Nd5!?	

This is the move that has attracted all the attention. It facilitates more tactics than the old main line which continued: 13 Bf4 Nbc6 14 Nxc6 Nxc6 15 0-0 0-0 16 Nd5 Ra7 17 Kh1 Rd8 18 Qf3 Qf5 19 Nxe7+ Nxe7 20 Qe3 Qd7 21 Bd6 Rb7 22 Qf3 Nd5 23 Bc5 Rc7 24 b4 Rc6 25 Qd3 ½-½ Sax-Nunn, London 1980.

13	...	Bc5

It is easy to go wrong:

a) 13...♘bc6 14 ♘b6 ♕d8 15 ♘xc6 +–.

b) 13...♗h4+ 14 g3 ♕c4 15 ♘f3 is good for White.

c) 13...♖a7 14 ♕h5 ♘bc6 15 ♘f5 0-0 (Morozevich-Mitenkov, USSR 1991) 16 ♗e3! ±.

14 b4   ♗a7 (D)

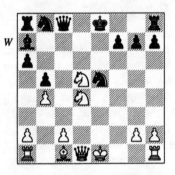

An instinctive reaction which allows White to maintain the pressure. Other poor replies are 14...♗xd4 15 ♕xd4 ♘bc6 16 ♕c5 ♕g4 17 ♗f4 and 14...♗xb4+ 15 ♘xb4 ♕c3+ 16 ♕d2 ♕xa1 17 0-0 when White is winning.

The right way is for Black to counterattack with 14...♕d7! which ensures a myriad of complications. In Yagupov-Moiseev, Podolsk 1992, White proceeded in robust fashion; his notes demonstrate a better treatment: 15 ♘f3 ♗d6! (not 15...♘xf3+ 16 ♕xf3 ♗a7 17 ♗b2 0-0 18 0-0-0! +–) 16 0-0 (16 ♘b6? ♗xb4+ 17 ♗d2 ♘xf3+ 18 gxf3 ♕xd2+ 19 ♕xd2 ♗xd2+ 20 ♔xd2 ♖a7 ∓)

16...♘bc6 17 ♘b6 ♕a7 18 ♗e3 ♖d8 19 ♘c4 (19 ♘xe5 ♗xe5 20 ♕f3 ♘d4 21 ♕e4 ♕e7! 22 ♔h1 ∞) 19...♕e7 (19...♕c7? 20 ♗b6 +–; 19...♕d7?! 20 ♘xd6+ ♕xd6 21 ♕xd6 ♖xd6 22 ♗c5 ±) 20 ♘xd6+ ♖xd6 21 ♕e1 ♘d7 (21...♘xf3+ 22 ♖xf3 ♖e6 23 ♕c3 {23 ♕f2 ♘e5 24 ♖g3 ♘d7 25 ♗d4 f6 ∞} 23...f6 {23...♘e5 24 ♖g3} 24 a4 ±) 22 ♕c3 (22 ♘h4! g6 23 ♕g3 ♖e6 24 ♗h6 ±) 22...0-0 23 ♖ae1 ♖e6 24 ♘g5 (24 ♘d4 ♘xd4 25 ♗xd4 ♖e8 26 ♖xe6 fxe6 is unclear) 24...♖g6! (24...♖e5 25 ♕d3 g6 26 ♗d2 ±) 25 ♗c1 ♘ce5 (25...♕xb4!? 26 ♕h3 h6 27 ♘e4 ♘de5 28 ♔h1 ∞) 26 ♘h3 ∞ ½-½.

15 ♗f4   ♕d7

In answer to 15...♕c4 White's superior development is evident upon 16 ♘f5 ♕e4+ 17 ♕e2 ±.

16 ♗xe5

The plausible 16 ♘f3 falls in with Black's plans: 16...♘bc6! 17 ♗xe5 0-0-0 18 ♗xg7 ♖he8+ 19 ♔f1 ♕xd5 20 ♕xd5 ♖xd5 ∞.

16 ...   ♕xd5

17 ♗xg7

Morozevich gives 17 ♕e2 as an adventurous alternative. Black's position rapidly becomes critical: 17...0-0 (17...♕c4 18 ♕xc4 bxc4 19 ♗xg7 +–) 18 0-0-0 ♗xd4 (both 18...♕c4 19 ♕f3 ♘d7 20 ♗xg7 and 18...♕xa2 19 ♘f5 f6 20 ♗xf6 ♖xf6 21 ♖d8+ win for White) 19 ♖d4 with a clear plus for White.

17 ...   ♕xg2

18	♕e2+	♕xe2+
19	♔xe2	♗xd4
20	♗xd4	

The situation has clarified somewhat. White has emerged with a slight advantage thanks to his dominant bishop.

20	...	♖g8
21	a4	♘c6
22	♗c5	0-0-0
23	axb5	♖ge8+
24	♔f3	axb5
25	♖hd1! *(D)*	

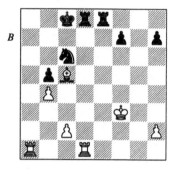

It is a correct policy to offer the trade of rooks because the white king would then have easier access to the kingside.

25	...	♔c7
26	h4	♘e5+
27	♔f4	♖xd1

A scheme to snare the king is harmless: 27...♘g6+ 28 ♔g5 h6+ 29 ♔h5! ±.

28	♖xd1	♘d7
29	♗d4	♔c6
30	♖a1?!	

Morozevich prefers 30 c3 intending ♖g1-g7 as a clear winning attempt.

30	...	♔d5
31	c3	♖e4+
32	♔g3	♖e6?!

Black should continue actively with 32...♘e5! intending ...f5-f4 which would ensure equality.

| 33 | ♖a7 | ♔c6 |
| 34 | h5 | |

Now ...♖g6+ is ruled out and the king can make progress.

34...♔d6 35 ♔f4 h6 36 ♔f5 ♖e1 37 ♖a6+ ♔d5 38 ♖xh6 ♘e5 39 ♖f6!

The passed pawn ensures victory.

39...♘f3 40 ♗c5 ♖h1 41 ♔f4 ♘e1 42 ♔g5 ♔c4 43 ♖xf7 ♔xc3 44 h6 ♘d3 45 h7 ♔c4

There is no respite: 45...♘xb4 46 ♗xb4+ ♔xb4 47 ♖f4+ ♔c3 48 ♖h4 or 45...♘xc5 46 bxc5 b4 47 c6 and White wins.

46 ♗d6 ♖g1+ 47 ♔h6 ♔d5 48 ♖f5+! 1-0

Game 9
Velimirović – Gutman
Metz 1988

1 e4 c5 2 ♘f3 d6 3 d4 cxd4 4 ♘xd4 ♘f6 5 ♘c3 a6 6 ♗c4 e6 7 ♗b3 b5 8 ♗e3

A relatively rare choice which has enjoyed limited success. Some even more obscure 8th move alternatives are examined in the next game.

8   ...   ♗b7 *(D)*

A critical test of the line is to dare to take the e-pawn. On 8...b4 9 ♘a4 ♘xe4 play could continue:

a) 10 ♘xe6! fxe6 (10...♗xe6 11 ♗d5 +−) 11 ♘b6 ♗b7 12 ♘xa8 ♗xa8 13 ♗xe6 ± Milić.

b) 10 ♘b6!? ♕xb6 11 ♘xe6 ♕xe3+ 12 fxe3 fxe6 (12...♗xe6? 13 ♗d5 +−) 13 ♕f3 d5 14 ♗xd5 exd5 15 ♕h5+ is unclear, according to Velimirović.

c) 10 0-0 ♘f6 11 ♖e1 ♗e7 12 ♘b6! ♕xb6 13 ♘xe6 ♕b7 14 ♘xg7+ ♔d8 15 ♗xf7 ∞ Konikowski-Klusek, Corr 1975.

9 f4   ♘bd7

Once again capturing the e-pawn is hazardous while Black's development is lagging: 9....♘xe4 10 ♘xe4 ♗xe4 11 0-0 or 9...b4 10 ♘a4 ♘xe4 11 0-0 when White has sufficient compensation for the pawn.

An important alternative is 9...♗e7 when after 10 0-0 a main line is entered:

a) 10...♘c6 11 a3 (11 ♘xc6 ♗xc6 12 f5 b4 13 ♘a4 exf5 14 exf5 {14 ♘b6?! ♗xe4! 15 ♗a4+ ♔f8 16 ♘xa8 ♕xa8 17 ♕e2 h5 ∓ Ceschia-Gaprindashvili, Reggio Emilia 1982/83} 14...♖b8 15 ♕d4 0-0 ± Glek-Grigorian, Kuibyshev 1981) 11...0-0 (11...♘xd4 12 ♕xd4 0-0 13 f5 e5 14 ♕d3 ♖ac8 15 ♖ad1 h6 ∞ Ulybin-Gelfand, USSR 1986) 12 ♕f3 ♘a5 (12...♘xd4 13 ♗xd4 ♖c8 14 ♖ad1 a5! 15 ♘xb5 ♗xe4 16 ♕e2 d5 17 ♘a7 ♖c7 18 ♘b5 = Sznapik-Ftačnik, Trnava 1984) 13 ♗xe6 fxe6 14 ♘xe6 ♕d7 15 ♘xf8 ♖xf8 16 ♖ad1 ♕e6 with equality; Božek-Cvetković, Lesko 1985.

b) 10...♘bd7 11 ♗xe6?! fxe6 12 ♘xe6 ♕c8 13 ♗d4 (13 ♘xg7+ ♔f7 14 ♘f5 ♗f8 15 e5?! ♖g8 16 ♘h4 ♕c6 ∓ Witomski-Larsen, Corr 1986) 13...♖g8 14 ♘d5 ♗xd5 15 exd5 ♘f8 16 ♖e1 ♘xe6 17 ♖xe6 ♖f8 18 ♕e2 ♖f7 ∓ Thorsen-Poulsen, Corr 1985.

c) 10...b4 and now:

c1) 11 ♘d5?! exd5 12 e5 dxe5 13 fxe5 0-0! (13...♘e4 14 ♘f5!) 14 ♘f5 ♘e8 15 ♗xd5 ♘c6 16 ♖f3? ♖b8! 17 ♗f4 ♗c5+ 18 ♔h1 ♘e7 0-1 de Firmian-H.Olafsson, New York 1987.

c2) 11 e5 bxc3 12 exf6 ♗xf6 and now:

c21) 13 bxc3 0-0 (13...♕c7!?) 14 ♕d2 ♗e4 (14...♕c7 15 ♖ad1 and now 15...d5!? 16 g4 =, A.Ivanov-Oll, USSR 1985, should be preferred to

15...♘d7?! 16 f5 e5 17 ♘e6! fxe6 18 fxe6 ♘c5 19 e7+ ♖f7 20 ♖xf6! ♘xb3 21 ♖xf7 ± Velimirović-Andersson, Moscow 1982) 15 ♖ad1 ♕a5 16 c4 (16 ♘e2 d5 17 ♘g3 ♗xc3 18 ♕e2 g6 19 ♘xe4 dxe4 20 f5! gxf5 21 g4! ± Inkiov-Andersson, Bor 1983) 16...♕xd2 17 ♖xd2 ♖c8 18 f5 e5 19 ♘e2 ♗e7 20 ♘g3 ♗c6 21 f6! ♗xf6 22 ♖xd6 ♗e7 23 c5! ♗xd6 24 ♖xf7 ♔h8 25 cxd6 ♘d7 26 ♗e6 ♖d8 27 ♘f5 ♘f8 28 ♗b3 ♗e4? (28...♖d7!?) 29 ♖xg7! ♘g6 30 ♗g5 ♗xf5 31 ♗f6 1-0 Canda-Diaz, Managua 1984.

c22) 13 f5 e5 14 ♗a4+ (14 ♘e2 cxb2 15 ♖b1 0-0 16 ♖xb2 ♕c7 17 ♗d5 ♗xd5 18 ♕xd5 ♘c6 with equality; de Firmian-Pinter, Copenhagen 1985) 14...♔e7 (14...♘d7!?) 15 ♘e2 cxb2 16 ♖b1 ♗c6 (Honfi-Božek, Wroclaw 1984) 17 ♗xc6 ♘xc6 18 ♘c3 ∞.

c23) 13 ♗a4+ ♘d7 14 f5 exf5 15 ♘xf5 0-0 16 bxc3 ♘c5 17 ♗b3 ♗xc3 18 ♖b1 ∞ Honfi-Pinter, Budapest 1983.

d) 10...♘xe4? 11 ♘xe4 ♗xe4 12 f5 e5 13 ♗xf7+ ♔xf7 14 ♕h5+ ♔g8 15 ♘e6 g6 16 ♕h6 ♗f8 17 f6! +–.

10 0-0 *(D)*

10 ...   ♖c8

A critical reply is 10...b4 11 ♘a4 and now:

a) 11...♘xe4 12 f5 e5 13 ♕h5 ♕e7 14 ♘e6 ♘df6 (14...♘ef6 15 ♕h4 fxe6 16 fxe6 ♘b8 17 ♗g5 ±) 15 ♘b6! ♗c6 (15...♘xh5 16 ♗a4+

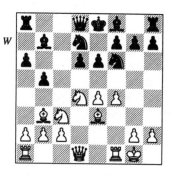

♕d7 17 ♗xd7+ ♔e7 18 ♘a8 fxe6 19 fxe6! ±) 16 ♕e2 fxe6 (16...♗b5 17 ♗c4!) 17 ♘xa8 ♗xa8 18 fxe6 ♕b7 19 a3 d5 20 axb4 ♗xb4 21 ♖xa6 ♗c5 (21...0-0 22 ♖b6 +–; 21...♗e7 22 ♗a4+ ♔f8 23 ♗c6 +–) 22 ♖xa8+ ♕xa8 23 ♕b5+ 1-0 Afek-Magem, Calella 1985.

b) 11...♗xe4 12 f5 e5 13 ♘e6! fxe6 14 fxe6 ♘b8 (14...♘c5 15 ♖xf6!) 15 ♘b6 ♗e7 (15...♘c6? 16 ♖xf6 gxf6 17 ♗d5 +–; 15...♖a7 16 ♗a4+ ♗c6 {16...♔e7 17 ♖xf6! gxf6 18 ♕g4! ♗a8 19 ♖f1 +–} 17 ♘d5 ♘xd5 18 ♗xc6+ ♘xc6 19 ♕d5 ♖c7 20 ♗b6 ∞ Velimirović) 16 ♗a4+ ♗c6? (16...♘c6 17 ♖xf6 ♗xf6 18 ♕g4 ±) 17 ♘xa8 ♗xa4 18 ♗b6 ♕c8 19 ♖xf6 ♗xc2 20 ♖c1 ♗xf6 21 ♖xc2 ♕b7 22 ♕xd6 ♗e7 23 ♘c7+ ♔f8 24 ♖f2+ 1-0 Velimirović-Suba, Pinerolo 1987.

10...♗e7 transposes to the note 'b' to Black's 9th move.

11 ♕e2

The queen wishes to stay on the d1-h5 diagonal in order to reserve

attacking options. Moreover, after
...b4 the pawn on a6 will come under
scrutiny. In Velimirović-Portisch,
Szirak 1987, White unwisely sought
to initiate a brash attack: 11 f5?! e5
12 ♘e6 fxe6 13 fxe6 ♘c5 14 ♘d5
♗xd5 15 ♗xd5 ♗e7 16 g4 0-0 17
g5 ♘xd5 18 ♕xd5 ♕c7 19 ♖f5 ♕b7
—+.

11 ...   b4
12 ♘a4

The game Velimirović-Vaulin,
Belgrade 1993, saw another instruc-
tive approach that is supplemented
by Black's analysis: 12 e5!? dxe5
(12...bxc3 13 exf6 ♘xf6 ±) 13 fxe5
♘xe5 14 ♖ad1 ♘ed7 (14...♕c7?! 15
♗a4+ ♘ed7 16 ♖xf6 gxf6 17 ♘xe6
fxe6 18 ♖xd7 ♕xd7 19 ♗xd7+
♔xd7 20 ♘a4 intending ♘b6+ ±;
14...bxc3 15 ♘xe6 fxe6 16 ♖xd8+
♖xd8 17 ♗f4 ♗c5+ 18 ♔h1 0-0 19
♕xe5 {19 ♗xe6+ ♔h8 20 ♕xe5
♘e4!} 19...♗d5 ±) 15 ♘a4!? (15
♘xe6 fxe6 16 ♗xe6 bxc3 and now:
17 ♗xd7+ ♕xd7 18 ♖xd7 ♔xd7 19
♖d1+ ♘d5 20 bxc3 ♔c7 ∞; 17
♗g5!? ♗e7 18 ♖xd7 ♕xd7
{18...♘xd7? 19 ♕h5+ g6 20 ♗f7+
♔f8 21 ♕h6#} 19 ♗xd7+ ♔xd7 20
♖d1+ ♔e8 21 ♖e1 ♖c7 22 ♕e5 ♔d8
23 ♖d1+ ♖d7 24 ♕b8+ ♗c8 25
♕b6+ ♔e8 26 ♖xd7 ♔xd7 27 bxc3
∞) 15...♕a5 16 ♘xe6 fxe6 17 ♗d4
e5 18 ♘b6 ♗c5 19 ♘xd7 ♘xd7 20
♖f7 ♗xd4+ 21 ♖xd4 ♗c6 22 ♖d1
♖f8 23 ♖xg7 ♔d8 24 ♗e6 ♖c7 25
♕e3! ∞.

12 ...   ♕a5

Or 12...♘xe4 13 f5 e5 14 ♘e6
♕h4 (14...fxe6 15 ♕h5+ g6 16 fxg6
+—) 15 ♘xf8 ♔xf8 16 a3 ∞. Black
can also consider 12...♗e7!? intending to whisk the king to safety when
White has the slightly better
chances.

13 a3   bxa3
14 ♖xa3   ♕h5

Black appears to have found a
remedy to thwart the attack. He offers an exchange of queens which, if
avoided, allows the awkward ...♘g4
or even ...♘xe4.

15 ♕xh5   ♘xh5
16 f5   e5
17 ♘e6! (D)

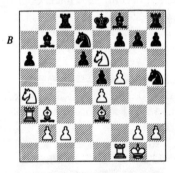

A remarkable way to continue the
attack. White sacrifices a knight to
disrupt Black's defences and secure
an enduring initiative.

17 ...   fxe6

17...♗xe4 only helps White – after 18 ♘xf8 ♔xf8 19 ♘c3 ♗b7 20
♗d5 the important a-pawn will fall,

allowing the queen's rook to infiltrate with advantage.

18	fxe6	♘df6

18...♘b8 is not possible because it allows White to unleash a discovered attack: 19 e7! ♗xe7 20 ♗f7+ ♔d8 21 ♗xh5 ♖xc2 22 ♗b6+ ♔d7 (22...♔c8 23 ♗g4+ ♘d7 24 ♖f7 ±) 23 ♗g4+ ♔c6 24 ♗d1 ♖c4 25 ♗e3 ±.

19	♘b6	♖c7

19...♖b8? allows White a bind on the position: 20 ♘d5 ♘xd5 21 exd5 ♘f6 22 ♗a4+ ♔e7 23 c4 ♗c8 24 ♗g5 intending 25 ♖af3 and ♖xf6, which is in White's favour according to Baljon.

20	♘d5	♘xd5
21	exd5	♘f6
22	c4	♗e7
23	♗a4+	♔f8
24	♖b3!	

The rook is well placed to exploit Black's cramped conditions by being a useful addition to the manoeuvre ♗a7-b8, removing the rook from the defence of b7.

24	...	♔g8
25	♗a7 *(D)*	
25	...	♗f8!

A necessary retreat to stem the tactics. For example:

a) 25...♗xd5? 26 cxd5 ♖xa7 27 ♖b8+ ♗f8 28 ♗d7! and 29 e7 winning.

b) 25...♗c8? 26 ♖b8 g6 {26...h6 27 ♗b6 ♖xc4 28 ♗b3 ♖b4 29 ♖xc8+ ♔h7 30 ♗c2+ ±} 27 ♗b6

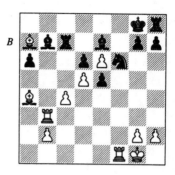

♖xc4 28 ♗b3 ♖b4 29 ♖xc8+ ♔g7 30 ♖c7 ♖e8 31 ♗e3! ♖xb3 32 ♗g5! +− Baljon.

26	♗b8	♖xc4
27	♖xb7	♖xa4
28	e7	♗xe7
29	♖xe7	h6?!

It is logical to give the king an escape square but 29...h5! is the answer to the situation. The crucial difference is that Black can activate his king's rook: 30 ♗xd6 ♘xd5 31 ♖a7 (31 ♖e8+ ♔h7 32 ♖xe5 ♘f6 33 ♗e7 ♔g6 =) 31...♖h6! 32 ♗xe5 ♖g6 =.

30 ♗xd6 ♘xd5 31 ♖a7 ♘e3 32 ♖f3 ♘g4 33 h3 ♖a1+ 34 ♖f1 ♖xf1+ 35 ♔xf1 ♘e3+ 36 ♔e2 ♘c4 37 ♗c7!

Now 38 b3 is the threat, so Black is obliged to allow a trade of pawns. White is still clinging to the advantage due to Black's dormant rook.

37...♘xb2 38 ♗xe5 ♘c4 39 ♗d4 ♖h7 40 ♖a8+ ♔f7 41 ♖xa6

The knight is running out of squares and the threat of ♔d3 means that the rook must come to its support.

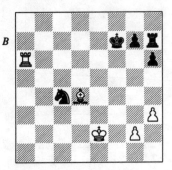

41...♖h8 42 ♔d3 ♖c8 43 ♖a7+ ♔e6 44 ♖xg7 ♘e5+ 45 ♔e4

White has won a pawn, which is sufficient advantage to win considering the activity of his pieces and the weakness of the h6-pawn.

White rounded up the other pawn and completed the technical part of the game as follows:

45...♘f7 46 ♖g6+ ♔e7 47 ♗e3 ♘d6+ 48 ♔d5 ♘f5 49 ♗xh6 ♔f7 50 ♖a6 ♖c2 51 g4 ♘e7+ 52 ♔e4 ♘g6 53 ♗g5 ♖c4+ 54 ♔d5 ♖b4 55 ♖a7+ ♔g8 56 ♗h6 ♘h4 57 ♖g7+ ♔h8 58 ♖e7 ♖b3 59 ♗e3 ♔g8 60 ♔e4 ♔f8 61 ♖d7 ♔g8 62 ♖d3 ♖b4+ 63 ♗d4 ♘g2 64 ♖d2 ♘h4 65 ♖b2 ♖a4 66 ♖b6 ♔h7 67 g5 ♔g8 68 ♖f6 ♖b4 69 ♖f4 ♘g6 70 ♖f5 ♖a4 71 ♖f6 ♘h4 72 ♖b6 ♔f7 73 g6+ ♘xg6 74 ♖f6+ ♔g7 75 ♖a6+ ♖xd4+ 76 ♔xd4 ♔h6 77 ♔e4 ♔h5 78 ♖a5+ ♔h4 79 ♔f5! ♘e7+ 80 ♔f6 1-0

Game 10

Djurhuus – Tisdall
Gausdal 1994

1 e4 c5 2 ♘f3 d6 3 d4 cxd4 4 ♘xd4 ♘f6 5 ♘c3 a6 6 ♗c4 e6 7 ♗b3 b5 8 f3!? (D)

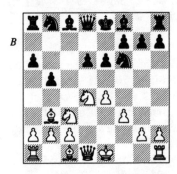

A logical if somewhat unusual move. White supports the e4 pawn and has aspirations of ♗e3, ♕d2 and g4.

Other ideas:

a) 8 ♗g5 and now:

a1) 8...b4 9 ♗xf6 ♕xf6 10 ♘a4 ♘d7 11 ♕d2 ♖b8 12 0-0 ♗b7 13 f4 ♗e7 14 f5 e5 15 ♘e6!? ♕h6 16 ♘c7+ ♔d8 17 ♕xh6 gxh6 18 ♘d5 ± Meister-Dvoirys, Voronezh 1988.

a2) 8...h6!? 9 ♗xf6 ♕xf6 10 ♕d3 ♘d7 11 0-0-0 ♗b7 12 f3 ♘c5 13 ♕e2 ♗e7 14 ♔b1 0-0 = Cueto-Livshits, Santiago 1990.

a3) 8....♗e7 9 ♕f3 and now:

a31) 9...0-0? 10 e5 dxe5 11 ♘xe6 ♗xe6 12 ♕xa8 +−.

a32) 9...♗b7? 10 ♗xe6! ♕b6 11

0-0-0 fxe6 12 ♘xe6 ♔f7 13 ♗e3
♕c6 14 ♘g5+ ♔e8 15 ♘d5 ±.

a33) 9...♕b6 10 0-0-0 ♕b7
(10...0-0 11 g4! ±; 10...♗b7 11 ♕h3
♘c6 12 ♗e3 ♘xd4 13 ♗xd4 ♕c7
14 f3 ∞ Doncević-Stern, Kecskemet
1984) 11 ♖he1 b4?! 12 ♘f5! exf5 13
♗xf6 ♗xf6 14 exf5+ ♔f8 15 ♕d3
♘c6 16 ♕xd6+ ♗e7 17 ♕d5 ♗g5+
18 f4! ♗xf4+ 19 ♔b1 g6 20 f6 ♗g4
21 ♖e7! ♗e6 1-0 Lazarev-Moiseev,
USSR 1989.
  b) 8 ♕e2 ♗e7 *(D)* and now:

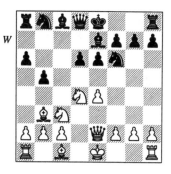

  b1) 9 g4 b4 (9...0-0 10 g5 ♘fd7
11 ♗xe6 fxe6 12 ♘xe6 ♕e8! 13
♘c7 ♕g6 14 ♘xa8 ♘e5 15 f4 ♗g4
∓ Cuesta-Vera, Cuban Ch 1985) 10
♘a4 d5 11 e5 ♘fd7 12 g5 ♗b7 13 f4
♘c6 14 ♗e3 ♕a5 15 c3 ♘xd4 16
♗xd4 ♗c6 17 ♕d1 0-0 18 0-0 ♖ab8
19 ♗c2 g6 20 ♖f3 ∞ Djurhuus-de
Firmian, Gausdal 1994.
  b2) 9 ♗e3 0-0 10 0-0-0 b4 11
♘a4 ♕a5 12 c3 bxc3 13 ♘xc3 ♗b7
14 f3 ♘c6 15 ♔b1 ♖ab8 16 ♕d2
♔h8 17 h4 ♖fc8 18 g4 ♘e5 with an

edge for Black; Bönsch-Adamski,
Dečin 1976.
  b3) 9 ♗g5 and now:
  b31) 9...0-0 10 0-0-0 (10 f4 b4
11 ♘a4 ♗b7 is level) 10...♘fd7
(10...♘xe4? 11 ♕xe4 ♗xg5+ 12 f4
d5 13 ♘xd5 exd5 14 ♗xd5 ♖e8 15
♗xf7+! ♔xf7 16 ♕xa8 ♗xf4+ 17
♔b1 ±) 11 ♗e3 b4 12 ♘a4 (Eppin-
ger-Chandler, Bundesliga 1987)
12...♗b7 ∞.
  b32) 9...♕a5 10 ♗d2 (10 f4!?)
10...♕c7 11 a4 b4 12 ♘a2 ♕b6 13
♕e3 ♘c6 14 ♘xc6 ♕xc6 ∓ Don-
chev-Dorfman, Lvov 1983.
  b33) 9...b4 10 ♘a4 ♗d7 11 f4
♕a5 12 e5 ♗xa4 (12...dxe5 13
♕xe5 ♕xe5 14 fxe5 ♘g4 15 ♗xe7
♔xe7 16 ♘b6 ♖a7 17 ♘c4 ± Don-
chev-Savon, Varna 1982) 13 exd6!
♗xd6 (13...♗xb3 14 ♘xb3 ±) 14
♘xe6 ♗xb3 (14...fxe6 15 ♕xe6+
♗e7 16 ♕f7+ ♔d8 17 0-0-0+ ♘bd7
18 ♖he1 ±) 15 ♘xg7+ ♔f8 16 ♗h6
♔g8 17 ♘e8 ♘bd7 18 ♘xd6 ♗e6
19 ♕f3 ♕d5 20 ♖d1! ± Horvath-
Vegh, Hungary 1986.
  c) The obscure 8 a3 makes room
for the bishop. This is considered
rather a slow way of handling the
position. For example:
  c1) 8...♗e7 9 ♗e3 0-0 10 ♕e2
♗b7 11 f3 ♘bd7 12 g4 ♘c5 13 ♗a2
♖c8 ∞ Rajna-Barczay, Hungary
1977.
  c2) 8...♗b7 and now:
  c21) 9 f3 ♗e7 10 ♗e3 0-0 11 0-0
♘bd7 12 ♕d2 (12 ♗xe6!? fxe6 13

♘xe6 ∞) 12...♘e5 13 ♕f2 ♕c7 14 ♖ac1 ♔h8! 15 ♘ce2 ♖g8! 16 ♔h1 g5 17 h3 ♖g6 18 ♘g3 ♖ag8 19 ♘xe6? fxe6 20 ♗xe6 ♘xe4 21 fxe4 ♖xe6 0-1 Garcia-Fischer, Havana OL 1966.

c22) 9 ♕e2 ♘c6 (9...♘bd7 10 ♗g5 ♕a5 11 0-0 b4 12 ♘d5 exd5 13 exd5+ ♔d8 14 axb4 ♕xb4 15 ♘c6+ ♗xc6 16 dxc6 ♘c5 ∞ Ibragimov-Mosionzhik, USSR 1962) 10 ♘xc6 ♗xc6 11 ♘d5 ♘d7 12 0-0 ♗b7 13 ♘c3 ♗e7 14 ♗f4 0-0 15 ♖ad1 ♕c7 16 ♖d3 ♖fd8 17 ♖fd1 ♘e5 18 ♖h3 g6 19 ♗c1 ♘c4 20 f4 d5 = Pilnik-Sanguinetti, Mar del Plata 1965.

8 ...   ♗b7
9 ♗e3   ♘bd7

A search through the archives reveals that the knight can also be developed on c6. For example: 9...♗e7 10 ♕d2 0-0 11 g4 ♘c6 12 0-0-0 ♘d7 (12...♘a5 13 h4 ♘xb3+ 14 axb3 ♖c8 15 h5 ∞ Ivanović-Messing, Yugoslav Ch 1968; 12...b4!? Milić) 13 h4 ♖c8 (13...♘de5 14 ♕e2 ♘a5! =) 14 g5 ♘de5 15 ♕e2 ♘xd4 16 ♗xd4 ♘c4 17 f4 ♕c7 18 g6 e5 19 ♗xc4 ♕xc4 20 gxh7+ ♔h8 21 ♕xc4 ♖xc4 22 fxe5 dxe5 23 ♗xe5 ♗xe4 = Ljubojević-Portisch, Palma de Mallorca 1971.

10 ♕d2
White plans to castle queenside, which is consistent with his aggressive stance.

10 ...   ♘c5
11 0-0-0   ♗e7

12 g4   ♘fd7
The knight is now re-routed in a cumbersome bid to create some counterplay. It might be more appropriate to play 12...♘xb3+ 13 axb3 ♕c7 intending to meet g5 with ...♘h5.

13 g5   ♘xb3+
14 axb3   ♘c5
15 ♔b1   0-0
16 h4

White embarks on a convincing plan of storming the kingside, with the g- and h-pawns leading the way. White has gained the upper hand very quickly due to Black failing to adjust his plan on realizing that the e4 pawn is no longer a liability.

16 ...   b4
17 ♘a4   ♘xa4
18 bxa4   ♕a5
19 h5 *(D)*

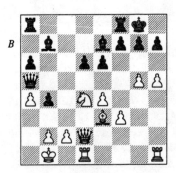

19 ...   ♕xa4
Material is not the main factor in deciding the race to deliver a decisive blow to the opposing king.

Black has remote chances to invade via a2 while White's forces are ominously gathering momentum.

20 g6   &f6

After 20...fxg6 21 hxg6 hxg6 22 ♘xe6 White has a clear advantage.

21 h6!   fxg6
22 hxg7   &xg7
23 ♕h2

With dual threats against d6 and h7 the queen is poised to take an influential role.

23 ...   h5
24 ♕xd6   ♖ac8

Now the pressure against c2 is designed to restrict the knight's movement, while ...&xd4 is always a possibility. This, however, is all to no avail.

25 ♕xe6+   ♔h7
26 ♕e7   &a8 (D)

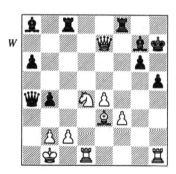

27 ♖xh5+!

Bravo!

27 ...   gxh5
28 ♖g1   ♖g8
29 &h6!   1-0

Game 11
Fischer – Gadia
Mar del Plata 1960

1 e4 c5 2 ♘f3 d6 3 d4 cxd4 4 ♘xd4 ♘f6 5 ♘c3 a6 6 &c4 e6 7 &b3 b5 8 0-0   &b7

Nowadays, this is not a common approach but it has the benefit of inviting double-edged play.

9 f4

Fischer aims for a quick f5 to increase the scope of his light-squared bishop. The crucial question is whether the e-pawn is immune.

Nevertheless 9 ♖e1, considered in the next game, is superior.

9 ...   ♘c6?! (D)

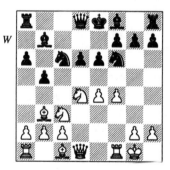

This natural reaction allows White to create a strong attack. A survey of the alternatives shows that Black should have adequate resources:

a) 9...♘bd7 and now:

a1) 10 f5 e5 11 ♘f3 ♘c5 12 &g5 ♘xb3 13 axb3 ♕b6+ 14 ♔h1 ♘xe4

15 ♘xe4 ♗xe4 16 f6 h6 17 ♗h4 (Honfi-Kadar, Pecs 1976) 17...gxf6 18 ♗xf6 ♖g8 19 ♕e2 ∞.

a2) 10 ♖e1 ♘c5 11 ♗d5! (11 e5 dxe5 12 fxe5 ♘xb3 13 axb3 ♗c5 14 ♗e3 ♘d5 15 ♘xd5 ♕xd5 = Minić-Bogdanović, Yugoslavia 1960) and now:

a21) 11...♕c8 12 b4 ♘cd7 13 ♗xb7 ♕xb7 14 a4 bxa4 15 ♖xa4 ♗e7 with equality; Cirić-Minić, Yugoslavia 1966.

a22) 11...exd5 12 exd5+ ♔d7 13 b4 ♘a4 14 ♘a4 bxa4 15 c4 ∞ ♔c7 16 ♕xa4 ♕d7 17 ♕a5+ ♔c8 18 ♗b2 ♗e7 19 c5 ± Pinter-Marjanović, Groningen 1974.

a23) 11...♕c7 12 b4 exd5 13 exd5+ ♘e6 14 ♗b2 ♘xd5 15 ♘xe6 fxe6 16 ♘xd5 ♕c6 17 ♖xe6+ ♔f7 18 ♖f6+! ♔g8 (18...gxf6 19 ♕h5+ ♔e6 20 ♖e1+ winning) 19 ♖xf8+! ♔xf8 20 ♗xg7+ ♔e8 (20...♔xg7 21 ♕g4+) 21 ♕h5+ ♔d8 22 ♗f6+ 1-0 Saverymuttu-Juhnke, West Germany 1971.

b) 9...b4 10 ♘a4 with the alternatives:

b1) 10...♗xe4 11 f5 (11 ♖e1 ♗e7 12 c3 d5 13 ♗e3 0-0 14 ♕e2 bxc3 15 bxc3 ♕d6 16 ♖ed1 ♘c6 17 c4 ♘xd4 18 ♖xd4 ♖ac8 19 ♖ad1 ♕c6 ∓ Mukhin-Grigorian, USSR Ch 1972) e5 12 ♗g5 ♗e7 13 ♗xf6 ♗xf6 14 ♕e1 d5 15 ♘e2 ♘c6 16 ♖d1 0-0 17 c4 bxc3 18 ♘axc3 ♕b6+ 19 ♕f2 ♕xf2+ 20 ♖xf2 ♘b4 = Browne-Saidy, USA 1967.

b2) 10...♘bd7 11 f5 e5 12 ♘e6 fxe6 13 fxe6 ♘c5 14 ♖xf6! ♕xf6 15 ♘xc5 ± Schran-Kjun, Corr 1966.

b3) 10...♘xe4 11 ♖e1 ♘d7 12 f5 e5 13 ♘e6 fxe6 14 ♕h5+ (Banas-Jankovec, Czechoslovakia 1973) 14...g6 ∞.

c) 9...♗e7 10 e5 (10 ♗e3 transposes to the note to Black's 9th move in Game 9; 10 ♗xe6?! fxe6 12 ♘xe6 ♕b6+ 13 ♔h1 ♘xe4 is good for Black) 10...dxe5 11 fxe5 ♗c5 (11...♘fd7 12 ♖xf7!, 11...♘d5 12 ♕f3 and 11...♘e4 12 ♗e3 are better for White) 12 ♗e3 *(D)* and now:

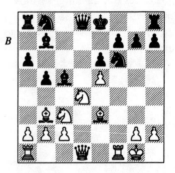

c1) 12...♗xd4 13 ♗xd4 (13 ♕xd4 ♕xd4 14 ♗xd4 ♘c6 15 ♗c5!? ♘xe5 16 a4 bxa4 17 ♗xa4+ ♗c6 18 ♗d4 ♗xa4 19 ♖xa4 ♘c6 20 ♗xf6 gxf6 21 ♖xf6 ♔e7 = King) 13...♘c6 14 ♖f4 ♕c7! 15 ♕f1 (15 ♕e2 0-0-0 16 ♖d1 ♘xd4 17 ♖fxd4 ♖xd4 18 ♖xd4 ♕c5 19 ♕e3 ♘d7 20 ♘e4 ♗xe4 21 ♖xe4 ♔b7 intending ...♖c8-c5 ∓ Nunn) 15...♘xe5?! (15...♘h5 =) 16 ♖xf6 gxf6 17 ♕xf6

🏰g8 18 ♕xe5 🏰xg2+ 19 ♔f1 ±
Savereide-Gallagher, Lewisham
1984.

c2) 12...♘c6 13 exf6 ♗xd4 (or
13...♘xd4 14 fxg7 🏰g8 15 🏰xf7
♘xb3 16 ♕h5 ♗xe3+ 17 ♔h1
♗xg2+ 18 ♔xg2 ♕g5+ 19 ♕xg5
♗xg5 20 🏰af1 ± Marjanović-Dieks,
Groningen 1972/3) 14 ♕e1 ♗xe3+
(14...♕b6 15 ♘d5! ♗xe3+ 16 ♘xe3
gxf6 17 ♔h1 0-0-0 18 🏰xf6 ±;
14...♗xf6 15 🏰d1 ± Nunn) 15 ♕xe3
♕d4 16 🏰ae1 🏰d8 (16...gxf6 17
♘e4 0-0-0 18 🏰xf6 ♘a5 19 ♕xd4
🏰xd4 20 ♘c5 ♗c6 21 🏰xf7 ♘xb3
22 cxb3 🏰g8 23 🏰e2 ± Perecz-
Kovacs, Hungary 1977) 17 ♘e4
gxf6 18 ♘xf6+ ♔e7 19 ♘d5+ (19 c3
♕xe3+ 20 🏰xe3 ♘a5 ∓) 19...🏰xd5
(19...♔e8!? 20 ♘f6+ =) 20 ♗xd5
♕xd5 21 🏰d1 ♘d4?! (21...♕e5!? ∞)
22 ♕f2 ♕xg2+ 23 ♕xg2 ♗xg2 24
♔xg2 ± Romanishin-Shashin, Daugavpils 1974.

10 ♘xc6   ♗xc6
11 f5!   e5

It would be problematic to try to
maintain the pawn on e6: 11...♕d7
12 fxe6 fxe6 13 ♗g5 (13 🏰xf6!?)
13...♗e7 (13...♘xe4 14 ♘xe4 ♗xe4
±) 14 ♗xf6 ♗xf6 15 ♕h5+ ♕f7 16
♕h3 ♗d7 17 e5! dxe5 18 🏰ad1 ±.

12 ♕d3   ♗e7
13 ♗g5 (D)

Fischer correctly intends to create
a bind on d5 by exchanging the
knight. Black is already facing a positional crisis.

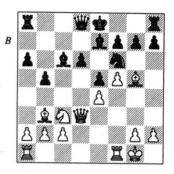

13	...	♕b6+
14	♔h1	0-0
15	♗xf6	♗xf6
16	♗d5	

The pieces are methodically
traded to leave a dominant white
knight.

16	...	🏰ac8
17	♗xc6	🏰xc6
18	🏰ad1	🏰fc8
19	♘d5	♕d8
20	c3 (D)	

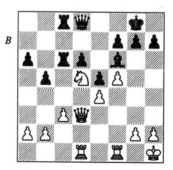

White has achieved a positional
advantage which is a model example
of what to aim for.

20	...	♗e7
21	♖a1!	f6
22	a4	

Now White must win a pawn.

22	...	♖b8?
23	♘xe7+	1-0

Game 12
Fischer – Rubinetti
Palma de Mallorca IZ 1970

1 e4 c5 2 ♘f3 d6 3 d4 cxd4 4 ♘xd4
♘f6 5 ♘c3 a6 6 ♗c4 e6 7 ♗b3 b5
8 0-0 ♗b7
9 ♖e1

This elastic continuation makes for a sophisticated tactical battle. The point is that in certain circumstances the e-file can be opened for an attack. It would be premature to start sacrificing immediately: 9 ♗xe6 fxe6 10 ♘xe6 ♕d7 11 ♘d5 ♔f7! 12 ♘g5+ ♔g8 13 ♘b6 ♕c6 14 ♘xa8 h6 15 ♘e6 ♕xe4 16 ♘f4 ♗xa8 ∓ Bielczyk-Diaz, Cienfuegos 1983.

9 ... ♘bd7

The hidden sting concealed in the apparently innocuous development of the rook is revealed if Black is not wary:

a) 9...♗e7? 10 ♗xe6! fxe6 11 ♘xe6 ♕d7 12 ♘xg7+ ♔f7 13 ♘f5 ♘c6 14 ♘d5! ♘xd5 15 ♕h5+ +−.

b) 9...b4? 10 ♘d5 ♘bd7 11 ♗g5 ±.

c) 9...♘c6?! 10 a4 b4 11 ♘xc6 ♗xc6 12 ♘d5 ♗e7 13 ♘xe7 ♕xe7

14 ♗g5 a5 15 ♗xf6 gxf6 16 ♕h5 ♕b7? 17 ♗xe6 ♕e7 18 ♗d5 ♕c7 19 ♖ad1 ♖a6 20 ♖d3 ♗xa4 21 b3 ♗c6 22 ♕f5 ♖f8 23 ♕xf6 ♕e7 24 ♕f5 ♔d8 25 ♗xc6 ♖xc6 26 ♕xa5+ 1-0 Emms-Quinn, Gausdal 1992.

10 ♗g5

Once again, White has toyed with a direct incursion into Black's camp: 10 ♗xe6 fxe6 11 ♘xe6 ♕c8 (11...♕b8!?) 12 ♗f4 ♔f7 13 ♘xf8 ♖xf8 14 ♗xd6 ♖e8 15 ♕d4 ♕c6 = Velimirović-Parameswaran, Lucerne OL 1982.

10 ... h6 (D)

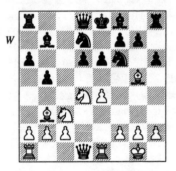

A natural reaction that poses the question of where to position the bishop. 10...♘c5?! to undermine e4 appears reasonable but is quickly routed: 11 ♗d5! ♕c7 (11...exd5 12 exd5+ ♔d7 13 b4 ♘a4 14 ♘xa4 bxa4 15 c4 ± Stean-Marjanović, Schilde 1971; 11...b4 12 ♗xb7 ♘xb7 13 ♘d5 exd5 14 exd5+ ♔d7 15 c3! b3 16 ♕xb3 ♘c5 17 ♕c4 ♕c8 18 ♘c6 h6 19 ♗xf6 gxf6 20

罝e3 含c7 21 b4 罝g8 1-0 Tal-Muk-hin, USSR 1972) 12 盒xb7 豐xb7 13 盒xf6 gxf6 14 豐h5 b4 15 ②d5 盒g7 16 豐h4 f5 17 ②xf5 exf5 18 exf5+ 盒e5 19 罝ad1 含d7 20 f4 f6 21 fxe5 fxe5 22 豐h6 a5 23 ②xb4 豐xb4 24 豐xd6+ 含c8 25 a3 豐c4 26 豐c6+ 含b8 27 b3 豐c3 1-0 Laketić-Lju-bičić, Kladovo 1990.

The alternative 10...豐b6 is dis-cussed in the next game.

11 盒h4

It might be even better to trade pieces with 11 盒xf6. Play might continue:

a) 11...②xf6 12 豐f3! 豐b6 13 罝ad1 0-0-0 14 a4 b4 15 ②a2 含b8 (15...罝d7 16 c4 盒e7 17 盒c2 罝c7 18 豐b3 d5 19 cxd5 exd5 20 e5 ②e4 21 盒xe4 dxe4 22 豐xf7 ± Kavalek-An-dersson, Tilburg 1980) 16 c3 ②xe4 17 a5 豐xa5 18 ②xb4 罝c8 19 罝xe4 f5 20 ②dc6+ 罝xc6 21 罝xe6 罝c8 22 盒d5 盒d5 23 ②xd5 1-0 Kinder-mann-Stangl, Altensteig 1989.

b) 11...豐xf6 12 a4 b4 13 ②a2 a5 14 c3 ±.

11 ... ②c5?!

The note to Black's tenth move would rightly suggest that the obvi-ous plan to put pressure on e4 is flawed. A more critical reaction stems from 11...g5!? 12 盒g3 ②e5 and now:

a) 13 盒xe6!? fxe6 14 ②xe6 豐c8 (14...豐d7 15 ②d5!) 15 ②xf8 罝xf8 16 豐xd6 ②c4 17 豐d4 豐c6 18 ②d5 ± Martinez-Alonso, Cuba 1986.

b) 13 ②f3 豐c7 14 ②xe5 (14 盒d5?! exd5 15 ②xe5 dxe5 16 盒xe5 豐xe5 17 exd5 盒d6 18 豐d4 ②d7 19 罝xe5+ 盒xe5 20 豐b4 0-0-0 21 a4 bxa4 ∓ Plaskett-Tukmakov, Malta 1980) 14...dxe5 15 豐f3 盒g7 16 h3 h5?! (16...0-0 and ...罝ad8 =) 17 罝ad1 b4? 18 ②d5! exd5 19 盒xe5! ± Honfi-Hradeczky, Budapest 1982.

12 盒d5! *(D)*

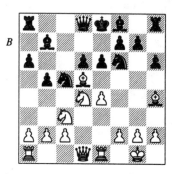

A clever way to thwart the attack on e4.

12 ... exd5

In the game Polgar-Filep, Hun-garian Ch 1969, Black rejected the sacrifice and still ended up with se-vere positional problems: 12...豐b6 13 盒xf6 gxf6 14 豐h5 0-0-0 15 盒xb7+ ②xb7 16 罝ad1 罝d7 17 罝e3 罝g8 18 h4! 含b8 19 b4 ±.

13 exd5+ 含d7

Not 13...盒e7 14 ②f5 and White is winning.

14 b4 ②a4
15 ②xa4 bxa4
16 c4

White has obtained a clear advantage. His pawns are set to advance against the wretched black king, whose defensive forces lack harmony.

16	...	♔c8
17	♕xa4	♕d7
18	♕b3	g5
19	♗g3	♘h5 *(D)*

The need to exchange pieces rather than develop is indicative of Black's plight.

20	c5!	dxc5
21	bxc5	♕xd5
22	♖e8+	♔d7
23	♕a4+	♗c6
24	♘xc6	1-0

Game 13
Adams – Sadler
Dublin Z 1993

1 e4 c5 2 ♘f3 d6 3 d4 cxd4 4 ♘xd4 ♘f6 5 ♘c3 a6 6 ♗c4 e6 7 ♗b3 b5

8	0-0	♗b7
9	♖e1	♘bd7
10	♗g5	♕b6
11	a4	b4 *(D)*

12 ♘d5!

A tremendous shot that aims to put White's lead in development to use by opening up lines to snare the black king.

12	...	exd5
13	exd5+	♘e5

13...♔d8 was seen in Golubev-Mantovani, Biel 1992, in a vain bid to escape White attentions: 14 ♘c6+ ♔c7 (14...♔c8 15 a5 ♕c7 16 ♕g4!! ♘xg4 17 ♖e8+ ♕d8 18 ♗xd8 ♘c5 19 ♖ae1 ♘e5 20 ♗b6+ ♔d7 21 ♖xa8 ♗xa8 22 ♗xc5 ±; 15...♕c5 16 c4! bxc3 17 ♖c1 ♗xc6 18 dxc6 ±; 15...♕b5 16 c4!? bxc3 17 ♖c1 ∞; 14...♗xc6 15 dxc6 ♕xc6 16 ♗d5 ♕c8 17 ♕h5 {17 ♗xa8 ♕xa8 18 ♕h5 ♕d5 19 c4 ♔c7! ∞} 17...♗e7 18 ♕xf7 ♖e8 19 ♗xa8 ♕xa8 20 ♕xg7 ♘e4! 21 ♗xe7+ ♖xe7 22 ♕g8+ ♖e8 23 ♕xh7 ∞ Golubev) 15 a5 ♕b5 16 ♘d4 ♕c5 17 ♗e3 ♗xd5 18 c4 bxc3 19 ♖c1! ♕xa5 20 ♖xc3+

♘c5?! (20...♔d8 21 ♗xd5 ♕xd5 22
♘c6+ ♔e8 23 ♗d4+ ♘e4 24 f3 ±)
21 ♗xd5 ♘xd5 22 ♕f3 ♘xc3 23
♕c6+ ♔b8 24 bxc3 ♔a7 25 ♖b1
♖b8!? 26 ♕xc5+! ♕b6 (26...♕xc5
27 ♘c6+ ♔a8 28 ♖xb8#) 27 ♘c6+
♔a8 28 ♖xb6 1-0.

14 a5

An important improvement that
aims to hound the queen. Up to this
point, Black was coasting along in
the knowledge that a well-known
game in the line continued 14 f4
0-0-0 15 fxe5 dxe5 16 ♖xe5 ♗c5!
17 c3 ♖he8 18 a5 ♕d6 19 ♖xe8
♖xe8 20 ♗xf6 ♕xf6 = de Firmian-
Kir.Georgiev, Niš 1981.

14 ...   ♕c5

If 14...♕c7 then 15 f4 regains
material without the pin on the d4
knight.

15 ♗e3! *(D)*

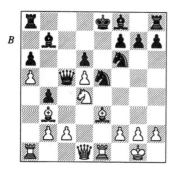

White boldly continues to add
more forces to the onslaught. The
immediate intention is to deter any
possible counterplay by ousting the
queen from the a7-g1 diagonal. Also
possible: 15 f4 0-0-0 16 fxe5 dxe5
17 ♖xe5 ♗d6 18 ♖f5 ±.

15 ...   ♕c8

Black is in all sorts of trouble:

a) 15...♘xd5? 16 ♗a4+ ♔d8 17
♘e6+ +−.

b) 15...♗e7 16 ♘c6 ♕b5 17
♘xe5 dxe5 18 ♗a4 +−.

c) 15...♗xd5 16 ♗a4+ ♘fd7 17
♘e6 ♕c8 (17...♕c4 18 b3 +−) 18
♘xf8 +−.

16 ♗a4+   ♔e7!?

There is nothing that can be done
to stem White's offensive. Upon
16...♘fd7 17 f4 Black can try:

a) 17...♘g6 18 ♘f5 ♗e7 (or
18...♔d8 19 ♗b6+ +−) 19 ♗d4
♔d8 20 ♖xe7 ♘xe7 21 ♘xd6 and
wins.

b) 17...♗xd5 18 fxe5 dxe5 19
♗f4 ♗c5 20 ♖xe5+ ♗e6 21 ♔h1
♗xd4 22 ♕xd4 0-0 23 ♖xe6 fxe6 24
♗xd7 ♖xf4 25 ♕xf4 ♕xd7 26
♕xb4 ± Adams.

17 f4   ♘xd5

In answer to 17...♘c4 White can
destroy Black's resistance by 18
♘c6+! ♗xc6 19 ♗b6+ ♘e5 20
♗xc6 ♖b8 21 fxe5 dxe5 22 ♕d4
♘d7 23 ♖xe5+ ♔d6 24 ♕f4 ♘xe5
25 ♕xb4#.

18 fxe5   dxe5
19 ♕h5   f6

Not 19...exd4 20 ♗xd4+ ♔d8
(20...♔d6 21 ♕e5#) 21 ♕xf7 ♗e7
22 ♗b6+ +−.

20 ♗f2!

A high-class quiet move. The intention is to pile on the pressure with ♗g3 and ♖ad1. In reply to 20...♔d6 21 ♕f7 or 20...♘f4 21 ♖xe5+! wins.

Less convincing is 20 ♘f5+ ♔e6 when the pace is slackening.

20 ...   g6
21 ♖xe5+   ♔f7

The other tries are also inadequate:

a) 21...♔d6 22 ♗g3 gxh5 23 ♖e6+ ♔c5 24 ♘b3+ ♔c4 25 ♖e4#.

b) 21...fxe5 22 ♕xe5+ ♔f7 23 ♕xh8 ♕g4 24 ♕xh7+ ♗g7 25 ♖f1 +−.

22 ♕f3   ♘c7
23 ♕b3+   ♔g7 (D)

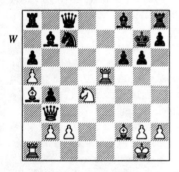

24 ♘f5+!

A dashing finale that rips open Black's remaining defences.

24 ...   gxf5
25 ♕g3+   ♔f7

Of course 25...♔h6 26 ♗e3+ ♔h5 27 h3 and mate to follow.

26 ♗b3+   ♘d5
27 ♖xd5   1-0

Game 14

Kasparov – Gelfand

Linares 1993

1 e4 c5 2 ♘f3 d6 3 d4 cxd4 4 ♘xd4 ♘f6 5 ♘c3 a6 6 ♗c4 e6 7 ♗b3 b5

8 0-0   ♗e7
9 ♕f3

This move first came to prominence in Fischer-F.Olafsson, Buenos Aires 1960. The immediate point is that it threatens the advance e5 with a discovered attack against the rook in the corner.

9 ...   ♕c7

Black aims to meet 10 e5 with 10...♗b7. 9...♕c7 and 9...♕b6 have emerged as the favoured responses, and both moves are comprehensively considered in this section. Less explored paths:

a) 9...♖a7 10 ♖e1 and now:

a1) 10...0-0 11 ♗g5 b4 12 ♘a4 ♗b7 13 ♕e3 ♖a8 14 e5?! (14 ♖ad1!?) 14...dxe5 15 ♕xe5 ♘c6 16 ♘xc6 ♗xc6 17 ♘c5 ♗d6 18 ♗xf6 gxf6 19 ♕h5 ♔h8 20 ♖ad1 ♖g8 21 ♘e4 ♖xg2+ 22 ♔xg2 f5 23 ♕xf7? ♕g5+ 24 ♔f1 ♗b5+ 25 ♖e2 fxe4 26 ♕xe6 ♗xh2 −+ Veingold-Borkowski, Saint John 1988.

a2) 10...♖c7 11 a4! b4 12 ♘a2 0-0 13 ♗d2 a5 14 c3 bxc3 15 ♘xc3 ♘bd7 16 ♘db5 ♖b7 17 ♖ad1 ♘c5 18 ♗c4 d5 19 exd5 exd5 20 ♘xd5 ♘xd5 21 ♗xd5 ♖d7 22 ♗f4 ♕b6 23 b3 +− Hernandez-Verduga, Mexican Ch 1990.

b) 9...♕d7 and now:

b1) 10 a4 b4 11 a5 0-0 12 ♘a4
♘c6 13 ♗e3?! (13 ♘b6! ♘xd4 14
♕d1 ♕b7 15 ♕xd4 ♖b8 16 ♖e1 ±)
13...♕b7! 14 ♘b6 ♖b8 15 ♘xc6
♕xc6 16 ♗d2 ♗b7 17 ♗xb4 ♘xe4
18 ♗a4 ♕c7 19 ♕e3 ♖fd8 20 c4 ∞
Bangiev-Rose, Corr 1987.

b2) 10 ♗g5 ♗b7 11 ♖ad1 ♘c6
12 ♕g3 0-0-0?! (12...♖d8!? 13 a3
0-0 14 ♖d2 ±) 13 ♘xc6 ♕xc6 14 a4
b4? (14...h6 15 axb5 axb5 16 ♗xf6
♗xf6 17 ♖fe1 ±) 15 ♖d4! ♕b6 16
♗e3 ♕a5 17 ♕xg7 e5 (17...bxc3 18
♕xf7 ♖he8 19 bxc3 ±; 17...♕h5 18
♗xe6+ fxe6 19 ♕xe7 ♖hg8 ±;
19...♘g4 20 ♖c4+ ♔b8 21 h3 ♘xe3
22 ♖xb4 +–) 18 ♘d5! exd4 19
♘xe7+ ♔b8 20 ♗xd4 +– Sikora-
Lerch–Ftačnik, Czechoslovakia
1988.

10 ♕g3

An interesting alternative is 10
♖e1, maintaining the tension, and
retaining the option of ♕g3. The
drawback is that Black can castle
and avoid being forced into playing
...♘e8. For example:

a) 10...0-0 and now:

a1) 11 a3 ♘c6 12 ♘xc6 ♕xc6 13
♕g3 ♘h5?! (13...♔h8!? 14 ♗g5
♘h5 15 ♕h4 ♗xg5 16 ♕xg5 ♘f6
17 ♖ad1 ♗b7 18 ♖d3 ♖ad8 and now
19 ♖h3!, Velimirović-Tukmakov,
Amsterdam 1974, gives White the
advantage in view of 19...♖g8 20
♖f3) 14 ♕h3 ♘f6 15 ♗g5 ♗b7 16
♖e3 ♖fe8 17 ♖ae1 ♔h8 18 ♕h4

♘g8 19 ♖g3 ♕c5 20 ♖ee3 h6?
(20...f6!) 21 ♗xe7 ♘xe7 22 ♕f4
♖f8 23 ♖h3 ♘g6 24 ♖xh6+! gxh6
25 ♕xh6+ ♔g8 26 ♗xe6! ♕e5 27
♕xg6+ ♕g7 28 ♕h5 fxe6 29 ♖g3
♖f7 30 ♕h6 +– Short-Ehlvest, Moscow rapid 1994.

a2) 11 ♕g3 ♔h8 12 ♗g5 ♗d7
13 ♕h4 ♘c6 14 ♘ce2 h6?!
(14...♘e5!?) 15 ♖ad1 ♘e5 16 f4
♘g6 17 ♕h3 e5 18 ♘f5 ♘xe4 19
♗xh6! ♗xf5 20 ♕xf5 ♕c5+ 21
♘d4 exd4 22 ♕xe4 gxh6 23 ♗xf7!
d3+ 24 ♔h1 dxc2 25 ♖c1 ♖xf7 26
♕xa8+ ♔g7 27 g3 ♕c4 28 b3 ♕d3
29 ♕g2 ♗f6 30 ♕xc2 ± Minasian-
Zagorskis, Frunze 1989.

b) 10...♘c6 11 ♘xc6 ♕xc6 12
♕g3 transposes to Game 17.

10 ...   0-0 (D)

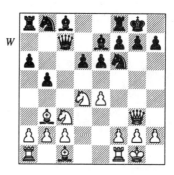

Instead the simplifying 10...♘c6
is considered in Game 17.

10...b4 may be over-ambitious:

a) 11 ♘a4 ♘xe4 (11...♘c6 12
♘xc6 ♕xc6 13 f3!? 0-0 14 ♗h6
♘e8 15 ♗e3 ♖b8 16 ♕f2 ♗d8 17

🗒fd1 a5 18 🗒ac1 ♗f6 19 c4 bxc3 20
♘xc3 ♕a6 21 ♘a4! ± Ehlvest-Tim-
man, Reykjavik 1988) 12 ♕xg7 ♗f6
13 ♕g4 d5 14 ♗e3 ♗d7 15 c4! bxc3
16 ♘xc3 ♘xc3 17 🗒ac1! e5 18 ♕f3
♕d6 19 🗒xc3 exd4 20 ♗f4 ♗e5
(20...♕b6 21 ♗c7 +−) 21 🗒e1 f6 22
🗒xe5+ fxe5 23 ♕h5+ ♔e7 24 ♗g5+
♔e6 25 ♕h6+ 1-0 Hoffmann-Re-
chel, Bochum 1989.

b) 11 ♘ce2 g6 12 ♗h6 (Fischer;
12 f3? e5 −+ Bellón-Verduga, Havana 1986; 12 c3?! ♘xe4 13 ♕e3
♘f6 14 cxb4 0-0 15 ♗d2 e5 16 ♘f3
♗b7 17 🗒ac1 = Fischer-F.Olafs-
son, Buenos Aires 1960) 12...e5!?
(12...♘xe4 13 ♕e3 ♘c5 14 ♗g7
🗒g8 15 ♕h6 ♗f8 16 ♗xf8 🗒xf8 17
♘f4 ♘c6 18 ♘xc6 ♕xc6 19 🗒fe1
♗b7 20 ♗d5 ± Dementiev-Mukhin,
USSR 1974) 13 ♗g7! 🗒g8 14 ♗xf6
♗xf6 15 ♘f5 🗒f8 16 ♘e3 ±.

11 ♗h6   ♘e8 (D)

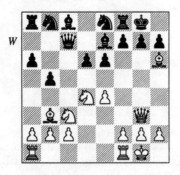

12 🗒ad1
A popular alternative is 12 🗒fe1
♗d7 and now:

a) 13 a4 b4 14 ♘ce2 ♔h8 15
♗g5 ♗xg5 16 ♕xg5 ♘f6 17 ♘g3
♘c6 18 ♘xc6 ♗xc6 19 🗒ad1 🗒ad8
20 🗒d3 h6 21 ♕f4 ♕e7 22 ♕h4 =
Kasparov-Gelfand, Paris Immopar
rapid 1991.

b) 13 🗒ad1 ♘c6 14 ♔h1 ♘a5 15
f4 ♘xb3 16 axb3 b4 17 ♘ce2 ♔h8
18 ♗g5 f6 19 ♗h4 e5 20 ♘f5 ♗xf5
21 exf5 ♕xc2 22 ♕g4 ♕xb3 23 fxe5
dxe5 24 🗒d7 ♗d6 25 ♘f4 🗒f7 26
🗒xf7 ♕xf7 27 ♘g6+ ♔g8 28 🗒e3
🗒c8 29 ♗e1 🗒c4 30 ♕h5 🗒c1?? 31
♕xh7+! 1-0 Rusinger-de Firmian,
Chiasso 1993.

12 ...   ♗d7
Not 12...♗b7? 13 ♗xe6! when
Black is busted.

In the game Ehlvest-Gavrikov,
USSR Ch 1988, White met the prophylactic 12...♗f6 by seeking to
trade pieces: 13 ♗g5 ♗xg5 14
♕xg5 ♕c5 15 ♕d2 ♗d7 16 🗒fe1
🗒a7 17 a3 🗒b7 18 ♘ce2 ♘c6 19
♘xc6 ♗xc6 20 ♘f4! ♘f6 (20...🗒e7
±) 21 ♕d4! ♕xd4 22 🗒xd4 🗒d7 23
♘xe6 fxe6 24 ♗xe6+ 🗒ff7 25 f3
and White was much better.

13 ♘f3
A clever way of conducting the
onslaught. The idea is to bring the
king's knight into play with ♗g5,
exchanging bishops and then install-
ing the knight on g5. In the game
A.Sokolov-Gelfand, USSR Ch
1989, White tried another plan: 13
f4 ♘c6 (13...b4!? 14 ♘ce2 ♔h8 15
♗g5 ♘c6 16 f5 ♘xd4 17 ♘xd4 ♘f6

18 ♕h4 ♖ae8 19 fxe6 fxe6 20 ♗xe6 ♗d8 21 ♕h3 ♖xe6 22 ♘xe6 ♕b6+ 23 ♔h1 ♖e8 ½-½ I.Almaši-Vaulin, Kecskemet 1993) 14 ♘xc6 ♗xc6 15 f5 ♔h8 16 ♗e3 b4 17 ♘a4 ♖b8?! (17...e5 18 c3 ±; 17...♘f6 18 fxe6 fxe6 19 ♕h3 ♘xe4 20 ♕xe6 ♗f6 ∞) 18 fxe6 fxe6 19 ♖xf8+ ♗xf8 20 ♖f1 ♕e7 (20...♘f6 21 ♘c5! ♘xe4 22 ♘xe4 ♗xe4 23 ♕f4 +–) 21 e5 ♗xa4 22 ♗g5 ±.

13 a3 is discussed in Game 16.

13 ... b4?! *(D)*

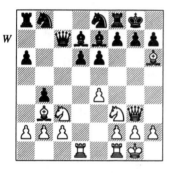

A natural way to continue but it merely aids White's attacking ambitions by driving another piece to kingside.

13...a5 is considered in the next game while 13...♘c6 has also been tested:

a) 14 ♘e2 a5 (14...♔h8 15 ♗g5 f6! is also unclear) 15 c3 a4 16 ♗c2 e5 17 ♘d2 ♗e6 18 ♗b1 ♔h8 19 ♗e3 ♘f6 20 f4 ♘h5 21 ♕f3 ♘xf4 22 ♘xf4 exf4 23 ♕xf4 a3 24 b3 ♗f6 25 ♘f3 ♘e5 26 ♗d4 ♗xb3 27 axb3

a2 28 ♗xa2 ♖xa2 29 ♘h4 ♕c8 30 ♘f5 ♕e6 ∞ Ashley-Arnason, Saint Martin 1993.

b) 14 ♗g5!? ♗c8 (14...♗xg5 15 ♘xg5 h6 16 ♘h3 ♖d8 17 ♖d2 ♗c8 18 ♖fd1 with the initiative) 15 ♗xe7 ♕xe7 (15...♘xe7 16 e5 d5 17 ♘e2) 16 e5 dxe5 17 ♘xe5 ♘xe5 18 ♕xe5 ♘f6 19 ♕d6 (19 ♖d3 ♗b7 20 ♖fd1 ♖ad8 = Bangiev) 19...♕b7 20 ♖d4 ♗d7 21 ♘e4 ♘xe4 22 ♕xd7 ♕xd7 23 ♖xd7 = Le Quang-Bangiev, Biel 1993.

14 ♘e2 a5
15 ♘f4! ♔h8

The game would come to an abrupt finish after 15...a4? 16 ♗xg7 ♘xg7 17 ♘h5 +–.

16 ♗g5 ♘f6

Black side-steps another trap: 16...♗xg5 (16...f6? 17 ♗xe6 fxg5 18 ♘g6+! hxg6 19 ♕h3#) 17 ♘xg5 a4 18 ♕h3 h6 19 ♗xe6! fxe6 20 ♘g6+ ♔g8 21 ♘xf8 ♔xf8 22 ♘xe6+ ±.

17 ♕h4! ♗b5?

This hastens Black's demise as it is essential to keep the bishop in reserve to counter sacrifices on e6. Kasparov's analysis demonstrates White's command of the position:

a) 17...a4 18 ♘h5 axb3 19 ♘xf6! (19 ♗xf6 ♗xf6 20 ♘xf6 h6 21 axb3) and now:

a1) 19...h6 20 ♗xh6 ♗xf6 21 ♘g5 ♗xg5 (21...♔g8 22 ♗xg7!) 22 ♗xg7+ ♔xg7 23 ♕xg5+ ♔h7 24 ♖d3 e5 25 ♖g3 +–.

b) 19...♗xf6 20 ♗xf6 gxf6 (or
20...♖a5? 21 ♘g5 ♖xg5 22 ♕xg5
♖g8 23 ♖d3 +–; 20...bxc2 21 ♘g5
h6 22 ♕xh6+ +–) 21 ♕xf6+ ♔g8
22 ♘g5! ♗b5 (22...♗c8 23 ♖d3
♖d8 24 ♕h6) 23 ♕h6 f6 24 ♕xf8+
♔xf8 25 ♘xe6+ ♔e7 26 ♘xc7 +–.

b) 17...♘c6!? 18 c3 (18 ♗a4
♖ae8) 18...bxc3 19 bxc3 intending
♗c2 gives White the better game.

18 ♘d4! *(D)*

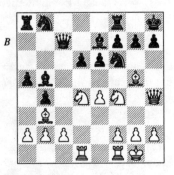

The rapid sharpening of the battle
is typical of Kasparov's energetic
play. Now 18...♗xf1 falls victim to
19 ♘dxe6! fxe6 20 ♗xe6 g6 (20...h6
21 ♗xh6 +–) 21 ♘xg6+ ♔g7 22
♕h6#.

18 ...   ♗e8
19 ♘dxe6!   fxe6
20 ♘xe6   ♕a7
21 e5!

Kasparov continues to follow up
his piece sacrifice with great precision, disdaining material gain in favour of bringing his queen's rook
into the fray.

21 ...   dxe5
22 ♘xf8   ♗xf8
23 ♗xf6   gxf6
24 ♖d8   ♘d7

There is no respite after 24...♘c6
(24...♕e7 25 ♖fd1 +–) 25 ♕xf6+
♗g7 26 ♕e6 ♘e7 27 ♖xa8 ♕xa8 28
♕xe7 +–.

25 ♕g4!   1-0

Game 15
Short – Kasparov
London PCA Wch (18) 1993

1 e4 c5 2 ♘f3 d6 3 d4 cxd4 4 ♘xd4
♘f6 5 ♘c3 a6 6 ♗c4 e6 7 ♗b3 b5 8
0-0 ♗e7 9 ♕f3 ♕c7 10 ♕g3 0-0 11
♗h6 ♘e8 12 ♖ad1 ♗d7 13 ♘f3

13 ...   a5!

This is Kasparov's prepared improvement over Gelfand's play in
the previous game.

14 a4

The text is a recommendation by
Gelfand. Kasparov has revealed an
incredible analysis continuing 14 e5
a4 15 ♖d4 axb3 (15...g6 16 ♗d5 ±)
16 ♗xg7 ♘xg7 17 ♖g4 bxa2 18
♖xg7+ ♔h8 19 ♘e4 a1♕ 20 ♖xh7+
♔xh7 21 ♘eg5+ ♗xg5 (21...♔g6
22 ♘xe6+ ♔f5 23 ♘fd4+ ♔e4 24
♕f3+ ♔xe5 25 ♕f5#) 22 ♘xg5+
♔g6 (22...♔h6 23 ♕h4+ ♔g6 24
♕h7+ ♔xg5 25 f4+ ♔g4 26 ♕h3#)
and White can only draw.

14 ...   b4
15 ♘e2   ♘c6
16 ♘f4   ♗f6 *(D)*

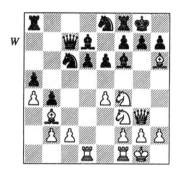

W

Black continues to defend with great verve. The automatic response to the pin 16...♔h8 is not so convincing: 17 ♗g5 ♗xg5 (17...f6? 18 ♗xe6 fxg5 19 ♘g6+ is winning for White) 18 ♘xg5 when White has threats against h7 and possible sacrifices on e6.

17 ♘d3

The robust nature of Black's position is evident after the alternatives:

a) 17 ♘h5 ♗xb2 18 e5 ♘xe5 and now:

a1) 19 ♘d4 ♘g6 ∓.

a2) 19 ♘xg7 ♘xf3+ –+.

a3) 19 ♘f6+ ♔h8 20 ♘xe8 (20 ♗xg7+ ♘xg7 21 ♕h4 ♘xf3+) 20...♘xf3+ 21 gxf3 ♖axe8 –+.

b) 17 ♘g5 (Plaskett) 17...♘e7 (not 17...♗xb2? 18 ♕h4 and White wins) 18 ♗xe6 fxe6 (18...♗xg5 19 ♕xg5 ♗xe6 20 ♗xg7 ♘xg7? 21 ♘h5 ♘g6 22 ♘f6+ ♔h8 23 ♕h6 mates) 20 ♘gxe6 ♕xc2 21 ♘xf8 ♔xf8 22 ♗g5 with a small advantage for Black.

c) 17 c3 ♔h8 (17...bxc3? 18 ♘h5!) 18 ♗g5 bxc3 19 ♘h5 cxb2 20 ♗xf6 gxf6 21 ♕f4 ♖g8 (or 21...♕d8!?) 22 ♘xf6 ♘xf6 23 ♕xf6+ ♖g7 24 ♕xb2 ♘e5 25 ♘xe5 dxe5 26 ♖d3 =.

17 ... e5
18 ♗e3 ♗e7!

Black regroups in order to contest the d5 square. In the event of 18...g6 White can instigate complications by 19 ♘d2 ♗e6 20 f4 (20 ♘c4 ♘d4 21 ♗xd4 ♗xc4 22 ♗e3 is level) 20...♗xb3 21 cxb3 exf4 22 ♘xf4! (22 ♗xf4 ♘e5 =) 22...♗xb2 23 ♘d5 and White has compensation for the pawn.

19 ♘d2 ♘f6
20 f3 *(D)*

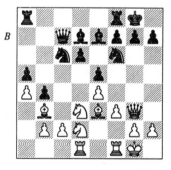

B

White is content to reinforce e4 to free the knight from its defence. Kasparov points out that 20 f4 is well met by 20...♘g4! when Black has at least equality.

20 ... ♖fe8
21 ♔h1 ♗e6

White has spent most of the game preventing the ...d5 break which Black is now on the verge of achieving. This signals that his attacking plan has been too slow.

22 ♖fe1

The best chance is to sharpen the position with 22 ♗xe6!? fxe6 23 ♕h3 ♗f8 24 f4 d5 25 fxe5 (25 f5 dxe4 26 ♘f2 ♘d4 27 ♗xd4 exd4 28 ♘dxe4 with good play) 25...♘xe5 (25...♘xe4 26 ♘f3) 26 ♗d4 ∞.

22 ...   ♖ac8
23 ♕f2   d5 (D)

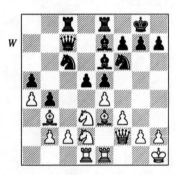

24 ♗b6

Worth considering is 24 exd5 (24 ♗g5?! ♘xe4! 25 ♘xe4 dxe4 ∓) 24...♗xd5 (24...♘xd5 25 ♗c5 ±) 25 ♘c4 e4 26 fxe4 ♘xe4 27 ♕f4 (27 ♕f5 ♗xc4 28 ♗xc4 ♘d6) 27...♕b7 28 ♘c5 when Plaskett claims that White is slightly better.

24 ...   ♕b8
25 ♗c5   ♗xc5
26 ♘xc5   ♘d4
27 ♘xe6   fxe6

28 exd5   ♘xb3!?

Kasparov avoids any risk by this exchange. If 28...exd5 29 ♘e4 ♘xb3 30 ♘xf6+ gxf6 31 ♖xd5?! (31 cxb3 and the black king is slightly exposed) 31...♘d4 32 ♕g3+ ♔h8 33 ♖d7 ♘e6 34 ♕h4 ♘g7 35 ♕xf6 ♖g8 when Black has the advantage.

29 ♘xb3   exd5
30 ♘xa5   ♕a8 (D)

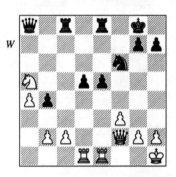

The passed a-pawn is a potential menace: 30...♕c7 31 ♘b3 ♕xc2 32 ♕xc2 ♖xc2 33 ♖b1 with an unclear game.

31 ♘b3

Of course, 31 ♕b6 ♖b8 32 ♕c5 ♖ec8 picks up a piece.

31 ...   ♕xa4
32 ♖a1   ♕c6
33 ♖e2   d4

½-½

The draw was agreed in view of the likely continuation 34 ♖ae1 ♘d5 35 ♖xe5 ♖xe5 36 ♖xe5 ♕xc2 37 ♕xc2 ♖xc2 38 ♖xd5 ♖xb2 39 h4

(39 ♘c1?! ♖b1 40 ♖c5 d3 wins for
Black) 39...♖xb3 40 ♖xd4 =.

Game 16
Short – Kasparov
London PCA Wch (20) 1993

1 e4 c5 2 ♘f3 d6 3 d4 cxd4 4 ♘xd4
♘f6 5 ♘c3 a6 6 ♗c4 e6 7 ♗b3 b5 8
0-0 ♗e7 9 ♕f3 ♕c7 10 ♕g3 0-0 11
♗h6 ♘e8 12 ♖ad1 ♗d7
    13 a3
Short varies from the previous
game and gives his bishop an es-
cape-square by pushing the pawn
just one square.
    13 ...   ♘c6
    14 ♘xc6   ♗xc6
    15 ♗f4 (D)

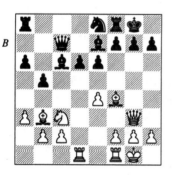

    White is relying on direct pres-
sure against d6. In the game Skro-
bek-Engel, Bannet Memorial 1991,
White advanced his f-pawn to take
part in an attack: 15 f4 ♔h8 16 ♗g5
a5 17 f5 b4 18 axb4 axb4 19 ♘e2
♗xg5 20 ♕xg5 ♘f6 21 fxe6 ±.

    15 ...   ♕b7
The pin is avoided by putting
pressure on e4. Black must be careful:
    a) 15...♗f6 16 ♖xd6! e5 17 ♖xf6
♘xf6 18 ♗xe5 +–.
    b) 15...♖d8 16 e5 dxe5 17 ♗xe5
♕b7 18 ♘e2 ♖xd1 19 ♖xd1 ♗f6 20
♗d4 ±.
    16 ♖fe1   a5
    17 e5   dxe5
Black wisely avoids a pawn structure reminiscent of the Advance
French, possible after 17...d5. This
can be met by ♘e2 and c3, followed
by ♗c2 and ♘d4 with bright prospects for White.
    18 ♗xe5
The outlandish 18 ♖xe5 is easily
rebuked: 18...♗f6 19 ♖c5 b4 20
♘a4 ♗e7 =.
    18 ...   ♗f6
Upon 18...♘f6 Kasparov was
worried about 19 ♖d4 ♖ad8 20 ♖h4
when White has excellent play on
the kingside.
    19 ♖d4   ♖d8 (D)

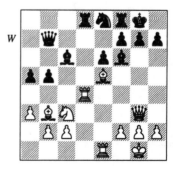

In a bid to extinguish the attack Black offers to trade his dormant rook for White's active one. Other moves:

a) 19...b4 20 axb4 axb4 21 ♗xf6 ♘xf6 22 ♘a2 and a pawn is lost.

b) 19...♗xe5 20 ♖xe5 (20 ♕xe5! ±) 20...b4 21 axb4 axb4 22 ♘a2 ♖xa2 23 ♗xa2 ♕a7 ∓.

| 20 | ♖xd8 | ♗xd8 |
| 21 | ♘e2 | a4 |

If 21...♗d5 then 22 ♖d1! ♘f6 (22...♗xb3?? 23 ♖xd8 ♗d5 24 ♖xe8 +−) 23 ♗xd5 exd5 24 ♘d4 when White is better.

22	♗a2	b4
23	axb4	♕xb4
24	♗c3	♕b7

The best continuation, as 24...♕c5 (24...♕d6 25 ♕xd6 ♘xd6 26 ♗b4 ♗e7 27 ♘d4 ±) 25 ♘f4 ♗c7 26 ♕g4 gives White the superior chances according to Adams.

| 25 | ♘d4 | ♘f6 *(D)* |

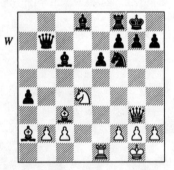

Kasparov is prepared to concede the bishop pair in order to deaden White's attack. His original intention had been 25...♗f6 26 ♘xc6 ♕xc6 27 ♗b4 ♕xc2 28 ♗xf8 ♔xf8 with adequate compensation, until noticing that the assessment is changed by 28 ♗b1! ♕xb2 29 ♗xh7+ ♔xh7 30 ♗xf8 when White has the advantage.

26 ♘xc6

It is tempting to sacrifice on e6 but there is no clear route to victory:

a) 26 ♗xe6 fxe6 27 ♘xe6 and now:

a1) 27...♖e8 28 ♘xd8 ♖xe1+ 29 ♗xe1 ♕e7 30 ♗a5 ±.

a2) 27...♕d7 23 ♘xf8 ♔xf8 ∓.

b) 26 ♖xe6 fxe6 27 ♘xe6 and now:

b1) 27...♕f7 28 ♘xg7 ♕xa2 29 ♘f5+ ♔f7 30 ♕g7+ ♔e6 31 ♘d4+ ♔d5 when Kasparov states that the king can flee from danger.

b2) 27...♗d5 28 ♗xd5 ♘xd5 29 ♗xg7 ♗h4! 30 ♕xh4 ♖e8. Short's analysis reveals that Black is winning.

26	...	♕xc6
27	♖d1	♗e7
28	h3	♖a8

Not 28...♖d8? 29 ♖xd8+ ♗xd8 30 ♗xf6 which picks up a piece.

29	♖d4	♘e8
30	♕d3	♗f6
31	♖c4	♕a6

Black has succeeded in defending as well as possible and avoids the latest trick: 31...♕b7 (31...♕b5? 32 ♗xf6 ♘xf6 33 ♖c8+) 32 ♗xf6

②xf6 33 ☖xa4! with a material advantage.

32	♗xf6	②xf6
33	♕d2	h6
34	☖d4	♕b6
35	c3	a3
36	bxa3	½-½

Game 17
Short – Kasparov
London PCA Wch (16) 1993

1 e4 c5 2 ②f3 d6 3 d4 cxd4 4 ②xd4 ②f6 5 ②c3 a6 6 ♗c4 e6 7 ♗b3 b5 8 0-0 ♗e7 9 ♕f3 ♕c7 10 ♕g3

10 ... ②c6

One of the main alternatives; Black aims to simplify the position.

11 ②xc6

White can also fight for an advantage with other moves:

a) 11 ②f5?! exf5 12 ♕xg7 ☖f8 13 ♗g5 b4 14 ②d5 ②xd5 15 ♗xd5 ♗xg5 16 ♕xg5 f4 and White's attack has evaporated; Guseinov-Magerramov, Baku 1986.

b) 11 ♗e3 0-0 12 ②xc6 ♕xc6 13 ♗h6 ②e8 14 a4 b4 15 ②d5! ♗d8 16 a5 ♕b7 17 ♗d2 exd5 18 ♗xd5 ♕a7 19 ♗xa8 ♕xa8 20 e5 dxe5 21 ♗xb4 f6 (J.Polgar-H.Olafsson, Egilsstadir 1988) and now 22 ♗xf8! ☖xf8 23 b4 gives White good play.

11 ... ♕xc6

12 ☖e1 *(D)*

It is now imperative that White defends e4; otherwise the pressure increases which ensures at least

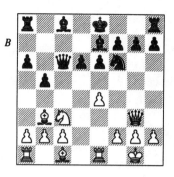

equality. For example: 12 ♗g5 ♗b7 13 ☖ad1 0-0 14 ☖fe1 ☖fd8 15 f4 ♕b6+ 16 ☗h1 b4 17 ②a4 ♕a5 18 c3 ♗c6 19 cxb4 ♕xb4 20 ②c3 a5 21 ♗h6 ♗f8 22 ♗g5 ♗e7 23 ♗h6 ♗f8 24 ♗g5 ♗e7 ½-½ Kuzmin-Polugaevsky, USSR 1977.

Black is at least equal after 12 ♕xg7 ☖g8 13 ♕h6 ②xe4 14 ②xe4 ♕xe4 15 f3 ♕g6.

12 ... ♗b7 *(D)*

The accepted way to try to avoid a hazardous defensive task. After 12...0-0 13 ♗h6 ②e8 14 ②d5 ♗d8 (14...☖a7?! 15 ②xe7+ ☖xe7 16 ☖ad1 ☖d7 17 ☖d3 ☗h8 18 ♗d2 ②f6 19 ♕h4 e5 20 ♗h6 ②e8 21 ♗d5 ♕c7 22 ♗xg7+! ②xg7 23 ☖h3 h5 24 ♕g5 ☖e7 25 ☖xh5+ ②xh5 26 ♕xh5+ ☗g7 27 ☖e3 ☖g8 28 ☖g3+ ☗f8 29 ♕h6+ ☖g7 30 ♕h8+ 1-0 Kudrin-Burgos, Saint Martin 1991) play might proceed:

a) 15 ②f4 ♗f6 16 c3 ☗h8 17 ♗g5 h6 18 ♗xf6 ②xf6 19 e5 dxe5 20 ☖xe5 ☖e8 21 ②d3 ♕d6 22 ☖c5 ♕xg3 23 hxg3 with an edge for

White; Yurtaev-Gavrikov, Moscow 1983.

b) 15 ♗g5 ♗xg5 16 ♕xg5 exd5 17 ♗xd5 ♕c5! 18 b4 ♕a7 19 ♗xa8 ♕xa8 ∓ Berkovich-Grigorian, Moscow 1981.

c) 15 a4 ♗b7 16 axb5 axb5 17 ♖xa8 ♗xa8 18 ♘b4! ♕c5 19 c3 intending ♗e3, f3 and ♗b3-c2-d3 with advantage according to Mikhalchishin.

d) 15 ♖e3 ♕b7 (15...♗b7? 16 ♖c3 ♕d7 17 ♖c7 +−; 15...♔h8 16 ♗g5 f6?! 17 ♖f3 ±; 15...♕d7 16 ♘f4 ♕e7 17 ♘h5 f6 18 ♖c3 ♔h8 19 ♗d2 ♗b7 20 ♘f4 ♘c7 21 ♖e1 ♗c8 22 ♕h3 ♕e8 23 ♖ee3 g5 24 ♖xc7! ♗xc7 25 ♘xe6 ♕e7 26 ♗c3 ± Gdanski-Jasnikowski, Polish Ch 1991) 16 ♘f4 ♔h8 17 ♗g5 ♗b6?! (17...f6? 18 ♗xe6 fxg5 19 ♘g6+ +−; 17...♗xg5 18 ♕xg5 ±) 18 ♖f3! ♕xe4 19 ♔f1 e5 20 ♘d5 ♗a5 21 ♘e7 ♘c7 22 ♘xc8 ♖axc8 (or 22...♖fxc8 23 ♖xf7 ±) 23 ♗e7 f5 24 ♗xf8 ♖xf8 25 c3 f4 26 ♕g4 b4 27 ♖e1 ♕c6 28 ♖h3 ♕e8 29 ♕f3 h6 30 ♕e4 bxc3 31 ♗c2 ♕b5+ 1-0 de Firmian-Browne, USA Ch 1989.

e) 15 c3 ♗d7 16 a4 ♕b7 17 ♘b4 bxa4 18 ♗xa4 ♗xa4 19 ♖xa4 ♕b5 20 ♖ea1 a5 21 ♘d3 ♖c8 22 ♗d2 = Zso.Polgar-Browne, New York 1989.

13 a3 *(D)*

A cautious continuation that aims for a solid game. The middlegame will involve patient manoeuvring.

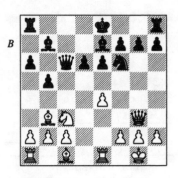

Other tries:

a) 13 a4? b4 14 a5 0-0 15 ♘a2 ♘xe4 16 ♕g4 f5 17 ♗xe6+ ♔h8 18 ♕e2 d5 0-1 Vavra-Vokac, Prague 1991.

b) 13 ♕xg7!? ♖g8 14 ♕h6 0-0-0 15 ♕h3 ♔b8 16 f3!? (16 a3 ♖g6 17 ♖e2 ♖dg8 ∞ Drozhdov-Shneider, USSR 1987) 16...♖g6 17 ♗e3 ♖dg8 18 ♖e2 ♘d7 19 ♘d5 exd5 20 ♗xd5 ♕c7 21 ♗xf7 ♗f6 22 ♖d1 ♗xb2 23 c4 ♗a3 24 cxb5 axb5 25 ♗xg8 ♖xg8 gave White a clear plus in Ivanchuk-Polugaevsky, Monaco blindfold 1993.

c) 13 f3 0-0 14 ♗h6 ♘e8 15 ♖ad1 (15 ♗g5 ♗xg5 16 ♕xg5 ♕c5+ 17 ♕e3 ♘c7 18 ♖ad1 ♖fd8 19 a3 a5 20 ♕xc5 dxc5 21 ♖xd8+ ♖xd8 22 ♖d1 ♖xd1+ ½-½ Bielczyk-Kuczynski, Bydgoszcz 1990) and now:

c1) 15...b4?! 16 ♘e2?! (16 ♘a4! followed by ♗e3, ♕f2 and c3 ±) 16...♕c5+ 17 ♔h1 ♗f6 18 ♘f4 = Rublevsky-Magerramov, USSR Ch 1991.

c2) 15...♖d8 16 ♔h1 (16 ♖d3
♔h8 17 ♗e3 ♘f6 18 ♖ed1 ♕c7 19
♗d4 ♗c6 20 a3 ♕b7 21 ♗xf6 gxf6
22 ♘e2 ♖g8 23 ♕f2 a5 24 c3 b4 25
axb4 ½-½ Prasad-Shneider, Calcutta 1991) 16...♗f6 (16...♔h8 17
♗g5 ♗xg5 18 ♕xg5 ♘f6 19 a4 {19
♕d2!?} 19...h6! 20 ♕d2 b4 21 ♘a2
a5 22 c3 bxc3 23 ♘xc3 ♗a6 ∓
Magomedov-Magerramov, USSR
1991) 17 ♗g5 ♖d7?! 18 ♗d5! ♕c8
19 ♗xb7 ♕xb7 20 ♗xf6 ♘xf6 21
♖xd6 ♘h5 22 ♕e5 ♕c7 23 ♖ed1 b4
± Magomedov-Magerramov, USSR
1991.

13 ...   ♖d8 (D)

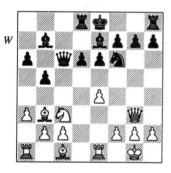

A refinement – the idea is to delay castling which makes it difficult
for White to develop his queen's
bishop to its best square. Alternatively:

a) 13...0-0 14 ♗h6 ♘e8 15 ♖ad1
and now:

a1) 15...♔h8 16 ♗f4 ♘f6 17
♕h4 ♘g8 18 ♕h5 ♘f6 19 ♕e2 a5 ∞
Sedishev-Vaulin, Sochi 1988.

a2) 15...♖d8 16 ♖d3 ♔h8 17
♗g5 ♗xg5 18 ♕xg5 ♘f6 19 ♕d2
♖d7 20 f3 ♖c8 21 ♖d1 ♘e8 22 ♕f2
with just a small edge for White;
Dolmatov-Polugaevsky, Moscow
TV 1987.

b) 13...♕c5!? 14 ♗e3 ♕h5 15 f3
(15 ♗f4 ♕c5 16 ♗e3 ♕h5 repeats)
15...0-0 16 ♕g5?! (16 ♘e2 ♕e5 17
♕xe5 dxe5 18 ♘c1! and ♘d3 ±)
16...♕xg5 17 ♗xg5 ♖fd8 = Garcia
Martinez-Magerramov, Andorra
1990.

14 f3

This cautious move has the benefit of supporting e4, while the opposing queen and bishop have little
chance to exploit the a8-h1 diagonal. The minus side is that it is no
longer possible to swing a rook to
the kingside via the third rank. It is
reckless to be too adventurous:

a) 14 ♕xg7?! ♖g8 15 ♕h6 d5!
16 exd5 ♘xd5 17 ♗xd5 ♖xd5 18
♘e4 ♖d1 19 ♖xd1 ♕xe4 20 f3
♖xg2+ 21 ♔xg2 ♕xf3+ 22 ♔g1
♕g2# – analysis by Short.

b) 14 ♘d5?! exd5 15 exd5 ♘xd5
16 ♕xg7 ♔d7! 17 ♕g4+ ♔c7 18
♗xd5 ♕xd5 19 ♖xe7+ ♔b8 is good
for Black, who threatens ...♖hg8.

14 ...   0-0
15 ♗h6   ♘e8
16 ♔h1

White wishes to avoid any awkward checks. It is worth noting the
course of the game Shtyrenkov-
Magerramov, Smolensk 1991,

which continued 16 ♘e2!? ♕c5+ 17 ♔h1 ♗f6 18 c3 ♗e5 19 f4 ♗f6 20 ♘d4 ♔h8 21 ♗g5 h6 22 e5 dxe5 23 ♗xf6 gxf6 24 ♕h4 exd4 25 ♕xh6+ ♔g8 26 cxd4 ♕xd4 27 ♖xe6 ♗xg2+ 28 ♔xg2 ♕xb2+ 0-1.

16	...	♔h8
17	♗g5	

The trade of bishops is a prelude to directing operations against d6.

17	...	♗xg5
18	♕xg5	♘f6
19	♖ad1	

White has a slight initiative although the obvious plan of doubling rooks on the d-file allows Black to adopt defensive measures.

19	...	♖d7
20	♖d3	♖fd8
21	♖ed1	♕c5
22	♕e3	♔g8 *(D)*

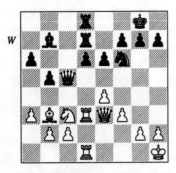

The exchange of queens would almost certainly lead to a draw, but Black bides his time by trying to improve his position gradually.

23	♔g1	♔f8

24	♕f2	♗a8
25	♘e2	g6?
26	♘d4!	

The immediate threat is 27 ♗xe6, against which Black must take precautions.

26	...	♕e5

Kasparov had planned to deal with this by prompting the trade of queens with 26...e5, but this can be met by 27 ♖c3! ♕a7 (27...♕b6? 28 ♘e6+ +−) 28 ♘c6 ♕xf2+ 29 ♔xf2 ♗xc6 (29...♖c8? 30 ♘xe5 ♖xc3 31 ♘xd7+ ♘xd7 32 bxc3 ±; 29...♖e8 30 a4 ±) 30 ♖xc6 a5 31 ♖b6 when the rook wins material.

The king side-step 26...♔g8 fails to 27 ♘xe6! ♕xf2+ 28 ♔xf2 fxe6 29 ♗xe6+ ♔g7 30 ♗xd7 ♖xd7 31 ♖xd6 ±.

27	♖e1	g5
28	c3! *(D)*	

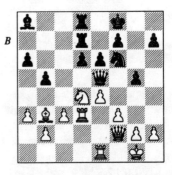

Short now embarks upon a shrewd scheme to undermine Black's queenside pawns by steering a rook to b4. Meanwhile, Black must be on guard against f4 and the subsequent concessions pose a long-term problem.

28	...	♔g7
29	♗c2	♖g8
30	♘b3	♔f8
31	♖d4	♔e7
32	a4	

The culmination of the first part of White's strategy, opening lines and creating weaknesses.

32	...	h5
33	axb5	axb5
34	♖b4 *(D)*	

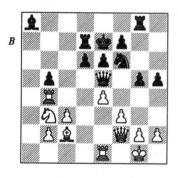

34 ... h4

Black's hopeful advance to stir up trouble indicates that his position is pitiful.

| 35 | ♘d4 | g4 |
| 36 | ♖xb5 | d5 |

A desperate resource, counting on 37 exd5 ♕xh2+ 38 ♔xh2 g3+ 39 ♔g1 gxf2+ 40 ♔xf2 ♗xd5 when prospects are still bleak for Black.

In any case there is no respite: 36...♕xh2+ 37 ♔xh2 g3+ 38 ♔g1

gxf2+ 39 ♔xf2 or 36...g3 37 hxg3! winning for White.

| 37 | ♕xh4 | ♕h5 |
| 38 | ♘f5+! | 1-0 |

Game 18
di Luca – Kinnunen
Corr 1991/93

1 e4 c5 2 ♘f3 d6 3 d4 cxd4 4 ♘xd4 ♘f6 5 ♘c3 a6 6 ♗c4 e6 7 0-0 b5

| 8 | ♗b3 | ♗e7 |
| 9 | ♕f3 | ♕b6 |

This is considered to be one of the main alternatives and was tipped to be employed by Kasparov in his match against Short. However, it only saw an appearance in one of the exhibition games when Short was understandably reluctant to reveal his opening preparation.

10 ♗e3

10 ♗g5 is a useful surprise weapon:

a) 10...♕xd4? 11 e5 ♘d5 12 ♗xe7 ♔xe7 13 ♖ad1 ♕c5 14 ♘xd5+ exd5 15 ♖xd5 ♕c6 16 exd6+ ♔d8 17 ♕xf7 is clearly better for White.

b) 10...♕a7?! 11 a3 ♗d7 12 ♖ad1 h6 13 ♗e3 ♕b7 14 ♕g3 ♘c6 15 f4 0-0-0 16 f5 ♘xd4 17 ♖xd4! h5 18 h3 h4 19 ♕e1 ♖h5 20 a4! ± Texeira-Castilho, Brazil 1989.

c) 10...b4?! 11 e5! ♗b7 12 ♘a4 ♕c7 (12...♕a7? 13 ♕d1 dxe5 14 ♘xe6 +–) 13 exd6 ♗xd6 14 ♕h3 ♘bd7?! 15 ♘xe6! fxe6 16 ♕xe6+

♚d8 17 ♗xf6+ gxf6 18 ♖ad1 ♗xh2+ 19 ♔h1 ♖e8 20 ♕xf6+ ♔c8 21 ♖xd7 1-0 Alvim-Valente, Corr 1988/89.

d) 10...♗b7?! 11 ♗e3 ♕c7 12 ♗xe6 fxe6 13 ♘xe6 when White has a promising attack according to Alvim.

e) 10...0-0 11 ♖ad1 ♗b7 12 ♖fe1 ♘bd7 13 ♕g3 b4 (13...♘c5 looks more sensible) 14 ♘a4 ♕c7 15 ♗h6 ♘e8 (15...♘h5) 16 ♗xe6!? fxe6 17 ♘xe6 ♕c4? 18 ♘xg7 (Alvim) gives White a decisive advantage (Nunn).

10 ...   ♕b7 *(D)*

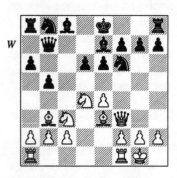

The queen looks out of place on b7, but it performs a useful role by putting pressure on e4. White has gained the move ♗e3 in comparison to other lines, but as it normally ventures out to g5 or h6, this is not an important tempo.

11 ♕g3

The pressure on the e-pawn has led White to try immediately to secure it with 11 ♖ae1?!, but this is unnecessary and misguided: 11...0-0 (11...b4? 12 ♘a4 ♘xe4 13 ♘b6! ♕xb6 14 ♘xe6 ♕b7 15 ♗d5! +−) 12 ♗g5 ♘bd7 (12...♗d7?! 13 e5! ♕xf3 14 ♘xf3 dxe5 15 ♘xe5 ±) 13 ♕g3 b4 14 ♘d5 (14 ♘a4? ♘xe4 15 ♖xe4 ♕xe4 16 ♘xe6 ♗xg5 17 ♘xf8 ♗f4 18 ♕h4 ♗b7 −+; 14 ♗d5? ♘xd5 15 exd5 ♗xg5 16 dxe6 ♘e5 17 ♕xg5 bxc3 −+) exd5 15 ♘f5 ♘e5 (15...♘b6?! 16 ♘xg7!) 16 ♗xd5 ♘xd5 17 ♗xe7 ♗xf5 18 ♗xd6 ♖fe8 19 ♗xe5 f6 20 exf5 fxe5 21 ♖xe5 ♖xe5 22 ♕xe5 ♘f6 23 h3 h6 ∓ Zapata-Browne, Las Vegas 1991.

11 ...   ♘bd7 *(D)*

The main alternatives 11...♘c6 and 11...♗d7 are discussed in the next game. There are other possibilities:

a) 11...b4 12 ♘a4 ♘bd7 (12...g6 13 ♖ad1 ♘bd7 14 f3 ♘h5 15 ♕e1 ±) 13 f3 0-0 *(D)* and now:

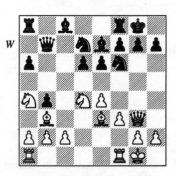

a1) 14 ♖ad1 ♔h8 15 ♖fe1 (15 ♖d2 ♘e5 16 ♘e2 a5 ½-½ Emms-

Szekely, Dublin 1991) 15...♖b8 16 ♔h1 ♘e5 17 ♘e2 ♕c7 18 c3 ♗d7 19 ♘f4 ♗xa4 20 ♗xa4 bxc3 21 bxc3 ♕xc3 22 ♗d4 ♕a5 23 ♗b3 ♕b5 24 ♘e2 ♖fc8 25 ♘c3 ♕a5 26 f4 ♘h5 27 ♕e3 ♘c6 28 ♘e2 ♘xd4 29 ♘xd4 ♕c3 30 ♖d3 ♕c5 31 ♕f3 ♘f6 32 f5 e5 33 ♘e2 ♕b4 34 ♘c3 d5 35 ♗xd5 ♘xd5 36 exd5 e4 37 ♖xe4 ♖xc3 38 ♖ed4 ♕d6 39 f6 ♗xf6 0-1 Short-Kasparov, London rapid 1993.

a2) 14 c3 bxc3 15 ♘xc3 ♘c5 16 ♕f2 ♗d7 17 ♖fd1 ♖fc8 with equality; Arakhamia-Zaichik, Moscow 1989.

a3) 14 ♘e2 ♘c5 15 ♘xc5 dxc5 16 ♕f2 ± Mikhalchishin.

b) 11...0-0 12 ♗h6 ♘e8:

b1) 13 ♘d5!? ♗d8 (13...exd5 14 ♗xd5 ♕a7 15 ♗e3) 14 ♘f4 ♔h8 15 ♗xe6 fxe6 16 ♘dxe6 gxh6 17 ♘xf8 ∞ Lepeshkin.

b2) 13 ♖ad1 ♗d7 14 ♖fe1 and now:

b21) 14...♘c6? 15 ♘d5! ♗d8 16 ♘f5! exf5 17 exf5 ♘e5 18 ♖xe5 dxe5 19 ♗xg7 ♘xg7 20 f6 ♗xf6 21 ♘xf6+ ♔h8 22 ♖xd7 ♖ad8 23 ♕h4 h5 24 ♕g5 +–.

b22) 14...♗f6 15 ♗g5 ♗xg5 16 ♕xg5 ♘c6 17 ♖e3 ♕a7 18 ♘ce2 ♘a5 19 ♕h4 ♘xb3 20 ♖h3 h6 21 axb3 ♕c5 22 ♖g3 ♔h7 23 ♖c3! ♕g5 24 ♕xg5 hxg5 25 b4! ± Kruppa-Gavrikov, Irkutsk 1986.

b23) 14...♔h8 15 ♗g5 ♗xg5 16 ♕xg5 ♘c6 17 ♘ce2 ♘f6 18 ♘g3 h6

19 ♕h4 a5 20 a3 ♘e5 = Hübner-Tisdall, Haifa 1989.

c) 11...♖g8?! 12 f4! b4 (or 12...♘xe4 13 ♘xe4 ♕xe4 14 f5 e5 15 f6! ±) 13 e5 bxc3 14 exf6 ♗xf6 (14...cxb2 15 ♕xg7!) 15 bxc3 ♕e7 16 ♖ab1 ♗b7 17 ♗a4+ ♔f8 18 ♖b6 ♕c7 19 ♖fb1 ♗d5 20 c4! ♗xc4 21 ♘c6 ± Mikhalchishin-Zaid, Alma-Ata 1977.

d) 11...g6 12 f3 and now:

d1) 12...0-0 13 ♖ad1 ♘bd7 14 ♗g5 b4 15 ♘ce2 ♘h5 16 ♕h4 ♗xg5 17 ♕xg5 ♘c5 18 ♗c4 ♘g7 19 b3 ± Mikhalchishin-Martinović, Lublin 1976.

d2) 12...♘bd7 13 ♖ad1 ♘c5 14 ♗h6 ♗d7 15 e5! ♘h5 16 ♕e1 dxe5 17 ♕xe5 f6 18 ♕e3 ♔f7 19 g4! ♘xb3 20 ♘xb3 ♘g7 21 ♗xg7 ♔xg7 22 ♘d5 ± Zaid-Anikaev, Lvov 1978.

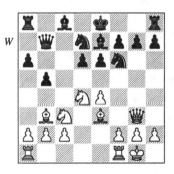

12 ♖fe1

In the game Kudrin-Freeman, Philadelphia 1991, White chose to bring the queen's rook to the centre:

12 ♖ae1 b4!? 13 ♘a4 ♘xe4 14 ♕xg7 ♗f6 15 ♕g4 h5 16 ♕d1 ♘e5 17 f3 ♘c5 18 ♘f5! exf5 19 ♘xc5 dxc5 20 ♗d5 ♕a7 21 ♗xa8 ♕xa8 22 ♗f4 ♗e6 23 ♗xe5 ♗xe5 24 ♖xe5 ♕c6 25 ♕d2 ♔f8 26 ♕d8+ 1-0.

12 ...   ♘c5
13 ♘f5   ♘xb3

Naturally, Black will not readily snatch the knight as it would only serve to open up the e-file for a dangerous offensive: 13...exf5? 14 ♗xc5 dxc5 15 ♕xg7 ♖f8 (15...♗e6 16 ♕xh8+ ♔d7 17 ♕g7 ♖g8 18 ♗xe6+ fxe6 19 ♕h6 b4 20 ♘a4 fxe4 21 ♘xc5+ +−) 16 exf5 c4 17 ♕xf6 ♖g8 18 ♘d5 ♗e6 19 ♕xe7+ ♕xe7 20 ♘xe7 ♔xe7 21 fxe6 winning for White.

14 ♘xg7+

14 ♘xe7 is also eminently playable after which a game Kir.Georgiev-Zaichik, Palma de Mallorca 1989, saw Black failing to cope with the assault: 14...♘xa1 (14...♕xe7 15 axb3 ♗b7 16 ♗g5! ±) 15 ♕xg7 ♖f8 (15...♘xc2 16 ♗g5 ♕xe7 17 ♕xh8+ ♔d7 18 ♗xf6 ♕e8 19 ♕xe8+ ♔xe8 20 ♖d1 ±) 16 e5! dxe5? (16...♘xc2! 17 ♗h6 ♘xe1 18 ♕xf8+ ♔d7 19 ♘ed5! ♘xd5 20 ♕xd6+ ♔e8 =) 17 ♗c5 ♘d7 18 ♘xc8? (18 ♘f5! ♘xc5 {18...exf5 19 ♖xe5+! ♘xe5 20 ♕xf8+ ♔d7 21 ♕e7+ ♔c6 22 ♕d6#} 19 ♘d6+ ♔e7 20 ♘xb7 ♗xb7 21 ♕xe5 ♘d7 22 ♕c7 ♘xc2 23 ♖d1 +−) 18...♖xc8 19

♗xf8 ♘xf8 20 ♘e4 ♕b6 21 ♕xe5 ♖xc2 22 ♖d1 ♘d7 23 ♘d6+ ♔d8? 24 ♕h8+ 1-0.

14 ...   ♔f8

Upon 14...♔d7 15 ♖ad1 White has sufficient compensation judging from analysis by di Luca:

a) 15...♘xe4 16 ♘xe4 ♕xe4 17 ♗f4 ♕g6 18 ♗xd6 ♕xg3 19 ♗xg3+ ♔c6 20 cxb3 ♖g8 21 ♖c1+ ♔b6 22 ♗c7+ ♔a7 23 ♘f5 ♗f6 24 ♘d6! +−.

b) 15...♖g8 16 axb3 ♘xe4 (or 16...♘h5 17 ♕f3!) 17 ♘xe4 ♕xe4 18 ♗g5 ♕c6 19 ♗xe7 ♔xe7 20 ♘f5+! ♔f8 21 ♕xg8+ +−.

c) 15...♘a5 16 e5 ♘e8 (16...♘d5 17 exd6 ♗xd6 18 ♗f4) 17 exd6 ♘xd6 18 ♗f4 ♕c6 19 ♗xd6 ♗xd6 20 ♘xe6 ♗b7 21 ♘e4 ♘c4 22 ♕g7! ±.

15 ♗h6   ♘xa1 (D)

16 e5!

This is the improvement that has revived interest in 14 ♘xg7+ as the threat of discovered check is more useful if the king's escape squares can be cut off. The search for material gains ends in vain after 16 ♘h5+ ♔e8 17 ♕g7 ♘xh5 18 ♕xh8+ ♔d7 ∓.

16 ...   ♘xc2

16...dxe5 is perilous on account of 17 ♖d1! ♗d7 (17...♘xc2 18 ♘xe6+ ♔e8 19 ♘g7+ ♔f8 20 ♘h5+ ♔e8 21 ♕g7 ♘d4 22 ♕xh8+ ♔d7 23 ♘xf6+ +−) 18 ♘h5+! ♔e8 19 ♕g7 ♔d8 20 ♘xf6 ♗xf6 21 ♕xf6+ ♔c7 22 ♕xe5+ +− Veličković.

17 ♖d1   ♘d7
18 ♘xe6+   ♔e8
19 ♘g7+   ♔d8

Black is routed after 19...♔f8 20 ♘f5+ ♔e8 21 exd6 ♕c6 22 ♕g7 ♗b7 23 ♕xh8+ ♗f8 24 ♘d5 +− di Luca.

20 exd6   ♗f6
21 ♗g5   ♖g8
22 ♕f4!   ♕xg2+

A stunning riposte. Black's only hope lines in gathering enough pieces for the queen and then trying to fend off the attack.

23 ♔xg2   ♖xg7
24 ♕e4   ♖xg5+
25 ♔f1   ♖b8
26 ♕xc2

The situation has clarified somewhat. Black has a rook and two pieces for the queen but in such a position it is insufficient compensation. Black's forces lack harmony and a combination of the exposed king and an opposing pawn on d6 present all sorts of problems.

26 ...   ♘f8
27 ♘e4   ♗h3+
28 ♔e2   ♖c8
29 ♕d2   ♖e5
30 f3 *(D)*

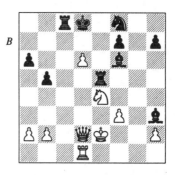

30 ...   ♘g6

di Luca points out that White can easily penetrate the heart of Black's camp after 30....♘e6 31 ♖c1 ♖xc1 (31...♘d4+ 32 ♔d3 ♖xc1 33 ♕xc1 +−; 31...♗g5 32 ♖xc8+ ♔xc8 33 ♕c3+) 32 ♕xc1 ♗g5 33 ♕c3 ♘f4+ 34 ♔d1 ♖d5+ 35 ♔c2 ♘e6 36 ♕a5+ +−.

31 ♖c1   ♗g5
32 ♕a5+   ♔e8
33 ♖xc8+   ♗xc8
34 ♕c7   ♗d7
35 ♕b8+   ♗d8
36 ♔d2   ♖f5

The rook is obliged to prevent both ♘f6+ and ♘c5-b7. Giving up the exchange fails to break White's grip on the position: 36...♖xe4 37 fxe4 ♘e5 (37...♗c6 38 ♕c8 ♗xe4

39 d7+ ♚e7 40 ♕xa6 ♚xd7 41
♕xb5+ ♗c6 42 ♕d3+ +–; 37...a5
38 ♕a8 ♘e5 39 ♕d5 ♘c4+ 40 ♚e1
♗h4+ 41 ♚e2 ♗g4+ 42 ♚d3
♘xb2+ 43 ♚c2 +–; 37...♘f8 38 b4
♗c6 39 ♕c8 ♗xe4 40 ♕xa6 +–) 38
♚c1 ♘c6 (38...♘f3 39 ♕a7 ♘xh2
40 ♕d4 f6 41 ♕d5 ♚f8 42 ♕h5
♘g4 43 ♕xh7 ♗e6 44 ♕h8+ ♗g8
45 ♕h5 +–) 39 ♕b7 +–.

37 b4   1-0

Game 19
Anand – Badea-Takacs
Prestwich 1990

**1 e4 c5 2 ♘f3 d6 3 d4 cxd4 4 ♘xd4
♘f6 5 ♘c3 a6 6 ♗c4 e6 7 0-0 b5 8
♗b3 ♗e7 9 ♕f3 ♕b6 10 ♗e3 ♕b7
11 ♕g3**

11 ...   ♘c6

The passive 11...♗d7 condemns
Black to a cheerless defence:

a) 12 f4 b4 13 e5 ♘h5 14 ♕h3
bxc3 and now:

a1) 15 ♕xh5 cxb2 16 ♖ae1! g6
17 ♕h6 ♗f8 18 ♕g5 ♗e7 = T.Hor-
vath-Psakhis, Lvov 1984.

a2) 15 f5! dxe5 (15...g6 16 fxe6
fxe6 17 exd6 ♗xd6 18 ♘xe6! ±;
15...exf5 16 exd6 ♗f6 {16...♗xd6
17 ♕xh5 g6 18 ♕h6 ♗f8 19 ♕f4 ±}
17 ♕xh5 0-0 18 ♘xf5 ♗xf5 19
♕xf5 cxb2 20 ♖ad1 ±; 15...0-0 16
exd6 ♗xd6 17 fxe6 ±) 16 fxe6 exd4
(16...♘f6 17 exd7+ ♕xd7 18 ♘f5 0-0
19 ♖ad1 ±) 17 ♕xh5 ♗b5 (17...0-0?
18 ♖xf7! ±; 17...♚d8 18 ♖xf7 cxb2

19 ♖b1 ±; 17...dxe3 18 ♖xf7 g6 19
♖xe7+ ±; 17...♕b5 18 exd7+ ♘xd7
19 ♕xf7+ ± Diaz Perez) 18 ♖xf7 g6
19 ♕e5 ♖g8 20 ♗g5 cxb2 21 ♖d1
♘c6 22 ♕e4 ♕c8 23 ♕h4 1-0 Diaz
Perez-Ojano, Pinar del Rio 1989.

b) 12 ♘f5 exf5 (12...b4?! 13
♕xg7! ♖g8 14 ♕xf6! ♗xf6 15
♘xd6+ ♚f8 16 ♘xb7 bxc3 17 bxc3
± Yurtaev-Isupov, USSR 1984) 13
♕xg7 ♖f8 14 ♗g5 and now:

b1) 14...♘xe4 15 ♗xe7 ♚xe7 16
♘d5+ ♚e8 17 f3 ♗e6 (17...♗c6 18
fxe4 ♘d7 19 ♖xf5 1-0 Delacroix-
Hugentobler, Corr 1989; 17...♕a7+
18 ♚h1 ♘f2+ 19 ♖xf2 ♕xf2 20
♕f6 1-0 Westerveld-Andriesse, Rot-
terdam 1988) 18 fxe4 ♘d7 19 ♕g5
f6 20 ♕g7 (20 ♕h5+ ♚d8 21 ♕xh7
fxe4 22 ♕e7+ 1-0 Vlad-Armas, Bucharest 1988) 20...♖f7 21 ♕g8+
♘f8 22 ♘c7+ ♖xc7 23 ♗xe6 ♖g7
24 ♕h8 ♖xg2+ 25 ♚xg2 ♕xe4+ 26
♚f2 ♕f4+ 27 ♚g1 ♕g4+ 28 ♚f2
♕f4+ 29 ♚e2 ♕e4+ 30 ♚d1 ♕d4+
½-½ Grilc-Stamenković, Cetinje
1990.

b2) 14...♘g8 15 ♗xe7 ♘xe7 16
♘d5 ♘g6 (16...♘g8 17 exf5 ♘c6
18 ♘f6+ ♘xf6 19 ♕xf6 ♘e7 20
♖fe1 ♗c6 21 ♕xd6 ♖d8 22 ♖xe7+
♕xe7 23 ♕xc6+ ♖d7 24 ♗e6! +–
Silva-Hawelko, Thessaloniki OL
1988) 17 ♘f6+ ♚d8 18 ♘xh7 ♖h8
19 ♗xf7 (19 ♘g5 ♗e8 20 exf5 ♖h5
21 ♘xf7+ ♗xf7 22 fxg6 1-0
Kuczynski-Cvitan, Warsaw 1990)
19...♖xh7 20 ♕xh7 ♘e7 21 ♖ad1

fxe4 22 罝xd6 含c7 23 罝fd1 &f5 24 &g6 1-0 J.Sørensen-Schandorff, Copenhagen 1990.

12 f4!? (D)

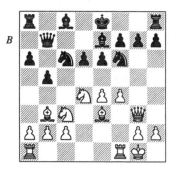

Anand has found a relatively simple plan to gain an advantage by trying to dominate the centre and reserve the option of e5.

The older moves deserve inspection:

a) 12 罝fe1 &d7 13 罝ad1 and now:

a1) 13...0-0 14 &h6 ②e8 15 ②d5! &d8 16 ②f5! exf5 17 exf5 ②e5 18 罝xe5 dxe5 19 f6 g6 20 ②e7+ 含h8 21 &xf8 ₩e4 22 &d5 ₩xc2 23 罝f1 罝b8 24 ₩xe5 1-0 Gurieli-Sakhatova, Erevan 1985.

a2) 13...b4 14 ②ce2 0-0 15 &h6 ②e8 16 &g5 &xg5 17 ₩xg5 ②f6 18 ②g3 h6 19 ₩h4 = Bouaziz-Marin, Szirak IZ 1987.

b) 12 ②xc6 ₩xc6 opens up possibilities of transposing, after a subsequent ...0-0 &h6, to the line 9...₩c7 10 ₩g3 ②c6 11 ②xc6

₩xc6. The move numbers will be different, since White has played &c1-e3-h6 instead of &c1-h6, and Black has played ...₩d8-b6-b7xc6 rather than ...₩d8-c7xc6. Alternatively, White may argue that the bishop can be useful on e3, giving rise to independent options. Play may continue:

b1) 13 a4?! b4 14 a5 0-0 15 ②a2 ②xe4 16 ②xb4 ₩b5 17 ₩f4 &b7 (17...₩xb4 18 罝a4) 18 c3 &g5 19 ₩g4 &xe3 20 fxe3 h5 21 ₩d1 ₩g5 22 ₩e2 h4 干 Howell-Popovych, New York 1990.

b2) 13 f3 0-0 and now:

b21) 14 罝fd1 罝d8 15 ₩f2 &b7 16 ②e2 ②d7 17 c3 ②e5 18 ②d4 ₩e8 19 ₩e2 罝ac8 20 a4! ②c4 (20...d5?! 21 axb5! axb5 22 罝a7 罝b8 23 f4 ②c4 24 e5 ±; 21...dxe4 22 bxa6 exf3 23 ②xf3 ②xf3+ 24 gxf3 &a8 ±) 21 &f2 g6 22 axb5 axb5 23 罝a7 罝c7 (23...&a8? 24 ②xb5 ₩xb5 25 &xc4 +-) 24 罝da1 e5 25 ②c2 罝a8 26 ②b4 罝xa7 27 罝xa7 ± Wahls-Armas, Bundesliga 1989/90.

b22) 14 ②e2 e5 (14...&b7 15 ②d4 ₩d7 16 &h6 ±) 15 &g5 ②h5 16 ₩h4 &xg5 17 ₩xg5 ②f6 18 ②g3 &e6 19 罝ad1 罝fd8 (19...₩c5+!?) 20 罝f2 h6 21 ₩e3 ₩c5 22 ②f1 ₩xe3 23 ②xe3 含f8 24 罝fd2 含e7 25 含f2 h5 26 h4 g6 27 c3 a5 28 &xe6 fxe6 29 c4 with a slight plus for White; Hübner-Armas, Bundesliga 1989.

b3) 13 罝fe1 &b7 and now:

b31) 14 ♗g5 (14 ♖ad1 see 'b4')
14...0-0 15 ♗h6 ♘e8 16 a3 ♔h8 17
♗g5 ♗xg5 18 ♕xg5 ♘f6 19 ♖ad1
♖ad8 20 ♖d3 ♖d7 21 f3?! (21 ♕d2
♖fd8 22 f3 ♕c5+ 23 ♔h1 ♗c6 ±)
21...♕c5+ 22 ♕e3 ♕xe3+ 23
♖dxe3 = Gdanski-Calinescu, Arn-
hem 1987/88.

b32) 14 a3!? 0-0 15 ♗h6 transposes to the position after 14 ♗h6 in
note 'a' to Black's 13th move in
Game 17.

b33) 14 f3 0-0 15 ♖ad1 (15 ♗h6
transposes to the position after 14
♗h6 from line 'c' in the note to
White's 13th move in Game 17)
15...a5!? 16 a4 ♗a6 17 ♗h6 ♘e8 18
♗g5 ♗xg5 19 ♕xg5 b4 20 ♘b1
♕b6+?! (20...h6!?) 21 ♕e3 ♕c7 22
♕d4 ♖c8 23 ♖e3 ± Henāo-Herrera,
Santa Clara 1990.

b4) 13 ♖ad1 ♗b7 14 ♖fe1 ♘xe4
15 ♘xe4 ♕xe4 and now:

b41) 16 ♗f4 ♕g6 17 ♗xd6 ♖d8
(17...♗xd6 18 ♖xd6 ♕xg3 19 hxg3
is also safe for Black; Wahls-Armas,
Germany 1990) 18 ♗xe7 ♕xg3 19
hxg3 ½-½ Rublevsky-Obukhov,
Smolensk 1991.

b42) 16 ♕xg7 ♗f6 (16...♔d7 17
♗xe6+ ♕xe6 18 ♗g5 ♗e4 19 ♗xe7
♖hg8 20 ♕xg8 ♖xg8 21 ♖xd6+
♕xd6 22 ♗xd6 ♖xg2+ 23 ♔f1 ♖g4
½-½ Kudrin-Browne, Saint Martin
1991) 17 ♕g3 0-0-0 (17...♗h4 18
♕h3 ♕g6 19 ♗xe6! +–; 18...♖g8
19 ♗g5!) 18 ♗b6! ♖dg8 19 ♖xe4
♖xg3 20 hxg3 ♗xe4 21 ♗d4 (21

♖xd6! ♗xb2 22 ♗d4 ♗xd4 23
♖xd4 ♗g6 24 ♖d6 ♔b7 ±)
21...♗xd4 22 ♖xd4 d5 23 f3 ♗g6 24
a4 ♔c7 25 ♔f2 = Verőci-Petronić–
Armas, Bad Wörishofen 1990.

12 ...   ♘xd4

Not 12...b4?! 13 ♘xc6 bxc3
(13...♕xc6?? 14 ♗a4) 14 ♘xe7 ±.

13 ♗xd4   b4
14 e5!   ♘h5
15 ♕g4 (D)

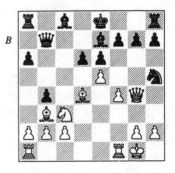

Anand himself suggests that 15
♗a4+ might be an improvement.
For example: 15...♔f8 (15...♗d7 16
♗xd7+ ♔xd7 17 ♕g4 ±) 16 ♕g4
bxc3 17 ♕xh5 ♕b4 (17...cxb2 18
exd6! bxa1♕ {18...♗xd6 19 ♖ad1
♕b4 20 ♗xb2! ±} 19 dxe7+ ♕xe7
20 ♖xa1 ∞) 18 bxc3 ♕xa4 19 exd6
♗xd6 (19...♗d8 20 ♕f3 ♖b8 21
♖ab1 ∞) 20 ♕g5 f6 21 ♗xf6 ♕d7
(21...♖a7 22 ♖ad1! ♕c6 23 ♗e5 ±)
22 ♖ad1 ♖g8 23 ♗e5 ♗c5+ 24 ♔h1
±.

15 ...   bxc3
16 ♕xh5   cxb2

17 ♗xb2   g6

17...d5? falls victim to 18 f5! with a clear advantage.

18 ♕h6   ♗f8
19 ♕h3   d5

Black would have good chances of equality after the refinement 19...♕b6+! 20 ♔h1 d5 when the bishop on b2 has a restricted role.

20 ♗d4!

The d-pawn is blocked in order to cancel out the possibility of ...d4 which would open up the a8-h1 diagonal.

20 ...   ♕c6
21 ♔h1   ♗d7
22 c3   ♗g7 *(D)*

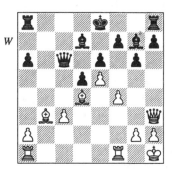

This is a natural reaction to guard the entry squares f6 and h6. However, Anand points out there is a need to simplify with 22...♗c5:

a) 23 f5 gxf5! (23...♗xd4 24 cxd4 exf5 25 ♕h6 ∞) 24 g4 0-0-0 ∞.

b) 23 ♗a4 ♕c7 24 ♗xd7+ ♔xd7 with an edge for White.

c) 23 ♕e3 is a small but safe positional advantage for White.

23 f5!   gxf5
24 g4!

Astutely offering another pawn which ensures the breakthrough.

24 ...   ♕c7
25 ♖ae1   ♗b5?

The best try is 25...0-0-0 26 gxf5 when White is clearly better.

26 gxf5!   ♗xf1
27 ♖xf1   ♕d7

27...0-0-0 (27...exf5 28 ♗a4+ ♔f8 29 ♕xf5 +−) 28 fxe6 fxe6 29 ♕xe6+ ♔b8 30 ♖f7 and White is better.

28 fxe6   ♕xe6

Or 28...fxe6 29 ♗a4! ♕xa4 30 ♕xe6+ ♔d8 31 ♗b6#.

29 ♕g2   1-0

3 Fischer Attack: Others

Waitzkin – Wojtkiewicz
New York 1993

1 e4 c5 2 ♘f3 d6 3 d4 cxd4 4 ♘xd4
♘f6 5 ♘c3 a6 6 ♗c4 e6 7 ♗b3

   7 ...   ♗e7
   8 g4 *(D)*

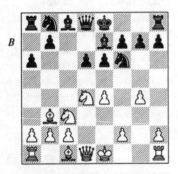

Velimirović was the main inspiration behind this daring way to handle the opening. The g-pawn is thrust forward in a bid to gain a territorial advantage. It is a reasonable continuation that has the benefit of avoiding a substantial amount of theory. The drawback is that it is very committal and without careful play can merely compromise White's pawn structure.

   8 ...   d5

A logical response that aims to open the centre in order to leave the g-pawn a bystander. The alternatives 8...0-0, 8...♘c6 and 8...h6 are discussed later in this chapter.

   9 exd5   ♘xd5
   10 ♘xd5

It is premature to give up the bishop: 10 ♗xd5 exd5 11 0-0 ♘c6 12 ♗e3 ♘e5 13 f3 ♘c4 ∓ Nikitin.

   10 ...   exd5
   11 ♘f5

White is obliged to maintain the initiative to justify g4. This has the benefit of luring Black into complications by utilizing the g-file. Nunn recommends 11 ♕f3 with play against d5 to gain an edge.

   11 ...   ♗xf5
   12 gxf5   d4
   13 ♕g4

After 13 ♕h5!? 0-0 14 ♗d2 (14 ♖g1!?) 14...♘d7 15 0-0-0 Black has some difficulties (Waitzkin).

   13 ...   ♗f6

Black is busted after 13...0-0? 14 ♗h6 ♗f6 15 ♖g1 +−.

   14 ♗f4   ♕e7+? *(D)*

Black seizes his chance to deprive White of his castling rights. In fact,

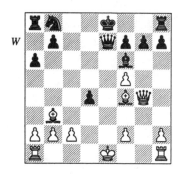

this can be achieved by 14...♕a5+ which also has the bonus that the king ends up on g2, when an extra tempo is required to place a rook on the g-file:

a) 15 c3?! dxc3? (15...0-0!) 16 ♗xf7+ ♔xf7 17 ♕h5+ ♔e7 18 ♕e2+ ♗e5 (18...♔d8 19 0-0-0+ ♘d7 20 ♖xd7+ ♔xd7 21 ♕e6+ ♔d8 22 ♖d1+ +−) 19 ♗xe5 cxb2+ 20 ♗c3+! ♔f7 21 ♕c4+ ♔e7 22 ♗b4+ (22 ♕e6+ ♔f8 23 ♕c8+ ♔e7 24 ♕xb7+ ♘d7 25 ♕xb2 +−) 22...♔f6 23 ♕e6+ +−.

b) 15 ♗d2 ♕e5+ 16 ♔f1 ♕b5+ 17 ♔g2 0-0 ∞ Waitzkin.

15 ♔f1   0-0
16 ♖g1

This rapid sharpening of the game is to White's advantage. A simplistic plan of attack is available in the form of trebling on the g-file or pinpointing h7 as a weakness. Black has problems in staging an adequate defence partly because f5 helps to avoid exchanges and also because of his lagging development.

16 ...   ♔h8
17 ♖e1   ♕d7
18 ♖g3

18 ♗g5 is worth consideration, and does have the merit of eliminating the defender of g7: 18...♗xf6 (18...♕d8!?) 19 ♕xg5 f6 20 ♕h5 ♘c6 21 ♖e4 (threatening 22 ♕xh7+ ♔xh7 23 ♖h4#) 21...h6 22 ♖eg4 ♘e5 23 ♖xg7 ♕xg7 24 ♖xg7 ♔xg7 25 f4 +−.

18 ...   ♘c6

After 18...g6 19 ♗g5 ♗xg5 20 ♕xg5 ♕xf5 21 ♕xf5 gxf5 22 ♖e7 ♘c6 23 ♖xb7 White has a superior ending.

19 ♖h3   g5

An unfortunate necessity, since 19...g6? 19 ♖xh7+ ♔xh7 20 fxg6+ fxg6 21 ♕xd7+ wins for White.

20 ♗xg5   ♗xg5
21 ♕xg5   f6
22 ♕h5   ♖ad8
23 ♖e4   ♕c7
24 ♖eh4 (D)

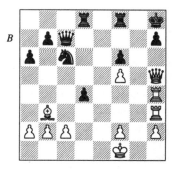

White has a strong bind on the

position with intense pressure against h7. This forces Black to adopt a defensive stance, with little hope of counterplay.

24...♖d7 25 ♕h6 ♖g7 26 ♖g3 ♕e7 27 ♖e4 ♘e5

Not 27...♕c7 28 ♕xf6!.

28 f4 ♖xg3 29 hxg3 ♘g4 30 ♖xe7 ♘xh6 31 ♗e6

White's extra material constitutes a winning advantage. This is enhanced by the text which cuts off the knight from returning to the fray.

31...♖d8 32 ♔e2 b5 33 ♖a7 ♘g4 34 ♖xa6 ♘e3 35 ♔d3 h5 36 ♖a7 ♘f1 37 ♖f7 ♘xg3 38 ♖xf6 ♔h7 39 ♖g6 ♘h1

The passed h-pawn is soon caught upon 38...h4 39 ♖g4! +–.

40 ♖g2 1-0

Game 21
Djurhuus – Van Wely
Gausdal 1994

1 e4 c5 2 ♘f3 d6 3 d4 cxd4 4 ♘xd4 ♘f6 5 ♘c3 a6 6 ♗c4 e6 7 ♗b3 ♗e7 8 g4

8 ... 0-0 (D)

Black decides to allow White to push the pawns in the hope that they can be exploited. The preliminary 8...h6 is a logical reaction to curb the effectiveness of g5. After 9 ♗e3 ♘c6 (9...b5 10 ♕f3 ♗b7 11 ♗xe6 ±) 10 ♖g1 play might continue:

a) 10...g5 11 ♕e2 ♕c7 12 0-0-0 ♖g8 (de Firmian-Gavrikov, Tunis IZ

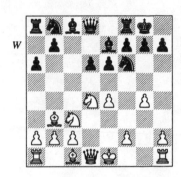

1985) and now 13 ♘xc6 bxc6 14 f4 gxf4 15 ♗xf4 e5 16 g5! with excellent play.

b) 10...♗d7 11 f4! g5 (11...h5!? 12 h3 hxg4 13 hxg4 ♖h3 14 ♕e2 ±) 12 f5 e5 (12...♕c8 13 fxe6 fxe6 14 ♘xc6 ♗xc6 {14...♕xc6 15 ♕d3} 15 e5! dxe5 16 ♕d3 ±) 13 ♘de2 ♘a5 14 ♘d5 ♘xb3 15 ♘xf6+! ♗xf6 16 axb3 ♗c6 17 ♘c3 ♕d7 18 ♕d2! ♗d8 19 h4 gxh4 20 ♗xh6 +– Donchev-Espig, Bulgaria-E.Germany 1982.

c) 10...♘a5 11 ♕e2 b5 12 h4! g6 (12...♗b7? 13 g5 hxg5 14 hxg5 ♘xe4 15 g6 ♘xb3 16 gxf7+ ♔d7 17 ♘xe6! ♔xe6 18 ♕g4+ ♔f7 19 ♕g6+ ♔f8 20 ♕xg7+ ♔e8 21 ♕xh8+ +–; 12...b4 13 ♘a4 ♘xe4?! 14 ♘xe6 ♗xe6 15 ♗b6 ♕c8 16 ♗xa5 +– Azmaiparashvili) 13 g5 hxg5 14 hxg5 ♘h5 15 f4 ♗d7 16 f5 ♕c8 17 0-0-0! ♘xb3+ 18 axb3 ♕b7 19 e5! dxe5? (19...d5! 20 f6 ±) 20 fxe6 fxe6 21 ♘f3 0-0-0 22 ♘xe5 ♖hg8 23 ♕g4 ♘g7 24 ♘xg6 ♗c6 25 ♗d4 ♘f5 26 ♘xe7+ ♕xe7 27

&f6 &xd1+ 28 &xd1 &c5 (or 28...&xf6? 29 gxf6 &xg4 30 f7 +−) 29 &e2 +− Azmaiparashvili-Gavrikov, USSR Ch 1986.

   9 g5   **&fd7**
  10 h4   **&c5**
  11 &e3

White prepares to castle queenside before advancing his g- and h-pawns any further.

  11 ...   **b5** *(D)*

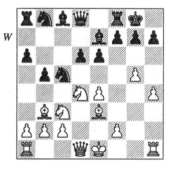

  12 &g4!

The queen is often developed at d2 or e2 but Black's move order allows this more active posting. It is useful to defend e4 against the threat of ...b4, and the long-term plan of h5 and g6 pinpoints the weak point e6.

  12 ...   **&bd7**
  13 0-0-0   **&e5**

Black's temporary initiative has little substance as the rest of his forces are not ready to participate in a counter-attack.

  14 &h3   **b4**
  15 &a4   **&c7**

This is an admission that something has gone wrong. The point of Black's knight tango was to snatch the e-pawn, which he has now rejected in view of 15...&xe4 16 f4! &d7 17 &c6 &e8 18 f5 when White dominates the board.

  16 h5   **&e8**

Black resolves to defend e6 but there is no time for ...&f8. After 16...&xe4 17 g6! &f6 (17...fxg6 18 hxg6 h6 19 &xe6 +−) 18 h6 (18 gxf7+ &xf7 19 &xe6 is also sufficient) 18...&xg6 19 hxg7 &xg7 20 &h6+ &g8 21 &g5 &d8 22 &d3 (intending &f3) 22...&b7 23 &xe6 White wins.

  17 g6   **&f6**

It is clear that if there are exchanges on g6 then e6 will be vulnerable and the open h-file will allow White to create mating threats: 17...fxg6 18 hxg6 h6 19 &xc5 dxc5 20 &xe6 &xe6 21 &xe6+ &h8 22 &xh6 +−.

  18 &xc5   **dxc5**
  19 h6 *(D)*

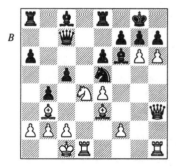

19   ...   fxg6
20   ♘xe6

A triumph for White's strategy. The pawn roller has succeeded in creating weaknesses and now the key defensive pawn is captured, which accelerates Black's demise.

20   ...   ♕f7
21   hxg7   h5

This is the only way to avoid mate, but it allows White to enter a superior ending.

22   ♘xc5   ♗xh3
23   ♗xf7+   ♔xf7
24   ♖xh3   ♘c4

An ambitious attempt to seize the initiative. The alternative is to settle for a robust defensive task, but this is also problematical: 24...♗xg7 25 b3 a5 26 ♗g5 ♖ec8 (26...♖ac8 27 ♘b7!) 27 ♖d5 intending f4 with a clear advantage.

25   ♗d4   ♗g5+
26   ♔b1   ♘d2+
27   ♔a1   ♖ad8

The only way to stay in the game as the variation 27...♘xe4 28 ♖f3+ ♘f6 (28...♔g8 29 ♖f8+! ♖xf8 30 gxf8♕+ ♖xf8 31 ♘xe4 +−) 29 ♗xf6 ♗xf6 30 g8♕+ ♖xg8 31 ♘e4 leaves Black a whole piece down.

28   ♖d3   ♘xe4
29   ♘xa6   ♗f4
30   ♘xb4   h4

A forlorn effort.

31 a4 g5 32 c4 h3 33 ♘d5 h2 34 ♖h1 ♖xd5 35 cxd5 ♖a8 36 b3 ♖d8 37 ♖xh3 ♘d2 38 ♔a2 1-0

Game 22

Yakovich – Zilbershtein
USSR 1987

1 e4 c5 2 ♘f3 d6 3 d4 cxd4 4 ♘xd4 ♘f6 5 ♘c3 a6 6 ♗c4 e6 7 ♗b3 ♗e7
   8 g4   ♘c6!?

Black continues developing and shows little concern for the unusual situation, perhaps assuming that the game will transpose to normal paths (i.e. the note to Black's 8th move in Game 21) after 9 ♗e3 h6.

9   g5   ♘xd4

The natural 9...♘d7? is severely punished by 10 ♗xe6! fxe6 11 ♘xe6 ±.

10   ♕xd4   ♘h5 (D)

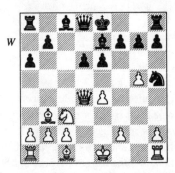

11   ♖g1

An acceptable way of defending the advanced pawn, especially as White intends to castle queenside.

11   ...   b5
12   ♗e3   0-0

It would appear that it is dubious to castle into the attack but Black has little choice. The king would have no shelter on the other wing and there is a need to bring the rest of the forces into play.

13 0-0-0 Rb8?!

The desire to push the a- and b-pawns is understandable, but the timing is wrong. It is better to avoid the pin on the d-file with 13...♕c7. White is on top after 13...♗b7 14 f4 and 13...♗d7 14 e5 d5 15 ♘e4!.

14 e5 d5

Certainly not 14...dxe5? 15 ♕h4 winning.

15 ♕h4 g6 (D)

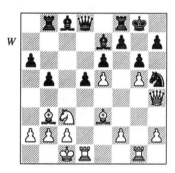

16 ♘e4! dxe4

A bold attempt to fend off the onslaught by trading the queen for the rook and knight. The perils that await Black if the offer is ignored is evident upon 16...a5? 17 ♘f6+ ♗xf6 18 gxf6 ♔h8 19 c3 a4 20 ♗c2 b4 21 ♕xh5! gxh5 22 Rg7 which gives White a winning game according to Yakovich.

17 Rxd8 Rxd8

18	♕xe4	♗b7
19	♕g4	♘g7
20	Rd1	

White has an interest in exchanging pieces as it would give the queen more freedom to infiltrate the opposition's camp.

20	...	♘f5
21	♗b6	Rxd1+
22	♔xd1	♗c6
23	♗a5	♗c5

It is futile to try to blockade the bishop: 23...b4 24 c3 bxc3 26 bxc3 when White has a passed pawn.

24	♔e1	♗d4
25	♕f4!	♗xb2
26	c3	♗a3
27	♗b4	♗xb4
28	♕xb4 (D)	

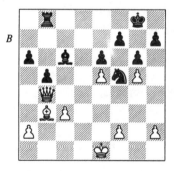

White has methodically traded pieces and is now ideally placed to force Black into submission by putting pressure on the queenside pawns.

28	...	♗f3
29	♕a5	Ra8

30 ♕b6   ♔f8

A precaution as the immediate 30...♘e7 falls victim to 31 ♗xe6! fxe6 32 ♕xe6+ ♔f8 33 ♕f6+ ♔e8 34 ♕xf3 +−.

31 a4   ♘e7

If 31...bxa4 32 ♗xa4 and the passed pawn is formidable.

32 axb5 axb5 33 ♕xb5 ♗c6 34 ♕b4 ♖d8 35 ♗a4 ♗xa4 36 ♕xa4 ♖c8 37 ♕d7!

The queen manages to paralyse the opposition by preparing to meet ...♖xc3 by ♕d8+. Now the c-pawn can romp towards the eighth rank.

37...♖a8 38 c4 ♖a1+ 39 ♔d2 ♖a2+ 40 ♔c3 ♖a8 41 ♔b4 ♖b8+ 42 ♔c5 ♘f5 43 ♔c6 ♔g7 44 c5 ♖b4 45 ♔c7 ♖d4 46 c6 ♖d5 47 ♔d8! ♘d4 48 ♔e7

Not 48 c7 ♘c6+!.

48...h6

There is no escape after 48...♘xc6+ 49 ♕xc6 ♖a5 50 ♕f3 ♖a7+ 51 ♔e8 or 48...♖xd7 49 cxd7 ♘c6+ 50 ♔d6 winning.

49 c7 1-0

Game 23
Fischer – Cardoso
New York (4) 1957

1 e4 c5 2 ♘f3 d6 3 d4 cxd4 4 ♘xd4 ♘f6 5 ♘c3 a6 6 ♗c4 e6

7 0-0   ♗d7

An unusual continuation that is similar to lines discussed in the note to Black's 8th move in Game 24

(Anand-Piket). It is less flexible than lines with 7...b5 or 7...♗e7 since the knight cannot now occupy d7.

8 ♗b3   ♘c6
9 ♗e3   ♗e7
10 f4   ♕c7?! (D)

Simple development fails to counter White's plan of f5 to undermine e6. A possible improvement: 10...b5 11 f5 ♘xd4 12 ♗xd4 e5 13 ♗e3 ♗c6 14 ♕d3 when White has a slight advantage.

11 f5   ♘xd4

It is a mistake to exchange on f5: 11...exf5 12 ♘xf5 ♗xf5 13 ♖xf5 when the open f-file and the light-squared bishop give White a clear advantage.

12 ♗xd4   b5
13 a3   e5

The less committal 13...0-0 is a reasonable alternative: 14 ♕e2 (14 fxe6?! fxe6 15 ♕e2 =) 14...♖ac8 15 ♖ae1 gives White a slight edge.

14 ♗e3   ♗c6
15 ♘d5

White declares his intention to try to secure d5 for his pieces.

15 ...   ♗xd5?

Certainly not obligatory, as the the weakness of e4 can be highlighted after 15...♕b7! 16 ♕d3 (16 ♘xe7 ♔xe7!) 16...♗xd5 17 exd5 0-0 18 a4 ♖fc8 ∞.

16 ♗xd5   ♘xd5
17 ♕xd5   ♖c8
18 c3   ♕c4
19 ♕b7! *(D)*

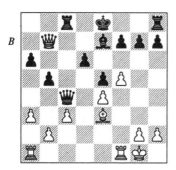

Black cannot castle and a6 is under threat. This can only be remedied by offering the exchange of queens, but White is left with the initiative.

Less good is 19 ♖ad1?! ♕xd5 20 ♖xd5 ♖c4 when the e-pawn falls.

19 ...   ♕c6
20 ♕xc6+   ♖xc6
21 a4

White intends to activate his rooks with the aim of creating a passed pawn on the queenside.

21 ...   ♔d7
22 axb5   axb5
23 ♖a7+   ♖c7
24 ♖fa1   ♖b8
25 ♔f2

The king joins in the struggle by starting the march to the queenside. The idea is that c4 can be eventually played intending to recapture with the king ensuring the b-pawn a free passage to the eighth rank.

25 ...   ♖bb7
26 ♖xb7   ♖xb7
27 ♔e2   ♗d8
28 ♔d3   h6
29 ♖a8   h5
30 b4!

Fischer conducts the ending in exemplary style. Black has to adopt a passive defence whilst White is able to dictate matters by creating and utilizing a passed b-pawn.

30...♗e7 31 ♖g8 ♗f6 32 ♖f8 ♔c6 33 c4! ♖d7 34 ♖a8 bxc4+ 35 ♔xc4 ♖c7 36 ♖a7

The trade of rooks means that Black will have difficulty in avoiding the entry of the opposing king.

36...♖xa7 37 ♗xa7 ♗d8 38 ♗e3 f6 39 b5+ ♔d7 40 ♔d5 ♗a5 41 ♗a7 ♗b4 42 ♗b8 ♗c5 43 g3

White is now poised to make a decisive incursion.

43...♔e7 44 ♔c6 g6 45 fxg6 f5 46 ♗xd6+ 1-0

4 The Sozin Attack

The contribution Fischer made to this line is immense. He played the system throughout almost the whole of his career. Indeed, he deserves to have this line named after him too, but since the name Sozin (who played the line in the 1920s) is well-established, I have preferred to reserve the name 'Fischer Attack' for ♗c4 specifically against the Najdorf, and refer to lines with an early ...♘c6 as the 'Sozin Attack'.

The search for less analysed lines has generated interest in the hitherto relatively obscure 9 f4. Anand, Judit Polgar and Short have successfully experimented with this move. White aims to expand on the kingside by playing ♕f3 and maintaining the option of g4. We shall investigate this line extensively. Other lines are covered to give White different options, including the way Kasparov handles the variation as White.

Game 24
Anand – Piket
Amsterdam 1990

1	e4	c5
2	♘f3	♘c6

3	d4	cxd4
4	♘xd4	♘f6
5	♘c3	d6
6	♗c4	e6
7	♗e3	a6

The slightly unusual 7...♗d7 is another possibility. After 8 ♗b3 ♗e7 9 0-0 0-0 play might proceed:
a) 10 f4 *(D)* and now:

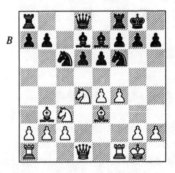

a1) 10...♘xd4 11 ♗xd4 ♗c6 12 ♕e2 (12 ♕e1 b5 13 ♖d1 b4 14 e5 bxc3 15 exf6 ♗xf6 16 ♕xc3 ♗xd4+ 17 ♕xd4 d5 18 f5 ♕b6 = Neukirch-Hartston, Hastings 1967; 12 ♕d3 b5 13 e5 dxe5 14 fxe5 ♘d7 15 ♘e4 ♗xe4 16 ♕xe4 ♘c5 17 ♕e3 ♕c7 = Minić-Sofrevski, Yugoslavia 1967) 12...b5 13 ♘xb5 ♗xb5 14 ♕xb5 ♘xe4 15 f5 and now:

a11) 15...♗f6 16 ♕d3! (16 ♖ad1 ♗xd4+ 17 ♖xd4 d5 18 ♖dd1 ♘d6 19 ♕c5 ♘xf5 20 ♗xd5 ♖c8 21 ♕xa7 ♕f6 22 ♗e4 ♕xb2 = Fedorov-Lysenko, USSR 1975) 16...d5 17 ♗xf6 ♘xf6 18 c4 dxc4 (or 18...♕b6+ 19 ♔h1 dxc4 20 ♕xc4 ±) 19 ♕xd8 ♖fxd8 20 ♗xc4 e5 21 ♖fe1 e4 22 ♖ad1 ± Fischer-Weinstein, USA Ch 1958/59.

a12) 15...d5?! 16 fxe6 fxe6 17 ♕c6! ± Penrose-Petersen, Varna OL 1962.

a13) 15...e5!? 16 ♗e3 ♗g5 17 ♕e2 ♗xe3+ 18 ♕xe3 ♘f6 19 ♖ad1 (19 ♔h1!?) 19...♕c7 20 h3 a5 21 a4 ♖ab8 22 ♖f2 ♕b6 23 ♖e2 ♖fc8 24 g4 ½-½ Chandler-Rachels, Manila IZ 1990.

a2) 10...♕c8 11 f5! ♘xd4 12 ♗xd4 exf5 13 ♕d3 fxe4 14 ♘xe4 ♘xe4 15 ♕xe4 ♗e6 16 ♖ae1! ♕d7 (16...♕c6 17 ♕f4! ♖ae8 18 ♕g3 g6 19 ♖xe6! 1-0 Janosević-Musil, Yugoslavia 1972) 17 ♗xg7! ♔xg7 18 ♕d4+ ♔g8 (18...♔g6 19 ♖e3 ♗g5 20 ♖g3 h6 21 h4 ±) 19 ♖e3 ±.

b) 10 ♕e2 and now:

b1) 10...♕a5 11 ♖ad1 ♖ad8 (11...♖ac8 12 ♘db5 ± Parma-Bradvarević, Yugoslav Ch 1963) 12 f4 ♘xd4 13 ♖xd4 ♗c6 14 f5! ± Jović-Sokolov, Belgrade 1965.

b2) 10...♘xd4 11 ♗xd4 ♗c6 12 ♖ad1 ♕a5 13 f4 e5 14 fxe5 (14 ♗f2? exf4 15 ♘d5 ♖ae8 ∓ Kots-Shamkovich, USSR Ch 1962) 14...dxe5 15 ♖f5 (15 ♗e3 or 15 ♗f2 ±) 15...♗c5

16 ♗f2 ♖ad8 (16...♕b6! =) 17 ♖f1 ♖d6 18 ♔h1 ♗xf2 19 ♕xf2 ♗xe4 20 ♘xe4 ♘xe4 21 ♖xf7! 1-0 Gligorić-Pomar, Torremolinos 1961.

8 ♗b3 ♗e7

It is also feasible to expand on the queenside with the aid of 8...♗d7. After 9 f4 b5 *(D)* play might proceed:

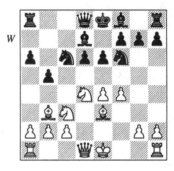

a) 10 ♕f3 ♘xd4 11 ♗xd4 ♗c6 12 0-0-0 b4 13 ♘d5!? exd5 14 exd5 ♗b5 15 ♖he1+ ♗e7 16 g4 ∞ Mikhalchishin.

b) 10 f5 ♘xd4 (10...b4 11 fxe6 fxe6 12 ♘ce2 ±) 11 ♕xd4 ♗e7 12 fxe6 ♗xe6 (12...fxe6 13 e5! dxe5 14 ♕xe5) 13 0-0-0 0-0 14 ♗xe6 fxe6 15 e5 dxe5 16 ♕xe5 ± Mikhalchishin-Saltaev, Groningen 1992.

c) 10 0-0 b4 (10...♕c7 11 f5 transposes to Game 23, Fischer-Cardoso) 11 ♘a4 ♖b8 12 c3 ♗e7 13 cxb4 (13 e5 ♘d5 14 ♗xd5 exd5 15 e6!? fxe6 16 f5 ∞ Kalegin-Dvoirys, USSR 1987) 13...♖xb4 14 ♘c2 (14 ♘c3 0-0 =) 14...♖b8 15 e5 dxe5 16

fxe5 ᐃxe5 17 ♗f4 ♛a5 18 ♖e1
♗xa4 19 ♖xe5 (A.Kovačević-
Ilinčić, Yugoslav Ch 1992) and now
19...♗b5! 20 a4 ♛b6+ 21 ♗e3 ♛c7
22 axb5 ♛xe5 23 bxa6 ♖xb3 24 a7
0-0 25 a8♛ ♖xa8 26 ♖xa8+ ♖b8
would have been good for Black.

9 f4 *(D)*

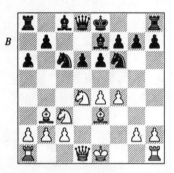

The starting point of the f4 variation.

9 ...   0-0

In the game Sigurjonsson-Ro-
batsch, Haifa OL 1976, Black tried a
premature thrust in the centre:
9...d5?! 10 e5 ᐃd7 11 ♛h5 ᐃc5 12
0-0 ᐃxb3 13 axb3 ♗c5 14 ᐃce2 ±.

10 ♛f3   ♛c7

For 10...ᐃxd4 and 10...♛a5 see
later games. Other moves fail to disturb White's equanimity:

a) 10...ᐃd7?! 11 0-0-0 ᐃc5 12
g4 ♗d7 13 g5 b5 14 ♔b1 ᐃxb3 15
axb3 ᐃxd4 16 ♗xd4 b4 17 ᐃa4 ±
Kupreichik-Mukhin, USSR 1973.

b) 10...e5 11 ᐃxc6 bxc6 12 fxe5
dxe5 13 0-0 (13 h3!?) 13...♖b8 14

♔h1 with an edge for White; Honfi-
Paoli, Timisoara 1972.

c) 10...ᐃa5 and now:

c1) 11 g4 ᐃd7 12 g5 ᐃxb3 13
axb3 ♖e8 14 h4 ♗f8 15 h5 e5 16
ᐃf5 exf4 17 ♛xf4 ᐃe5 18 ᐃd5
♗e6 19 0-0-0 ♗xd5 20 exd5 ♛c7
21 g6 fxg6 22 hxg6 hxg6 23 ♛h4!
♖ec8 24 ᐃd4 +−.

c2) 11 0-0-0 ♛c7 12 g4 ᐃxb3+
13 axb3 b5 14 g5 ᐃd7 15 f5 b4 16
ᐃa4 exf5 17 ᐃxf5 ᐃe5 18 ♛g2
♗b7 19 ᐃb6 a5 20 ᐃxa8 ♖xa8 21
♗d4 ♗f8 22 ♖hf1 ± Dominguez-
Panno, Mar del Plata 1962.

d) 10...♗d7 11 0-0-0 *(D)* and
now:

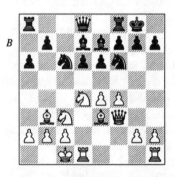

d1) 11...♛c7 12 g4 ᐃxd4 13
♗xd4 e5 14 fxe5 dxe5 15 ♛g3
ᐃxg4 16 ᐃd5 ♛d6 17 ♗c3 ♛h6+
18 ♗d2 ♛h4 19 ♖hg1 ♗d8 20
♛xh4 ♗xh4 21 ᐃb6 ᐃf6 22 ᐃxd7
ᐃxd7 23 ♗h6 ♗f2 24 ♖xg7+ ♔h8
25 ♖g2 1-0 Trepp-Kanel, Biel 1989.

d2) 11...♛a5 12 ♖he1 ᐃxd4 13
♗xd4 ♛h5 14 ♛g3 ♖ac8 15 ♔b1 b5

16 e5 dxe5 17 fxe5 ♘e8 18 ♘e4
♕g6 19 ♕f4 ♗c6 20 ♖d3 ♖d8 21
♗c5 ♖xd3? 22 ♗xe7 ♕xe4 23
♕xe4 ♗xe4 24 cxd3 ♗xd3+ 25 ♔c1
+− Trepp-D.Cramling, Biel 1986.
    d3) 11...♖c8 12 f5?! (12 g4! is
better) 12...♘xd4 13 ♗xd4 e5 14
♗e3 ♖xc3! 15 bxc3 ♗c6 16 ♔b2
♘xe4 17 ♕g4 d5 18 ♖d3 ♕a5 −+
J.Polgar-I.Ivanov, New York 1989.

11 0-0-0

The introduction of the flexible
text move has enhanced the reputation of the line. The exchange in the
centre favours White: 11...♘xd4 12
♗xd4 b5 13 e5 dxe5 14 ♗xe5 ♕b7
15 ♕g3 a5 16 a4 bxa4 17 ♗xa4 g6
18 ♖d3 ♘h5 19 ♕f2 ♖a6 20 ♖hd1
♖b6 21 b3 f6 22 ♗d4 ♖b4 23 g3
♕c7 24 ♘b5 ♕c6 25 ♖c3 ♕e4 26
♖c7 ♖xb5 27 ♗xb5 ♗d6 28 ♗d3
♕a8 29 ♖a7 ♕b8 30 ♗c5 ♘g7 31
♗c4 1-0 Soltis-Liberzon, Palma
1989.

The main alternative, the committal 11 f5, is examined in Game 27,
J.Polgar-Szekely.

11 ... b5
12 g4 ♘xd4

Baljon suggests an unclear position is reached after 12...b4!? 13 g5
(13 ♘xc6 ♕xc6 14 ♘d5?! exd5 15
g5 ♗g4! 16 ♕g2 ♗xd1 17 gxf6
♗xf6 ∓) 13...bxc3 14 gxf6 ♗xf6 15
♖hg1 (15 e5 ♘xd4 16 ♗xd4 dxe5
17 fxe5 ♗g5+ 18 ♔b1 ♗b7 ∓)
15...♗b7 16 f5.

13 ♖xd4! *(D)*

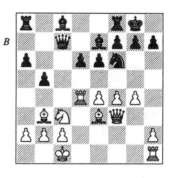

A surprising recapture that has
the benefit of making the standard
...b4 advance more complicated. After 13 ♗xd4 b4 14 ♘a4 ♗b7 Anand
judges the position to be unclear.

13 ... b4

A valiant attempt to seize the initiative by shedding a pawn. If
13...e5 then White makes use of the
important d5 square after 14 ♘d5
♘xd5 15 ♖xd5 exf4! (15...♗e6? 16
f5 ♗xd5 17 ♗xd5 ±) 16 ♗xf4 ♗e6
17 ♖d2 ± (Anand).

14 ♖xb4 d5
15 ♖d4 dxe4

White can go on the offensive
upon 15...♗c5 16 exd5 ♗xd4 17
♗xd4 when the pair of bishops rep-
resent a formidable force.

16 ♕e2 a5
17 g5 ♘d7
18 ♘xe4

The advantage lies with White
who remains a pawn up with actively placed pieces. Black has open
lines as compensation but it is difficult to provoke serious weaknesses.

18	...	♘b6
19	a4	♗a6
20	♕f2	♗c4

Black continues in an energetic manner by trading White's defensive bishop in an effort to undermine a4 and seek play against c2.

21	♗xc4	♘xc4
22	b3	♘xe3
23	♕xe3	e5!
24	♖c4	♗a3+! *(D)*

If 24...exf4?! then 25 ♖xc7 ♗a3+ 26 ♔d2 ±. Black's precise move-order means that the king cannot safely emerge on d2 while the queens remain on the board.

25	♔b1	exf4
26	♖xc7	

A speculative knight sacrifice fails to make an impression: 26 ♘f6+? gxf6 (26...♔h8? 27 ♕h3 +−) 27 ♕g1 ♕a7! ∓ (Anand).

26	...	fxe3
27	♖e1	♖fe8
28	♖c4	

Better than 28 ♖xe3 ♗d6!.

28	...	h6?!

White is just slightly better after 28...♖e5 29 ♖xe3 ♖ae8 30 c3 h6 31 h4 (Baljon).

29	♔a2	♗f8
30	gxh6	f5
31	hxg7	

The error of 28...h6?! is revealed; White has won a pawn by forcing the bishop to retreat.

31	...	♗xg7
32	♘d6	♖e5
33	♖f4?!	

It is even better to initiate direct action against Black's king with 33 ♖c7!. For example: 33...e2? 34 ♖g1 e1♕ 35 ♖cxg7+ ♔h8 36 ♘f7#.

33	...	♖d8
34	♘c4	♖e7
35	♖xe3	♖d1 *(D)*

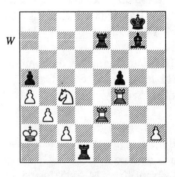

36	c3	♗xc3?!

This attempt at a combination only leads to a rapid defeat. Black should have tried 36...♖xe3, but even in this case 37 ♘xe3 ♖d2+ 38 ♔b1 ♗xc3 39 ♘c4 ♖xh2 40 ♖xf5 leaves White with a sizable advantage.

37	Xxc3	Xe2+
38	♘b2	Xdd2
39	Xg3+!	1-0

In view of 39...♔f7 40 Xxf5+ ♔e6 41 Xxa5 Xxb2+ 42 ♔a3 +–.

Game 25

Velimirović – Popović

Yugoslav Ch 1986

1 e4 c5 2 ♘f3 d6 3 d4 cxd4 4 ♘xd4 ♘f6 5 ♘c3 ♘c6 6 ♗c4 e6 7 ♗e3 a6 8 ♗b3 ♗e7 9 f4 0-0 10 ♕f3 ♘xd4 11 ♗xd4 ♕a5!? *(D)*

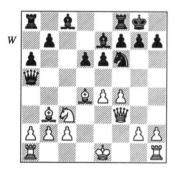

An ambitious move at this juncture that is designed to accelerate a queenside attack. A fianchetto is also feasible, as featured in the game Istratescu-Buturin, Bucharest 1992: 11...b5 12 a3 (12 ♗xf6 – Game 28) 12...♗b7 13 0-0-0 a5!? (13...♕c7?! 14 f5! ±) 14 ♗xf6 ♗xf6 15 ♘xb5 a4 16 Xxd6 ♕c8 (16...♕b8 17 ♗c4 Xc8 18 ♕d3 ♗a6 19 e5 ♗e7 20 Xxa6! Xxa6 20 ♘d6 ±) 17 ♗a2 ♕c5 18 ♕d3 ♗xe4 (18...♗a6 19 Xxa6 Xxa6 20 e5 ♗e7 21 ♘c3! Xa7 22 Xe1 ±; 18...♗c6 19 ♘c7 Xa7 {19...♗xb2+?! 20 ♔xb2 Xab8+ 21 ♔c1 ♗xe4 22 ♘a6! +–} 20 e5 ♗e7 {20...Xxc7 21 exf6 ♗e4 22 ♕xe4 ♕xd6 23 ♕xa4! ±} 21 ♘a6 ♕b6 22 ♘b4 ♗xd6 23 exd6 ±) 19 ♕xe4 ♕xb5 20 c3 Xab8 21 ♕c2 Xfc8 22 Xhd1 g6 23 X6d3! Xc7 24 g4 Xbc8 25 f5! exf5 26 gxf5 ♔g7 27 fxg6 hxg6 28 Xf3 Xc5 29 Xg1 ♕b6 30 Xgf1! ± (Istratescu).

12 f5

An idea that can be recognized as a standard feature to extend the influence of the light-squared bishop.

12 ... exf5

13 0-0!

This simple move gives White open lines and attacking chances in return for a pawn. The king has been whisked to safety leaving the queen on a5 a remote figure.

13 ... fxe4?!

A more solid reaction is 13...♗e6 14 exf5 ♗xb3 15 axb3 ±.

14 ♘xe4 ♘g4 *(D)*

The knight heads for e5 to lessen the influence of the d4 bishop. Black does not object to 15 ♗xf7+, when the pin against the queen will be awkward. On 14...♘xe4 then 15 ♗xf7+ ♔h8 16 ♕xe4 ±.

15 ♕xf7+!

A superb continuation that plunges Black into a tactical crisis.

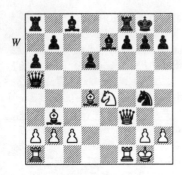

15 ...   Rxf7
16 Rxf7   ♘e5?!

The complications are immense and Black goes wrong. 16...♗f6? 17 Rxf6+ d5 18 Rd6 wins, so the critical line is reached after 16...d5!. For example: 17 Rxe7 ♔f8 18 Rxg7 (18 ♗c5 ♘f6 19 Rf1 ♕xc5+ 20 ♘xc5 ♔xe7 =) 18...dxe4 19 Rf1+ ♔e8 20 c3 ♘e5 (20...♗f5 21 Rg8+ ♔d7 22 Rxa8 ±; 20...♘h6 21 Rxh7 ♕g5 22 ♗b6! ♗d7 23 Rh8+ ♔e7 24 Rxa8 ±) 21 Rf6 ♗d7 (21...♘c6? 22 Rff7 +−; 21...♘d7? 22 Rg8+ ♔e7 23 Re6+ +−; 21...♗f5 22 Rxf5 ♘f3+ 23 Rxf3 exf3 24 Rg8+ ♔e7 25 Rxa8 ±) 22 a4! ♗xa4 (22...♕c7 23 ♗b6 ♕c8 24 Rg8+ +−) 23 Re6+ ♔f8 24 Rxe5 ♕xe5 25 ♗xe5 ♗xb3 26 Rxh7 ± (Baljon).

17 ♗xe5   dxe5
18 Rxe7+   ♔f8
19 Rf7+   ♔g8

A sad necessity for Black due to 19...♔e8 20 ♘d6+ ♔d8 21 Rd1 +−.

20 Rf6+   ♗e6
21 Rxe6   ♔h8

22 Rf1

With two pieces and a rook for the queen White is clearly better.

22 ...   h6
23 c3   Rd8
24 Rf7   ♕b5
25 h3   a5 (D)

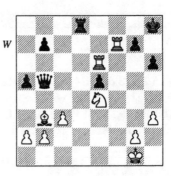

26 Rxh6+??

White wishes to finish in style by delivering mate on h7, but there is a flaw! It can only be assumed that both players were in desperate time-trouble, since the game concluded as follows:

26...gxh6 27 ♘f6 ♕d3 28 ♘g4 e4 29 Re7 Rf8 30 ♘e5 ♕f1+ 31 ♔h2 ♕f4+ 32 ♔g1 ♕e3+ 33 ♔h2 ♕f4+ 34 ♔g1 ♕e3+ ½-½

Game 26
Yakovich – Balashov
St. Petersburg 1993

1 e4 c5 2 ♘f3 ♘c6 3 d4 cxd4 4 ♘xd4 e6 5 ♘c3 d6 6 ♗e3 ♘f6 7 ♗c4 a6 8 ♗b3 ♗e7 9 f4 0-0

10 ♕f3   ♕a5

A contentious sortie, indicating that Black is in an aggressive frame of mind.

11 0-0-0 *(D)*

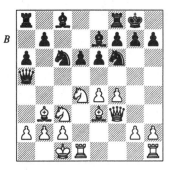

This accepts the challenge posed by the queen and aims to take advantage of its early outing. 11 f5 is incorrect in view of 11...♘e5! 12 ♕f4 (12 ♕g3? ♘xe4 –+) 12...♘h5 13 ♕f1 ♘g4 14 ♗d2 ♕c5 when Black is better.

11 ...   ♘xd4

12 ♖xd4

A familiar capture that can be seen from the game Anand-Piket. White reinforces the e-pawn and deters ...b5-b4. If 12 ♗xd4 then 12...e5! and ...♗g4 nets Black the exchange.

12 ...   ♗d7

Also worth considering 12...♘d7 13 g4 ♘c5 14 g5 ♘xb3+ 15 cxb3 ♗d7 ∞ Skrobek-Dorfman, Mexico 1977.

13 g4!

Invariably the right response in such situations. The kingside pawns are rapidly advanced to gain the initiative.

13 ...   e5 *(D)*

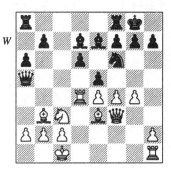

14 ♘d5!

White lands the first punch. With the rook and g-pawn under fire White has prepared the idea of discarding material, in order to seize the d5 square to launch an attack. In the game Panchenko-Kozlov, Pinsk 1986, White played a fine game based upon occupying d5: 14 ♖d5 ♘xd5? 15 ♘xd5 ♗d8 16 f5 ♖c8 17 f6 ♗e6 18 fxg7 ♖e8 19 g5 ♕b5 (19...b5? 20 ♗b6! ♗xb6 21 ♘f6+ ♔xg7 22 ♕h5 ♔f8 23 ♕h6+ ♔e7 24 ♗xe6 ♔xe6 25 ♘xe8+ ♔e7 26 ♘xd6 +–) 20 h4 ♕d7 (20...a5? 21 ♗b6 ♗e7 22 ♖f1 ♕d7 23 ♗xa5 is good for White) 21 h5 b5 (21...a5?! 22 a4!; 21...♔xg7?! 22 ♘f6 ±) and now White can win with 22 ♖g1 ♔xg7 23 ♘f6 ♕c6 24 ♘xe8+ ♕xe8 25 g6 fxg6 26 hxg6 hxg6 27 ♕h5 (analysis by Baljon). The reason why Black wished to repeat this line is a significant improvement revealed by Yakovich: 14...♕d8! 15 f5 ♘xd5 16 ♘xd5 ♗g5 when the complications slightly favour Black.

14 ...   exd4

Black accepts the challenge. The backward d-pawn comes under fire after 14...♕d8: 15 ♘xf6+ ♗xf6 16 ♖d2! (16 ♖xd6? ♗xg4! 17 ♖xd8 ♗xf3 18 ♖xa8 ♖xa8? {18...♗xh1 ∞ is better} 19 ♖f1 ♗xe4 20 fxe5 ±) 16...exf4 17 ♗xf4 ♗g5 18 ♖xd6 ± (Yakovich).

15 ♘xe7+   ♔h8
16 ♗xd4   ♕d8

Black's perilous state is revealed immediately if the pawn is snatched: 16...♗xg4 (16...♘xg4 17 ♖g1 +—) 17 ♕g3 ♗h5 18 ♗xf6 gxf6 19 ♕h4 ♔g7 20 ♘f5+ +—.

17 g5!

White must press on with his attack before Black can regroup. If 17 ♗xf6 gxf6 18 ♘d5 ♗e6 and the initiative is slipping away.

17 ...   ♘e8

After 17...♕xe7 18 gxf6 gxf6 19 ♕c3 Black is routed.

18 ♘d5   ♗e6
19 ♕h5

White has marshalled his attack carefully and now pinpoints h7 as the weakest point.

19 ...   ♖c8
20 f5 (D)

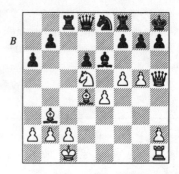

20 ...   ♗xd5
21 g6!   1-0

In view of 21...♖xc2+ (21...fxg6 22 fxg6 h6 23 ♕xh6+ ♔g8 24 ♕h7 mate) 22 ♔d1! ♖c1+ 23 ♔xc1 ♕c7+ 24 ♔d2 and White wins.

Game 27
J.Polgar – Szekely
Hastings 1988/89

1 e4 c5 2 ♘f3 d6 3 d4 cxd4 4 ♘xd4 ♘f6 5 ♘c3 a6 6 ♗c4 e6 7 ♗b3 ♘c6 8 ♗e3 ♗e7 9 f4 0-0 10 ♕f3 ♕c7 11 f5!? (D)

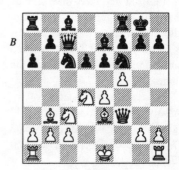

White continues in robust manner by immediately pressurizing e6. This line was particularly popular in the 1970s but has since faded, primarily due to the mushrooming of associated lines. It is a sound continuation that deserves a revival.

11 ...   ♘xd4
12 ♗xd4   b5

By analogy with other positions, Black must carefully judge when to give up the d5 square, since otherwise White may occupy it, enhancing the strength of his light-squared bishop. For example: 12...e5 13 ♗e3 b5 14 a3 ♗b7 15 0-0 ± Honfi-Blubaum, West Germany 1979.

13 a3

13 0-0-0 is worth consideration, and does have the merit of adventurously ignoring Black's ambitions on the queenside. A.Ivanov-Wessman, Reykjavik 1990, continued 13...b4 14 ♘a4 ♖b8 15 g4 e5 16 ♗f2 ♗b7 17 ♖he1 ♗c6 18 g5 ♘xe4 19 ♖xe4 ♗xg5+ 20 ♗e3 ♗xe3+ 21 ♕xe3 ♕d7 22 f6! gxf6 23 ♖g1+ ♔h8 24 ♕h6 1-0.

A kingside pawn assault has been tested: 13 g4 b4 (13...♗b7!? 14 g5? ♘xe4 is good for Black) 14 g5 ♘e8 15 f6 bxc3 16 fxe7 ♕xe7 17 ♖g1 cxb2 18 ♗xb2 e5 19 0-0-0 ♗e6 20 ♗a3 ♖c8 ½-½ Minić-Jansa, Budva 1963.

13 ...   ♖b8

The accepted continuation. Other tries are not convincing:

a) 13...exf5 14 exf5 ♗b7 15 ♕h3 ♘d7 16 0-0-0 ♗f6 17 ♗d5 ♖ac8 18 ♗xb7 ♕xb7 19 ♗xf6 ♘xf6 20 ♖xd6 ± Honfi-Jaschelin, Corr 1981.

b) 13...e5 14 ♗f2 (14 ♗e3) 14...♗b7 15 0-0 ♖ac8 16 ♖ae1 ♕b8 17 ♗h4 ± (Bednarski).

14 g4   b4
15 g5   ♘d7?

This natural response immediately leads to Black's downfall. The most precise move is 15...♘e8 when Vera-Lechtynsky, Bratislava 1983 continued 16 axb4 ♗xg5 ∞.

16 f6   bxc3 (D)

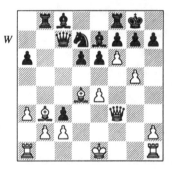

17 fxg7!

A nasty surprise for Black who was counting on 17 fxe7 ♖e8 18 0-0 ♖xe7 when f7 is safeguarded.

17 ...   ♘e5

If 17...♖e8, then 18 0-0! ♘e5 19 ♗xe5 ♗xg5 20 ♗xc3 wins.

18 gxf8♕+   ♔xf8
19 ♕xc3   ♕xc3
20 ♗xc3   ♗xg5
21 ♖d1

With a material advantage the ending is clearly better for White. The next stage of Judit's campaign is to maintain her initiative by targeting the weak pawn on d6 before Black can drum up counter-play based on White's relatively exposed king.

21	...	♔e7
22	♗a5	♖b7
23	♔e2	♘g6
24	h4! *(D)*	

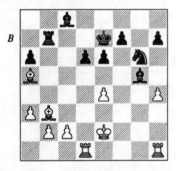

White's relentless aggression affords Black no opportunity to regroup. The h-pawn is taboo because of 24...♗xh4 (24...♘xh4 25 ♗b4) 25 ♗b4 ♖b6 26 e5! +–.

24...♗f6 25 h5 ♘e5 26 ♗b4 ♖b6 27 ♖hg1 ♗b7 28 ♗a5 ♖xb3

A sign of sheer desperation, but 28...♖c6 29 ♖g8 (with the idea 29 ♗d8+) 29...♖c8 (29...♔d7 30 ♗a4 +–) 30 ♖xc8 ♗xc8 31 ♗b4 was no better. Now White clinically exchanges the major pieces and prepares to create a passed pawn.

29 cxb3 ♗xe4 30 ♗b4 ♗d5 31 ♖xd5 exd5 32 ♗c3 ♔e6 33 b4 d4 34 ♗xd4 ♘f3 35 ♔xf3 ♗xd4 36 ♖g2 h6 37 a4 ♔d5 38 ♖c2 1-0

Game 28

Short – Kasparov
London PCA Wch (12) 1993

1 e4 c5 2 ♘f3 d6 3 d4 cxd4 4 ♘xd4 ♘f6 5 ♘c3 a6 6 ♗c4 e6 7 ♗b3 ♘c6 8 f4 ♗e7 9 ♗e3 0-0 10 ♕f3 ♘xd4 11 ♗xd4

| 11 | ... | b5!? *(D)* |

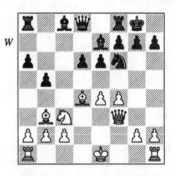

Kasparov revives an unusual line which invites a tactical response.

12 ♗xf6!?

A preliminary measure before utilizing the discovered attack. 12 e5?! is an inaccuracy from which Black can profit: 12...dxe5 13 fxe5 (13 ♗xe5 ♕b6 14 0-0-0 ♗b7 15 ♕g3 ♖ad8 is slightly better for Black – Shamkovich) 13...♕xd4 14 exf6 ♗c5 15 fxg7 ♖d8 16 ♖d1 ♕e5+ 17 ♕e4 ♖xd1+ 18 ♔xd1

♕xe4 19 ♘xe4 ♗e7 ∓ Hermlin-
Shamkovich, USSR 1972.

For the insipid 12 a3, see the note
to Black's 11th move in Game 25.

12 ...   ♗xf6

Or 12...gxf6 13 f5! tying Black
up.

13 e5

White is obliged to complicate,
since otherwise there is no justifica-
tion for giving up the bishop pair.

13 ...   ♗h4+
14 g3   ♖b8

In Pekarek-Bagaturov, Brno 1991,
Black chose a less convincing continuation: 14...♕b6 15 gxh4 dxe5 16
fxe5 ♗b7 17 ♕f2 ♕c7 18 ♖f1
♕xe5+ 19 ♕e2 ♕d4 20 ♕d2 ♕e5+
21 ♕e2 ½-½.

15 gxh4

White must accept the sacrifice as
otherwise the open nature of the position will favour Black's bishops,
e.g. 15 0-0-0 ♗b7 16 ♘e4 ♗e7 ∓
Hmadi-de Firmian, Tunis 1985.

15 ...   ♗b7
16 ♘e4   dxe5
17 ♖g1   g6!

This is the novelty that Kasparov
had prepared – a cunning, non-forc-
ing move ruling out threats against
the weak point g7. White conse-
quently has a free move, but nothing
constructive can be gained from it.
The alternatives are weak:

a) 17...♕xh4+? 18 ♕g3 ♕xg3+
19 ♘xg3 exf4 20 ♘h5 g6 21 ♘f6+
♔g7 22 ♘d7 +−.

b) 17...♕d4? 18 ♘f6+ ♔h8 19
♕g3 +−.

c) 17...f5? 18 ♗xe6+ ♔h8 19
♕g3 +−.

18 ♖d1   ♗xe4

If 18...♕e7 19 ♕e2! ♗xe4 transposes to the game.

19 ♕xe4   ♕xh4+
20 ♔e2! (D)

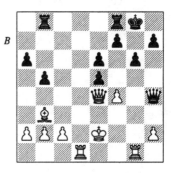

20 ♔f1 ♖bd8! highlights White's
unconnected rooks; for example 21
c3 ♖xd1+ 22 ♗xd1 ♖d8 23 ♗e2
exf4 gives Black excellent compensation.

20 ...   ♕xh2+?!

A signal that Black is prepared to
enter the ending. Keeping the queens
on the board appears to maintain
Black's initiative, e.g. 20...exf4 21
h3 a5 22 a3 a4 23 ♗a2 b4 24 axb4
♖xb4! 25 ♕xb4? f3+ 26 ♔xf3
♕xb4 −+. However, 24 ♗c4! offers
equal chances.

21 ♖g2   ♕xf4
22 ♕xf4   exf4
23 ♔f3

The potential pawn avalanche looks imposing but the situation is not so clear-cut. To a certain extent the pawns are static, White's bishop is useful and there is the possibility that the c-pawn will become passed.

23 ...   Rfd8

Not 23...e5? 24 Rg5 Rbe8 25 Rde1 which picks up two pawns.

24 Rxd8+   Rxd8
25 Kxf4   Kf8
26 Ke3! (D)

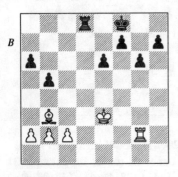

White's king is flexibly placed, ready to support the c-pawn or to drop back to the kingside if Black over-reaches.

26 ...   Ke7
27 c4   h5

There were a few commentators who preferred 27...f5 as a winning attempt. Kasparov decided this was a risky idea and concentrated on securing the draw.

28 a4   bxa4
29 Bxa4   h4
30 c5   Rh8

31 Rc2   h3
32 Bc6   e5!

Black's plan is lock out the bishop by creating a pawn wall.

33 Kf2   h2
34 Rc1   a5

A precise move which stops White supporting his c-pawn with b4.

35 Bd5   Rd8 (D)

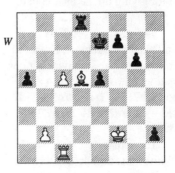

36 Bg2

In reply to 36 Bb7 to march the c-pawn forward, Kasparov noted the resource 36...Rd2+ 37 Ke3 Rxb2 38 c6 Rc2 39 Rxc2 h1Q 40 c7 Qe1+ 41 Kd3 Qd1+ 42 Kc3 Qd4+ =.

36 ...   Rd2+
37 Kg3   Kd7
38 Ra1

A draw is also the result after 38 c6+ Kc7 39 Rc5 f5! 40 Rxe5 f4+ 41 Kh3 f3 42 Bxf3 Rd3.

38 ...   f5
39 Kxh2   Rxb2
40 Rxa5   e4

½-½

Game 29

Short – Kasparov

London PCA Wch (14) 1993

1 e4 c5 2 ♘f3 d6 3 d4 cxd4 4 ♘xd4
♘f6 5 ♘c3 a6 6 ♗c4 e6 7 ♗b3 ♘c6
8 ♗e3 ♗e7 9 f4 0-0
    10 0-0 *(D)*

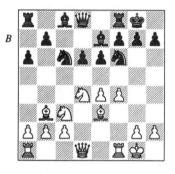

Short relies on an established system that can involve f5 or e5. Early pioneers of the system included Boleslavsky and Ragozin, whose games inspired Fischer to adopt it.

10 ...   ♘xd4

Other lines fail to give White any difficulties:

a) 10...d5?! 11 e5 ♘d7 12 ♕h5 ♖e8 13 ♘xd5! exd5 14 ♕xf7+! ♔xf7 15 ♗xd5+ ♔g6 16 f5+ ♔h5 17 ♗f3+ ♔h4 18 g3+ ♔h3 19 ♗g2+ ♔g4 20 ♖f4+ 1-0 Troinov-Popov, Bulgaria 1962.

b) 10...♘a5?! and now:

b1) 11 g4!? d5 12 e5 ♘d7 13 ♕f3 ♕c7 14 h4 ♘c4 15 ♗xc4 dxc4 16 a4 b6 17 h5 ♗b7 18 ♕g3 h6 with

equality; Fischer-Evans, USA Ch 1958/59.

b2) 11 ♕f3 ♕c7 12 g4 (12 f5!? e5 13 ♘de2 ♘xb3 transposes to 'b3' in the note to Black's 11th move in Game 3) 12...b5 (12...♘c4 13 ♗xc4 ♕xc4 14 g5 ♘d7 15 ♕h5 ± Pogats-Negyesy, Budapest; 12...♘xb3 13 axb3 d5 14 e5 ♘d7 15 g5 ♘c5?! 16 ♕h5 ♘e4 17 ♖f3! ♘xc3 18 ♖h3 ± Vasiukov-Gurgenidze, Kharkov 1967) 13 g5 ♘d7 (13...♘e8 14 f5) 14 ♘xe6 fxe6 15 ♗xe6+ ♔h8 16 ♘d5 ♕d8 17 ♕h5 ♘c5 18 ♗xc8 ♖xc8 19 f5 ♗xg5 20 ♗xg5 ♕e8 21 ♕xe8 ♖fxe8 22 f6 ♘d7 23 f7 ♖xe4 24 ♘b6 +– Boleslavsky-Aronin, USSR Ch 1949.

c) 10...♗d7 and now:

c1) 11 f5!? ♘xd4 (11...♕c8? 12 fxe6 ♗xe6 13 ♘xe6 fxe6 14 ♘a4 +– Fischer-Larsen, Denver Ct (3) 1971) 12 ♗xd4 b5 13 a3 ♕c7 = Hartston-Suetin, Hastings 1967/68.

c2) 11 ♕f3 ♘a5 (11...♖c8 12 f5 e5 13 ♘de2 ♘a5 14 g4 ±; 11...b5 12 e5 ♘xd4 13 ♗xd4 dxe5 14 fxe5 ♗c6 15 ♕d3 ♘d7 16 ♘e4 ♗xe4 17 ♕xe4 ♘c5 = *ECO*; for 11...♕c7 see 'd') 12 f5 ♘xb3 13 cxb3 b5 14 b4 ♖c8 15 ♖fd1 ♕c7 16 a3 ♕b8 with equality; Smailbegović-Toran, Sarajevo 1960.

d) 10...♕c7 11 ♕f3 ♗d7 (11...b5 12 e5! ♘xd4 13 ♗xd4 ♗b7 14 exf6 ♗xf3 15 fxe7 ♕xe7 16 ♖xf3 with an edge for White – Kasparov and Nikitin) and now:

d1) 12 ♖ad1 b5 (12...♖ac8 13 f5! e5 14 ♘de2 ♘a5 15 g4 ♘xb3 16 axb3 ♗c6 17 g5 ♘e8 18 ♘g3 ± Keres-Palmason, Munich OL 1954) 13 a3 ♘xd4 14 ♗xd4 ♗c6 with an equal game – Boleslavsky.

d2) 12 f5 ♘xd4 13 ♗xd4 b5 (13...e5 14 ♗f2! ♗c6 15 g4 ±) 14 a3 a5 15 g4 b4 16 axb4 axb4 17 ♖xa8 ♖xa8 18 g5 bxc3 19 gxf6 ♗xf6 20 ♗xf6 gxf6 21 fxe6 ♗xe6 22 bxc3 ± Khenkin.

11 ♗xd4   b5
12 e5

This is the modern method of treating the line. White invites a double-edged game. The alternative, 12 a3, is considered in the next game.

Other replies are less convincing:

a) 12 f5 b4 13 ♘a4 e5 14 ♗e3 ♗b7 ∓.

b) 12 ♕f3 ♗b7 13 a3 a5! 14 ♖ae1 b4 15 axb4 axb4 16 ♘b1 d5 17 exd5?! (17 e5 ♘e4 18 f5!? ∞) 17...♗xd5 18 ♗xd5 exd5 19 c3 ♘e4 20 ♖d1 f5 ∓ Radulov-Bobotsov, Varna 1967.

12 ...   dxe5
13 fxe5   ♘d7

The retreat 13...♘e8 has been tested: 14 ♘e4 ♗b7 15 ♕d3 ♗xe4 16 ♕xe4 g6 17 a4 ♘g7 18 g4 b4 19 ♖ad1 ♕c7 20 ♖d3 ♖ad8 21 ♖fd1 ± Mortensen-Fishbein, Herning 1991.

14 ♘e4 (D)

Not 14 ♖xf7? ♖xf7 15 ♗xe6 ♘xe5 −+.

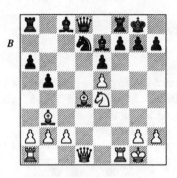

Also possible is 14 ♕g4, though this is not as clear as the text:

a) 14...♘c5 and now:

a1) 15 ♗e3 ♕c7 16 ♖ae1 ♘xb3 17 ♗h6 ♗c5+ 18 ♔h1 g6 19 ♗xf8 ± Kuznetsov-Yalundin, Russia 1993.

a2) In Yuneev-Aseev, Daugavpils 1989 White's attack evaporated after 15 ♘e2 ♘xb3 (15...♗b7 16 ♘g3 ♗e4!? 17 c3 ♗g6 18 ♖d1 ♖c8 19 ♗f3 ♘d3 20 a4 ♖c4! ∞ Lendwai-Blasek, Gelsenkirchen 1991) 16 axb3 ♕d5 17 ♘c3 ♕d7 18 ♗e3 ♕c7 19 ♕g3 ♗c5 20 b4!? ♗xe3+ (20...♗xb4 21 ♗h6 f5 22 ♘xb5 ♕b6+ 23 ♔h1 ♖f7 24 ♘d6 ♗xd6 25 exd6 ∞ Aseev) 21 ♕xe3 ♗b7 22 ♖f4 ♖fd8 23 ♖af1 ♖d7 24 ♖g4 ♖ad8 =.

b) 14...♗b7 15 ♖xf7!? ♔xf7 (15...♖xf7? 16 ♕xe6 +−) 16 ♗xe6+ ♔e8 17 ♕h5+ g6 18 ♕xh7 ♕c7 19 ♕xg6+ ♔d8 20 ♖d1 ♔c8 21 ♗e3 ♖d8 22 ♕g7! ♗b4 (22...♗f8 23 ♗xd7+ ♕xd7 24 ♖xd7 ♗xg7 25 ♖xg7 +−) 23 ♘d5 (23 ♖xd7!? ♖xd7 24 ♕g8+ ♕d8 25 ♗xd7+ ♔xd7 26

♕g4+ +−) 23...♗xd5 24 ♖xd5 ♖b8
25 c3 ♗f8 26 ♕f7 ♖b7 27 ♖xd7
♖xd7 28 ♕xf8+ ♔d8 29 ♕xd8+
♔xd8 30 ♗xd7 ♖xd7 31 ♗d4 1-0
I.Kuznetsov-Molev, Russia 1994.

14	...	♗b7
15	♘d6	♗xd6
16	exd6	♕g5
17	♕e2	

White is obliged to watch out for
mate on g2. The course of the game
depends on the value of the passed
pawn, compared to Black's kingside
pawn majority where the e- and f-
pawns can be advanced to join in the
attack. The alternative 17 ♖f2 is feasible. After 17...a5 (17...♖ad8 18
♕e2 ♗d5 {18...♘b8?! 19 ♗e3!
♕e5 20 ♗b6 ♕xe2 21 ♖xe2 ♖d7
22 a4 ±} 19 ♖d1 ♗xb3 20 axb3 e5
21 ♗e3 ♕g6 22 c4 f5 ∞ Naivelt-
Dvoirys, USSR 1985; 17...e5 18
♗c3 e4 19 ♕f1 ♕g6 20 ♖e1 ±) 18
a4 *(D)* play might proceed:

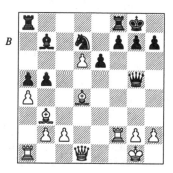

a) 18...b4 19 ♕e2 (one uninfor-
mative example runs 19 ♕d2 ♕xd2
20 ♖xd2 ♖fd8 ½-½ de Firmian-
Tringov, Niš 1981) 19...♖a6 20 ♕b5
♕xb5 21 axb5 ♖xd6 22 ♗e3 ♖a8 23
♗f4 ♖d4 24 ♗e3 ♖d6 25 ♗f4 ♖d4
26 ♗e3 = Winants-Tukmakov, Wijk
aan Zee 1993.

b) 18...♖a6 and now:

b1) 19 axb5 ♖xd6 20 ♕d2 ♕xb5
21 ♕c3?! (21 ♖xa5 ♕c6 22 ♕f4!?
e5 23 ♗xf7+ ♔h8 24 ♖xe5 ♘xe5 25
♕xe5 ♖f6! 26 ♕xf6 gxf6 27 ♗xf6+
♕xf6 28 ♖xf6 ♔g7 =) 21...e5 22
♗e3 ♘f6! ∓ Bosch-Cifuentes, Hol-
land 1991.

b2) 19 ♕e2 bxa4 20 ♖xa4 ♖xd6
21 h4 ♕e7 22 c3 ♗d5 23 ♗c2 e5 24
♗e3 g6 25 h5 ♖b8 26 c4 ♗c6 27
♖a2 ♕h4 28 c5 ♖f6 29 b3 ♖b4 30
♗d1 = Martens-Lendwai, Vienna
1991.

c) 18...e5 19 ♗c3 b4 20 ♗d2
♕g6 21 c3 ♘c5 22 ♗c2 ♗e4 23
♗e1 ♗xc2 24 ♕xc2 ♕xd6 25 cxb4
♘d3 26 bxa5 ♘xf2 ∓ Yilmaz-
Panchenko, USSR 1991.

| 17 | ... | e5 *(D)* |

The most forcing continuation.
Alternatively:

a) 17...♗d5?! 18 ♖ad1 ♗xb3 19
axb3 ♖ac8 (19...e5 20 ♗c3 ♕d8 21
♕d2 ♕b6+ 22 ♔h1 ♕c6 23 ♗a5 f5
24 ♕d5+ ♕xd5 25 ♖xd5 ± Sax-Gy-
orkosu, Hungary 1992) 20 c4 ♖c6
21 ♖d3 g6 22 ♖g3 ♕d8 23 c5 e5 24
♗xe5 ♖xc5 25 ♗f4 ♖e8 26 ♖e3
♖xe3 27 ♕xe3 ♖f5 28 ♖e1 ♘f8 29
♕e7 ♕c8 30 ♗h6 +− Moutousis-Ti-
moschenko, Vrnjačka Banja 1990.

b) 17...a5!? 18 a4 (18 c3 ♖a6 19 ♖ad1 ± Sax-Jasnikowski, Næstved 1988) 18...b4 19 ♖ad1?! (19 ♗c4! with the idea ♗b5) 19...♗a6 20 ♗c4 ♗xc4 21 ♕xc4 ♖ac8 22 ♕e2 ♖c6 ∓ Am.Rodriguez.

c) 17...♖ad8 18 ♖ad1 e5 19 ♗e3 ♕g6 ∞ Shamkovich.

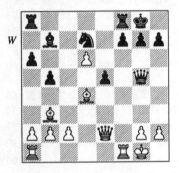

18 ♗c3

This is slightly unusual, with 18 ♗e3 to dislodge the queen normally being preferred. For example: 18...♕g6 19 ♖ad1 ♔h8 20 h4 ♘f6 (20...f5 21 h5 ♕f6 22 a4 f4 23 ♕g4 ♗c6 24 ♗e6 ♖ad8 25 ♗f2 ♕h6 26 ♗h4 ♘f6 27 ♕g5 = Browne-Donner, Wijk aan Zee 1974) 21 d7! ♕g3 (21...♖fd8 22 ♖d6! ♖xd7? 23 ♖fxf6! +−; 21...♖ad8 22 ♗c5 ♖g8 23 ♗e7 ±; 21...♗c6 22 ♖d6! ±) 22 ♖xf6 gxf6 Zapata-Am.Rodriguez, Bucarmanga 1992) and now 23 ♕f2! ♕g7 (23...♕g4 24 ♕xf6+ ♔g8 25 ♖d2 ♖ad8 26 ♗xf7+ +−; 23...♕xf2+ 24 ♔xf2 ♔g7 25 ♖d6 ±) 24 ♗c5 ♖fd8 25 ♗e7 f5 26 ♖d6

♔g8 27 ♗f6 ♕g4 28 ♗xe5 gives White a clear advantage according to Am.Rodriguez.

18 ... ♕g6
19 ♖ad1 ♔h8
20 ♗d5

The precautionary measure to free the f-pawn is immediately useful in the line 20 ♗a5 f5 21 a4 f4 22 ♗d5 ♗xd5 23 ♖xd5 e4 and the pawn roller is a menace.

20 ... ♗xd5
21 ♖xd5 ♕e6
22 ♖fd1 ♖fc8 (D)

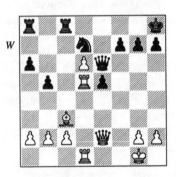

The point of Kasparov's odd-looking sequence ...♖fc8-c6 is to lessen the effectiveness of 23 a4 bxa4 24 ♖a5 when the queenside pawns come under pressure.

Previously played was the more straightforward 22...f5 23 a4 bxa4 24 ♗xe5 ♖ae8 25 c4 ♘xe5 26 d7 ♘xd7 27 ♕xe6 ♖xe6 28 ♖xd7 ♖c6 29 ♖1d4 ½-½ Christiansen-Spassov, Indonesia 1982.

23 ♗a5 ♖c6

24 b3   Xac8
25 ♗c7   Xe8

Now that his passed pawn is
guarded by the bishop, White's pri-
ority is to open lines, whereupon the
threat of further pawn advances
would prove decisive. The urgency
for Black to create kingside counterplay is now acute. Although optically not far-advanced, Black's
attack will be aided by the inability
of the bishop on c7 to come to the
defence of White's king.

Kasparov suggests 25...f5! to
speed up the counter-attack.

26 c4   bxc4
27 bxc4   f5
28 h3

A quiet move to avoid the threat
of back-rank mates. For example: 28
♕c2 e4 29 ♕a4 e3 30 ♕xc6 e2 31
Xe1 ♕e3+ 32 ♔h1 ♕f2 and Black
wins.

28 ...   h6
29 ♕c2   e4
30 ♕a4   Xc5
31 Xxc5   ♘xc5
32 ♕c6   ♘d7
33 ♕d5   ♕g6 *(D)*
34 ♕d2?

This timid move allows Black to
seize the initiative. The logical 34 c5
intending c6 is the most dangerous
continuation. Initially, Kasparov
proclaimed the position lost, but
later two astounding defences were
discovered, which enable Black to
salvage a draw:

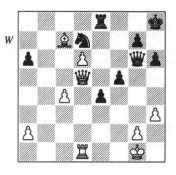

a) 34...f4 35 c6 and now:

a1) 35...♘f6? 36 ♕c4 f3 37 ♕c2
e3 38 ♕xg6 f2+ 39 ♔h2 e2 40 ♕b1
exd1♕ 41 ♕xd1 Xe1 42 ♕f3 f1♕
43 ♕xf1 Xxf1 44 d7 +—.

a2) 35...f3 36 g4 ♘f6 37 ♕f5
♕f7! (Lau; 37...♕xf5? 38 gxf5 e3
39 Xb1 +—) 38 ♕f4 (38 d7 ♕xa2 39
dxe8♕+ ♘xe8 40 ♕f8+ ♔h7 41
♕f5+ =) 38...♕xa2 39 ♕d2 ♕xd2
40 Xxd2 e3 41 Xb2 e2 42 ♗a5 ♘e4
43 Xxe2 (43 ♗e1 f2+! 44 ♗xf2
♘xd6 45 ♗e1 Xc8 46 Xc2 ♘b5 =
Timman) 43...fxe2 44 d7 Xf8 45 c7
Xf1+ and Black delivers perpetual
check (Lau).

b) 34...Xe5 35 ♕a8+ ♔h7 36 c6
Xb5! and now:

b1) 37 ♔h1 Xb2 38 Xg1 ♘e5!
39 d7 ♘xc6 40 ♕xa6 (40 d8♕
♘xd8 41 ♕xd8 Xxa2 —+) 40...Xd2
41 ♕c8 ♕e6 42 d8♕ ♘xd8 —+.

b2) 37 cxd7 Xb2 38 g4 fxg4 39
♕e8 ♕f5 40 ♕f8 (40 Xf1 ♕c5+ 41
♔h1 ♕c2 —+) 40...♕xf8 41 Xf1
♕g8 42 d8♕ ♕xa2 43 d7 gxh3 44
♕h8+ ♔xh8 45 d8♕+ ♔h7 46 ♕d6

♜g2+ 47 ♔h1 ♜g6 48 ♛h2 ♛g2+
49 ♛xg2 hxg2+ −+.

b3) 37 ♛xa6! ♜b2 38 ♛f1 f4 39
cxd7 f3 40 g4 (40 d8♛ ♜xg2+ 41
♔h1 ♛g3 −+) 40...♛f6 41 ♗b6! (41
d8♛ f2+ 42 ♔h2 ♛f4+ 43 ♔g2
♛f3+ 44 ♔h2 ♛xd1 45 ♛f8 ♛xf1
46 ♛f5+ with a draw − Kasparov)
41...♜xb6 (41...♛f4 42 ♗f2 e3 43
♛d3+ +−) 42 d8♛! ♛xd8 43 ♛e1
♜xd6 44 ♜xd6 ♛xd6 45 ♛xe4+
♔h8 46 ♛a8+ ♔h7 47 ♛xf3 ♛d4+
48 ♔g2 ♛d2+ 49 ♛f2 ♛d5+ = Timman.

34	...	♜e5
35	♛e3	♛e6?!

Kasparov rightly states that Black
is much better after 35...♛f7! threatening ...f4 and ...♛xc4.

36	♜c1	♜c5
37	♜c2	♔g8
38	a4	♔f7
39	♛f2	e3

½-½

Game 30

Moutousis – Tukmakov
Haifa 1989

1 e4 c5 2 ♞f3 d6 3 d4 cxd4 4 ♞xd4
♞f6 5 ♞c3 a6 6 ♗c4 e6 7 0-0 ♞c6
8 ♗e3 ♗e7 9 ♗b3 0-0 10 f4 ♞xd4
11 ♗xd4 b5

    12   a3 *(D)*

A prudent continuation to defend
against ...b4.

12	...	♗b7
13	♛d3	

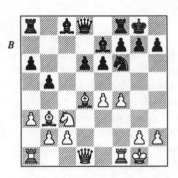

The queen soon becomes exposed
here, which suggests 13 ♛e1 or 13
♛e2 as alternatives.

13	...	a5!?

The threat of ...b4 now has to be
dealt with. Larsen has suggested
13...♜c8 with an exchange sacrifice
in mind if appropriate.

14	e5	dxe5
15	fxe5	♞d7
16	♞xb5	♞c5 *(D)*

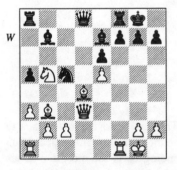

    17   ♛e3

White wishes to maintain the tension, but he was probably wrong to
forego the accepted continuation 17

&xc5. For example: 17...&xc5+ 18
&h1 ♕g5 (18...♕xd3 19 cxd3 &a6
20 ♘c7 &xd3 21 ♖fc1 &e3!
{21...♖ab8? 22 ♘xe6! fxe6 23
&xe6+ &h8 24 ♖xc5 ♖xb2 25 &f7!
+–} 22 ♖c3 ♖ad8 23 ♖d1 &b6 =)
19 ♕e2?! (19 ♕g3 ♕xg3 20 hxg3
&a6 21 a4 &xb5 22 axb5 &d4 23 c3
&xe5 24 g4 &c7 =) 19...♖ad8 20
♖ad1 ♖xd1! 21 ♖xd1 h5 22 ♘d6
&a8 23 &c4 h4 24 h3 &e3 25 ♕g4
♕xe5 26 ♕xh4 g5 27 ♕g4 &c5 28
♘b5 &g7 29 ♘d4 ♖h8 30 ♘f3
&xf3 31 ♕xf3 &d6 32 ♕c3 ♕xc3
33 bxc3 &e5 34 ♖d7 &f6 35 &g1
&xc3 36 &e2 &e5 37 &f1 ♖c8 38
&h5 ♖c7 39 ♖xc7 &xc7 40 a4 &e7
41 &e2 f5 42 &d3 &e5 43 c4 &d6
44 &f7 &g3 45 c5+ ½-½ Fischer-
Spassky, Reykjavik Wch (4) 1972.

17 ... &xb3
18 ♕xb3 a4
19 ♕d3 ♕d5

Black dominates the a8-h1 diagonal; the mate threat provides time
to centralize his rooks. Pinning
White's knight is a less effective
plan: 19...&a6 20 ♖ad1 ♕b8 21 c4
&xb5 22 cxb5 ♖a5 = (Gligorić and
Wade).

20 ♖f2 ♖fd8
21 ♖d1 &a6
22 ♘c7

If 22 c4 &xb5 23 cxb5 &c5 24
&xc5 (24 ♖fd2 ♕xe5 –+) 24...♕xd3
25 ♖xd3 ♖xd3 26 b6 (26 &d6 ♖b3
–+) 26...♖c8! ∓.

22 ... &xd3

23 ♘xd5 ♖xd5
24 ♖xd3 ♖ad8
25 ♖f4

Certainly not 25 ♖fd2? (25 c3
♖xe5) 25...&g5 26 ♖d1 ♖xd4 27
♖xd4 &e3+ and Black wins.

25 ... &g5
26 ♖g4 ♖xd4
27 ♖xg5 ♖xd3
28 cxd3 ♖xd3
29 ♖g4 ♖d1+
30 &f2 ♖d2+
31 &f3 ♖xb2
32 ♖xa4 h5
33 ♖a7

This error ensures White a dour
defensive task. Despite the vulner-
ability of e5, Tukmakov mentions
that 33 h4 would hold the draw because the king with e4 and f4 at its
disposal could more easily support
the e5-pawn.

33...g5! 34 a4 &g7 35 h3 ♖b3+
**36 &f2 &g6 37 ♖a8 ♖a3 38 ♖a7
♖c3 39 ♖a5 ♖c4 40 &f3 &f5 41
g3?!**

A technical draw results from 41
♖a7 &xe5 42 ♖xf7 ♖xa4.

After the text Black can test
White's resources further.

**41...♖c3+ 42 &g2 ♖c2+ 43 &g1
♖a2 44 ♖a7 &xe5 45 ♖xf7 ♖xa4 46
♖g7 &f5 47 ♖f7+ &e5 48 ♖g7 &f6
49 ♖g8 g4**

49...h4 50 gxh4 gxh4 51 &f2 ♖a3
52 &g2 =.

**50 ♖h8! ♖a1+ 51 &g2 ♖a2+ 52
&h1!**

52 ♔f1 gxh3 53 ♖xh5 h2 −+; 52 ♔g1 gxh3 53 ♖xh5 ♖g2+ −+.

52...♔g6 53 hxg4 hxg4 54 ♖g8+ ♔f5 55 ♖f8+ ♔e4 56 ♖f4+ ♔e3 57 ♖xg4 e5 58 ♖g8 ♔f3 59 ♔g1 e4 60 ♖f8+ ♔e3 61 g4 ♔d3 62 ♖d8+ ♔e2 63 ♔g2 e3 64 ♔g3 ½-½

Game 31
Fischer − Bielicki
Mar del Plata 1960

1 e4 c5 2 ♘f3 d6 3 d4 cxd4 4 ♘xd4 ♘f6 5 ♘c3 a6 6 ♗c4 e6 7 ♗b3 ♘c6 8 f4 ♘a5

After 8...♗e7, 9 ♗e3 transposes to normal lines although White tried an independent line in the game Kaiszauri-Sax, Groningen 1972: 9 f5 ♘xd4 10 ♕xd4 exf5 11 exf5 ♗xf5 12 0-0 ♗e6 ∞.

An early sortie by the queen cannot be recommended: 8...♕a5 9 0-0 ♘xd4 (9...d5 10 ♘xc6 bxc6 11 f5 ♗c5+ 12 ♔h1 0-0 ±) 10 ♕xd4 d5 11 ♗e3 ♘xe4 12 ♘xe4 dxe4 13 f5! ♕b4 14 fxe6 ♗xe6 15 ♗xe6 fxe6 16 ♖xf8+ ♕xf8 17 ♕a4+ 1-0 Fischer-Dely, Skopje 1967.

9 f5 ♘xb3?!

This appears to be a rather basic continuation, but will attract considerable attention from those who wish to eliminate the b3-bishop immediately in a vain attempt to handicap a future attack. This game is especially important since the same position can also arise from the

move-order 1 e4 c5 2 ♘f3 d6 3 d4 cxd4 4 ♘xd4 ♘f6 5 ♘c3 a6 6 ♗c4 e6 7 ♗b3 ♘bd7 8 f4 ♘c5 9 f5.

10 axb3 ♗e7
11 ♕f3 *(D)*

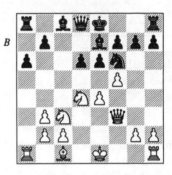

The queen takes up a familiar role on f3. Compared to other lines White has increased flexibility, because Black has no queen's knight to exert pressure on e4 (from c5) or occupy e5.

11 ... 0-0
12 ♗e3 ♗d7

Black tried to improve by 12...e5 in Romanishin-Dorfman, USSR 1976, preferring to engineer a rapid pawn sacrifice for double-edged play: 13 ♘de2 d5!? 14 exd5?! (14 0-0-0! dxe4 {14...d4? 15 ♘xd4 exd4 16 ♗xd4 ♕a5 17 e5 ±} 15 ♘xe4 ♕a5 16 ♔b1 ±) 14...e4 15 ♕h3 ♘xd5! 16 0-0-0 ♗xf5 17 ♕h5? (17 ♖xd5 ♗xh3 18 ♖xd8 ♖axd8 19 gxh3 f5 ∓; 17 ♕xf5 ♘xe3 18 ♖xd8 ♘xf5 19 ♖xa8 ♖xa8 20 ♘xe4 ∓) 17...♘xe3! 18 ♖xd8 ♖axd8 19 ♘g3

♗g6 20 ♕a5 b5! 21 h4 h6 22 ♕b6
♘d5 23 ♘xd5 ♖xd5 24 ♘e2 ♖fd8
25 g3 ♗h5 26 ♘c3 ♖5d6 27 ♕b7
♗f3 28 ♖e1 ♖6d7 29 ♕xa6 b4 30
♘e2 e3 31 ♔b1 ♖a8 32 ♕c4 ♖da7
0-1.

13 g4

Fischer flings the g-pawn up the
board with immense venom. White
is on the verge of dictating matters
by employing the standard attacking
plan of advancing the g- and h-
pawns, aided by bringing the
queen's rook to g1.

13	...	e5
14	♘de2	d5!?
15	exd5	e4

The only way to make a battle of
it is to deflect White's forces away
from the onslaught. Black has sacri-
ficed a pawn to conjure up some activity on the queenside.

| 16 | ♕g2 | ♗b4 |
| 17 | 0-0-0 | |

Bolstering the d-pawn and seeking out the next target, which is on
e4.

17	...	a5
18	g5	♘e8
19	f6	a4 *(D)*

There is little choice for Black.
The emphasis must be on seeking a
crack in White's defences as the alternative is dire: 19...gxf6? 20 gxf6+
♔h8 21 ♘xe4 ♘xf6? 22 ♘xf6 ♕xf6
23 ♗d4 +–.

20 ♘a2 ♗d6 21 b4 ♕c7 22 ♔b1
♖c8 23 ♘ec3 a3 24 b3

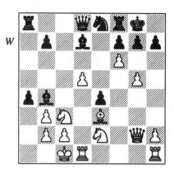

White has contained Black's latest surge of aggression at the cost of
weakening the dark squares around
his king. However, this is difficult to
exploit and ♗c1 is always a safe
move to avoid a calamity.

24...♗e5

24...♗xb4 25 ♘xe4 (25 ♘xb4?
♕xc3) 25...♗d6 26 ♘xd6 with a
clear advantage for White.

25 ♘xe4 ♗f5 26 fxg7 ♔xg7 27
♗c5 ♘d6 28 ♘xd6 ♗xd6 29 ♕f2

White neatly answers the question of how to defend against the
attack on c2 by going on the offensive.

29...b6 30 ♗d4+ ♔g6 31 ♖c1
♗e5 32 ♖hf1 ♗xd4 33 ♕xd4
♗xc2+ 34 ♔a1

Black has finally captured c2, but
at too high a price. His bishop is
pinned and the remote attacking
chances have faded, while White is
on the verge of snaring the enemy
king.

34...f5 35 gxf6 ♕d6 36 ♖g1+
♔f7 37 ♖g7+ ♔e8 38 ♕e3+ 1-0

5 The Velimirović Attack

This system is an important off-shoot from the Sozin Sicilian which owes its credibility to the grandmaster Dragoljub Velimirović. It has the same theme as previous games but with the difference that White plays ♕e2 and castles queenside. The idea is that e5 or f5 can give Black central footholds, so White instead sounds the charge with g4-g5. The attack can be reinforced by h4-h5 and g6, sacrificing pawns to open lines. If Black's king remains in the centre, then White often routinely sacrifices on d5 or f5.

```
               Game 32
           Golubev – Kožul
              Skopje 1991

   1  e4            c5
   2  ♘f3          d6
   3  d4            cxd4
   4  ♘xd4         ♘f6
   5  ♘c3          ♘c6
   6  ♗c4          e6
   7  ♗e3          ♗e7
   8  ♕e2  (D)
   8  ...           ♕c7
   9  0-0-0         a6
  10  ♗b3          0-0
```

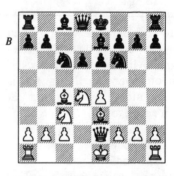

11 ♖hg1

A clear signal that the g-pawn is to be advanced to aid the attack, which also allows the rook in certain circumstances to be brought into play via ♖g3-h3. Other moves:

a) 11 g4 and now:

a1) 11...♘xd4 12 ♖xd4 ♘d7 13 g5 ♘c5 14 ♖g1 (14 ♕h5!? is also possible) 14...♗d7!? 15 ♖g3 g6 16 h4 f5! 17 exf5 ♖xf5 18 h5 ♗e8 19 hxg6 ♗xg6 20 ♘e4 ♘xb3+ 21 axb3 d5 22 ♘f6+ ♗xf6 23 gxf6 ♕e5 24 ♕d2 ♖c8 25 f4 ♕xf6 26 ♖d3 e5 –+ Koyas-Atalik, Katerini 1993.

a2) 11...♘d7 12 g5 ♘c5 13 ♔b1 ♘xb3 14 cxb3 ♗d7 15 ♖c1 ♖ac8 16 f4 ♖fe8 17 h4 ♗f8 18 h5 ♘xd4 19 ♗xd4 ♗c6 20 g6 h6 21 gxf7+ ♕xf7 22 ♖hg1 b5 23 b4 was unclear in the game Arakhamia-Cebalo, Aosta 1990.

a3) 11...♘a5 12 g5 ♘xb3+ 13 axb3 ♘d7 14 h4 b5 15 g6! ♘f6 (15...♘c5 16 b4 ♘a4 17 ♘xa4 bxa4 ± Romanishin-Vaiser, USSR 1982; 15...♘e5 16 gxh7+ ♔h8 17 f4 ♘d7 18 ♖dg1 ± Skroberg-Jankovec, Zilina 1976; 15...hxg6 16 h5 g5 17 ♖hg1 b4 18 ♗xg5 ♗xg5 19 ♖xg5 ± Dely-Paoli, Debrecen 1970; 15...b4? 16 gxf7+ wins for White) 16 gxh7+ ♔h8 17 b4? (17 ♖dg1!) 17...d5 18 e5 ♘xh7 19 f4 ♗xb4 20 ♖d3 ♗d7 21 ♖g1 ♗c5 22 ♕h5 b4 23 ♘b1 ♖ac8 24 ♖g2 ♗a4 25 b3 ♗xd4 26 ♗xd4 ♗xb3! 27 ♖xb3 ♕c4 28 ♕g4 ♖g8 29 ♗c3 bxc3 30 ♖g1 d4 31 ♖b7 (Hon-D.Cooper, Hastings 1991/92) and now 31...d3! is winning for Black.

b) 11 f4 ♘xd4 12 ♖xd4 b5 (also possible is 12...♘d7!?) 13 f5!? exf5 14 exf5 ♗xf5 15 g4 ♗e6 16 g5 ♘d7 17 ♕h5 ♗f5?! (17...♘e5!?) 18 ♖f1 ♗g6 19 ♕d1! ♘c5 20 ♗d5 ♖ab8 21 h4 b4 22 h5 ♗xc2 23 ♕xc2 bxc3 24 ♕xc3 ♘e6 25 ♖c4 ♕d7 26 h6 ♗d8 27 g6! 1-0 Lukin-Shirov, Daugavpils 1989.

11	**...**	**♘d7**
12	**g4**	**♘c5**
13	**g5** *(D)*	
13	**...**	**b5**

This is the usual reply, but Black should consider 13...♗d7 which has the virtue of connecting the rooks. For example:

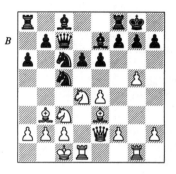

B

a) 14 f4 b5 15 f5 b4! 16 g6 ♘xb3+ 17 axb3 fxg6 18 fxg6 bxc3 19 ♕h5 hxg6 20 ♖xg6 ♖f7 21 ♖h6 gxh6 22 ♖g1+ ♗g5 23 ♗xg5 ♖g7! ∓ Benjamin-Liberzon, 1980.

b) 14 ♖g3 ♖fc8 15 ♕h5 g6 16 ♕h6 ♗f8 17 ♕h4 and now:

b1) 17...b5 18 ♖h3 ♘xb3+ 19 axb3 ♗g7!? 20 ♕xh7+ ♔f8 21 f4 ♘e7 22 ♘f3! e5 (22...b4 23 ♗d4! e5 24 fxe5 dxe5 25 ♗xe5 ± Donchev-Semkov, Varna 1978) 23 f5 gxf5 24 ♘h4 f4 25 ♘f5! +− Kasparov.

b2) 17...♘e7 18 ♘de2 (18 ♕h6! ♗f8 19 ♕h4 ♗e7 =) 18...h5 19 f4 b5 20 f5 ♘xb3+ 21 axb3 b4 22 ♘f4 bxc3 23 bxc3 ♕a5! 24 fxg6 fxg6 25 ♘xg6 ♔g7 26 ♘xe7 ♘xe7 27 ♗d4+ e5 28 g6 ♘g8! ∓ Kasparov.

b3) 17...♘xd4 18 ♖xd4! ♘xb3+ 19 axb3 e5?! (19...♗e7 20 f4 {20 ♕h6 =} 20...h5 21 f5 b5 22 ♖d2 a5 ∞ Marković) 20 ♖d2 ♗e6 (Velimirović-Marković, Vrnjačka Banja 1992) 21 ♖h3! h5 22 gxh6 ♔h7 23 ♖f3 intending ♕f6 and h4-h5, with a small advantage for White.

14   ♕h5   b4 *(D)*

Black has attempted to defend the position in a variety of ways:

a) 14...♖e8?! 15 ♗d5! g6 16 ♕h6 ♗d7 17 ♖g3 ♗f8 18 ♕h4 ♗e7 19 ♖f3! ♘e5 20 ♖h3 h5 21 ♗xa8 ♖xa8 22 ♘ce2 ♖c8 23 ♘f4 ♔f8 24 ♘xh5 gxh5 25 ♕xh5 ♘g6 26 ♖f3 ♔g8 27 ♖xf7 ♔xf7 28 ♕h7+ ♔e8 29 ♕xg6+ ♔d8 30 ♕g8+ ♗e8 (Renet-Piket, Groningen 1984) 31 e5! +–.

b) 14...♖d8? and now:

b1) 15 ♖g3 g6 16 ♕h6 ♗f8 17 ♕h4 b4 18 ♘xc6 ♕xc6 19 ♗d4 ♗g7 20 ♗xg7 1-0 J.Hartston-Alexandria, wom IZ Menorca 1973.

b2) 15 ♘xc6 ♕xc6 16 ♗d5 exd5 17 ♘xd5 ♕e8 18 ♘f6+ ♗xf6 19 gxf6 g6 20 ♗xc5 ♕f8 21 ♗b6 ♖e8 22 f3 +– Djurhuus-Kaspersen, Copenhagen 1988.

c) 14...g6 15 ♕h6 ♖e8 16 ♖g3 (or 16 ♘xc6 ♘xb3+ 17 axb3 ♕xc6 18 ♗d4 ♗f8 19 ♕h4 b4 {Sharif-Radashkovich, Netanya 1977} and now 20 ♖g3! transposes to Pereira-Varabiescu below) 16...♗f8 17 ♕h4 b4 (17...♗e7 18 ♘f5 ♘xb3+ 19 axb3 h5 20 ♘h6+ ♔g7 21 f4 ♗f8 22 f5 ♔h7 23 ♘g4 ± Dussol-Mattern, Strasbourg 1975) 18 ♘xc6! (18 ♖h3 h5 19 gxh6 bxc3 {Magerramov-Tal, clock simul 1974} 20 ♘xc6 ♘xb3+ 21 axb3 e5!) 18...♘xb3+ 19 axb3 ♕xc6 (20...bxc3 20 ♗d4! e5 21 ♘xb4!) 20 ♗d4 h5 21 gxh6 e5 22 ♘d5 exd4 23 ♖dg1! ♖a7 24 ♘f6+

♔h8 25 ♖xg6 fxg6 26 ♖xg6 ♗e6 27 ♕g5 ♗e7 28 h7 1-0 Pereira-Varabiescu, Corr 1981.

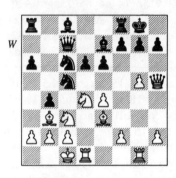

15   ♘xc6

The modern treatment is an improvement on the alternatives, which lack knockout potential:

a) 15 ♖g4? bxc3 16 ♖h4 ♘xb3+ 17 axb3 h6 18 ♘xc6 ♕xc6 19 ♖g1 ♕e8! 20 ♖hg4 f5! is winning for Black; Ioffe-Pukshansky, USSR 1980.

b) 15 ♖g3? bxc3 16 ♖h3 ♘xb3+ 17 axb3 h6 18 ♘xc6 ♕xc6 19 ♖g1 ♕xe4! 20 gxh6 g6 21 h7+ ♔h8 22 ♗h6 cxb2+ 23 ♔b1 ♗b7 0-1 Markland-Dubinin, Corr 1980.

c) 15 ♘a4!? ♗d7 16 ♘xc5 ♘xd4 16 ♘xd7 ♘xb3+ 17 axb3 ♖fc8 with equality; Heim-Spassov, Norway 1975.

15   ...   ♘xb3+

After 15...♕xc6 play has transposed to the next illustrative game.

16   axb3   ♕xc6

17   ♗d4

17 ♘d5?! was answered challengingly by 17...exd5 in Espig-Beliavsky, Sukhumi 1972, allowing Black to fend off the attack after 18 ♗d4 ♕d7! 19 ♗xg7 ♔xg7 20 ♕h6+ ♔h8 21 g6 fxg6 22 ♖xg6 ♖f7 23 ♖dg1 ♗b7 24 ♖g7 ♗g5+! –+.

17 ...   ♗d7 *(D)*

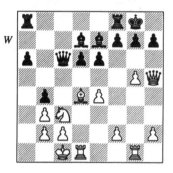

There have been assorted unsuccessful attempts to revive dubious lines:

a) 17...♗b7?! 18 ♘d5! exd5 19 ♖d3! ♖fc8 (19...♗c8 20 ♕h6 +–) 20 c3 dxe4 (20...♔f8 21 ♖f3 ♔e8 22 ♖xf7! ♔d7 {22...♔d8 23 ♕xh7 ♕e8 24 ♗b6+} 23 g6 h6 24 ♕f5+ ♔d8 25 ♗xg7 +–) 21 ♖h3 ♔f8 22 g6! fxg6 23 ♕xh7 ♔e8 24 ♖xg6 bxc3 25 ♕g8+ ♔d7 26 ♕e6+ ♔d8 27 bxc3 ♗f8 28 ♕f7 ♗e7 29 ♕xe7+! ♔xe7 30 ♖g7+ 1-0 Howell-Wahls, Gausdal 1986.

b) 17...bxc3?! 18 ♕h6 e5 19 ♗xe5 cxb2+ 20 ♔xb2 dxe5 (or 20...♕xc2+ 21 ♔xc2 dxe5 22 ♕c6 ♗e6 23 ♔b2 ♖ab8 24 ♖g3 +–) 21

♕xc6 ♗e6 22 ♕c3 a5 23 ♕xe5 ♖fc8 24 f4 a4 25 ♖a1 a3+ 26 ♔b1 ♗b4 27 ♖g3 ♖d8 28 ♖d3 g6 29 f5 1-0 Ligterink-Weinstein, Wijk aan Zee 1975.

c) 17...♖d8?! 18 ♖d3 bxc3 19 ♖f3 e5 20 ♕xf7+ ♔h8 21 ♕xe7 ♖g8 22 g6 ♕xe4 (Grigov-Spassov, Bulgarian Ch 1975) 23 ♕xg7+! +–.

18 ♖g4

A blatantly aggressive manoeuvre intending ♖h4 which is difficult to refute. The tempting 18 ♗f6 is insufficient after 18...bxc3 (18...♖fc8! 14 ♗xe7 bxc3 ∓ Mochalov) 19 ♕h6 cxb2+ 20 ♔xb2 ♕xc2+ 21 ♔xc2 ♖fc8+ 22 ♔b2 gxh6 23 ♗xe7 h5 ∓ Rudnev-Mochalov, USSR 1976.

18 ...   ♖fc8

White stormed Black's defences in the game Plaskett-Wahls, Hastings 1988/89, after 18...bxc3 19 ♖h4 ♗xg5+ (19...h6 20 gxh6 +–) 20 ♕xg5 f6 21 ♕h5 cxb2+ 22 ♗xb2 h6? (22...♖fc8 23 c4! ±) 23 ♖g1 ♖f7 24 ♕xh6 ♔f8 25 ♖xg7 1-0.

19 ♖h4

Instead 19 ♗xg7 (19 ♖f4? e5!) is met by 19...bxc3! 20 ♗xc3 (20 bxc3? ♔xg7 21 ♕h6+ ♔h8 22 ♖h4 ♗xg5+ 23 ♕xg5 ♕xc3 and Black wins) and now 20...♕b5!? 21 ♗f6! is good for White (Nunn), so perhaps 20...♕c5!? is the best chance.

19 ...   ♗xg5+?

In return for relinquishing the bishop Black intends to stem the onslaught. The most accurate defence

is 19...♔f8! (19...h6? 20 gxh6 ♗xh4
21 ♕g4 ♔f8 {21...g5 22 h7+ +−} 22
♗xg7+ +−) 20 ♕xh7! (20 ♖f4!? is
also promising – Nunn) 20...♗xg5+
21 f4 e5 (21...♗h4? 22 ♗xg7+ +−;
21...♔e7 22 fxg5 bxc3 23 ♗xc3 +−;
21...♗f6 22 ♗xf6 gxf6 23 e5! ±) 22
fxg5 exd4 (22...bxc3 23 ♗xc3 is
also good for White) 23 ♕h8+ ♔e7
24 ♕xg7 ♗e6 25 ♖f1 intending
♖xf7+ gives White the advantage
according to Golubev.

> 20   ♕xg5   e5
> 21   ♖g1   g6
> 22   ♕f6! *(D)*

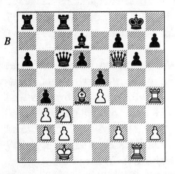

Black underestimated the power
of this move which sets up various
mating possibilities.

> 22   ...   bxc3

There is no way to alleviate the
pressure: 22...♗e8 (22...♗e6 23
♖xg6+!) 23 ♖xh7 ♔xh7 24 ♖g4 is
winning for White.

> 23   ♖xh7!   cxb2+
> 24   ♔xb2   ♕xc2+
> 25   ♔a1   1-0

Game 33

Hector – Plaskett
London 1991

1	e4	c5
2	♘f3	d6
3	d4	cxd4
4	♘xd4	♘f6
5	♘c3	♘c6
6	♗c4	e6
7	♗e3	♗e7
8	♕e2	0-0
9	0-0-0	a6
10	♗b3	♕e8!? *(D)*

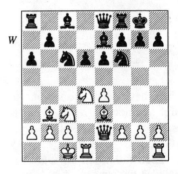

An unusual continuation that was
favoured by Beliavsky in the 1970s.
Black supports the knight on c6,
enabling the b-pawn to advance.

> **11   ♖hg1**

White adopts direct action to seek
an advantage. The g-pawn will be
advanced to instigate a kingside attack. 11 f4 is a major alternative:

a) 11...♗d8?! 12 ♘xc6 ♕xc6 13
e5 dxe5 14 fxe5 ♘e4 15 ♕g4 ±
Stean-Beliavsky, Teesside 1973.

b) 11...♘d7 12 g4 ♘c5 13 ♔b1 b5 14 f5 ♗f6 (14...♘xb3 15 axb3 ♗d7 ±) 15 fxe6 fxe6 16 ♘f5! ♘b7 17 ♘xd6 ♘xd6 18 ♖xd6 ♗e5 ± Velimirović-Spassov, Porec 1974.

c) 11...b5 12 f5 (12 ♘xc6 ♕xc6 13 e5 dxe5 14 fxe5 ♘d7 15 ♘d5!? ♗d8 ∞; 12 e5!? dxe5 13 fxe5 ♘xe5 14 ♗g5 ∞ Velimirović) 12...♘xd4 (12...b4 13 fxe6? bxc3 14 exf7+ ♖xf7 15 ♗xf7+ ♕xf7 16 ♘xc6 ♕xa2 –+ N.Foster-Plaskett, London Barbican rapid 1991) 13 ♖xd4 (13 ♗xd4? b4 14 ♘a4 e5 15 ♗f2 ♗b7 16 ♘b6 ♗xe4! 17 ♘xa8 ♕xa8 ∓) 13...exf5 14 ♖f1 ♘xe4 15 ♘xe4 fxe4 16 ♖xe4 ♗b7? (16...♗e6 17 ♗xe6 fxe6 18 ♖xe6 ♖xf1+ 19 ♕xf1 ♕f7 =) 17 ♖g4 d5 18 ♗d4 f6? 19 c3! ± Nunn-Large, British Ch 1979.

11 ...   ♘d7

The game Timoshchenko-Izvozchikov, USSR 1975, continued: 11...b5 12 g4 b4 13 ♘d5?! (13 ♘xc6!? ♕xc6 14 ♘d5 ±) 13...♘xd5 14 exd5 ♘xd4 15 ♖xd4 a5 16 dxe6 fxe6 17 ♗d2 ♔h8 18 ♗xe6 ♗h4 19 ♗c4 ½-½.

Also possible: 11...♘xd4 12 ♗xd4 ♘d7 13 g4 b5 14 g5 ♘c5 15 ♕h5 ♘xb3+ 16 axb3 e5 17 ♘d5 ♔h8 18 ♗b6 ♗e6 19 ♘c7 ♕c6 20 ♘xe6 fxe6 21 g6 h6 22 ♗e3 ♕xe4 23 ♗xh6 ♕h4 24 ♕xh4 ♗xh4 25 ♖xd6 ♗xf2 26 ♖g2 ♖f5 27 ♗g5 ♖xg5 ½-½ Lažić-Kosić, Yugoslav Ch 1990.

12 g4   ♘c5

13 g5

White has experimented with the waiting move 13 ♔b1, with Black responding energetically: 13...b5 14 ♘xc6 ♕xc6 15 ♗d4 ♘xb3 16 axb3 b4 17 ♘a4 e5 18 ♗e3 ♕xe4 19 ♘b6 ♗e6! ∓ Watson-Plaskett, British Rapidplay Ch 1987.

13 ...   b5

14 ♕h5!

The most aggressive way forward. There are other possibilities:

a) 14 ♔b1 ♗b7 (14...♗d7 15 ♕h5 ♘xb3 16 axb3 {16 cxb3! b4 17 ♘ce2 ♘xd4 ± Velasquez-Cifuentes, Santiago 1986} 16...♘b4 17 ♖g3 g6 18 ♕e2 e5 19 ♘f3 ♖c8 20 h4 ♗e6 21 ♘e1 ♕c6 22 ♕d2 ♕c7 23 ♘d3 ♘xd3 24 ♕xd3 ± Ghizdavu-Ostojić, Bucharest 1973) 15 ♕h5 b4? (15...♘xb3 16 axb3 b4 ∞) 16 ♖g3 bxc3 (16...♘xb3 17 ♖h3 h6 18 ♘d5! exd5 19 ♘f5 +–; 16...♘xd4 17 ♗xd4 f6 18 g6 ±) 17 ♖h3 h6 18 ♘f5! ♗xg5 (18...exf5 19 gxh6 +–) 19 ♗xg5 f6 (19...exf5 20 ♗xh6 +–) 20 ♘xh6+ gxh6 (20...♔h8 21 ♘f7+ ♔g8 22 ♗xf6! +–) 21 ♕xh6 ♕d7 22 ♖g1 1-0 Freitas Sampaio-Fraga Portilho, Corr 1990.

b) 14 ♘xc6 ♕xc6 15 ♗d4 ♗d7 16 ♗d5 exd5 17 ♘xd5 ♖fe8 18 ♕h5 ♖ac8 19 c3 ♘e6 20 ♗xg7! ♔xg7 21 ♘f6 ♗xf6 22 gxf6+ ♔h8 23 ♖d5! 1-0 Anand-Wegner, London 1987.

14 ...   b4 (D)

15 ♘xc6

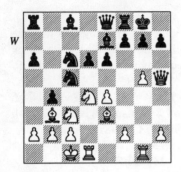

This is the critical line that has undermined the whole of Black's strategy. The older move poses no threat: 15 ♘a4 ♘xd4 16 ♗xd4 ♘xb3+! (16...♘xa4?! 17 ♕h6! e5 18 g6 gxh6 19 gxf7+ ♚h8 20 fxe8♕ ♖xe8 21 ♗xa4 ±) 17 axb3 e5 18 ♗e3 ♗b7 19 ♖g4 g6 20 ♕h6 f5 ∞ Velimirović.

15 ...   ♕xc6

After 15...♘xb3+ the game transposes to the previous game.

16 ♗d5!

A sparkling bishop sacrifice to maintain the initiative.

16 ...   ♕c7

Black's defences are demolished after 16...exd5 17 ♘xd5 ♗d8 18 ♘f6+ ♗xf6 (18...gxf6 19 gxf6+ ♚h8 20 ♕h6 +−) 19 gxf6 g6 (19...♘e6 20 ♖xg7+ ♘xg7 21 ♕g5 +−) 20 ♗xc5 dxc5 21 e5 ♚h8 22 ♕h6 ♖g8 23 ♖d8 +−.

17 ♗d4

It is essential that the onslaught continues in earnest as 17 ♗xa8 bxc3 allows Black good chances due

to ...♗d7 or ...♕b8 and the bishop leaves the board, while 17 ♖g4? fails to 17...bxc3 18 ♖h4 h6 19 gxh6 g6 which repels White's onslaught.

17 ...   bxc3

18 ♕h6!

The key to White's attacking plan is revealed. The queen is taboo due to 18...gxh6 19 gxh6 mating.

18 ...   f6 (D)

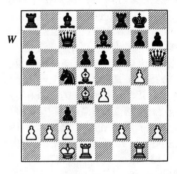

This is the only way to maintain the tension. For example: 18...e5 19 g6! hxg6 (19...gxh6 20 gxf7+ ♚h8 21 ♖g8+ ♖xg8 22 fxg8♕#) 20 ♖xg6 ♗f6 (20...♘e6 21 ♖xg7+ ♘xg7 22 ♖g1) 21 ♗xc5 dxc5 22 ♖xg7+ ♗xg7 23 ♖g1 +−.

19 gxf6?

White fails to fathom the myriad of complications and goes astray. Plaskett reveals that White can win, not by direct attack, but by liquidating to an ending: 19 ♗xa8! gxh6 20 gxf6+ ♚f7 21 ♖g7+ ♚e8 23 ♖xe7+ ♕xe7 23 fxe7 ♚xe7 24 e5! +−.

19 ...   ♗xf6

20 ♗xf6

White starts to drift. A better try is 20 ♗xa8 ♗xd4 21 ♖xd4 cxb2+ when Black has the advantage.

20	...	♖xf6
21	♕xf6	cxb2+
22	♕xb2	exd5
23	♖xd5	♗b7
24	♖xd6	

Not 24 ♖dg5? ♘d3+ –+.

24	...	♘xe4
25	♖b6	♘c3!

The threat of 26...♕f4+ is a bonus as the main idea is to block any ambitions on g7.

26	♖g3	♘e2+
27	♔b1	♗e4
28	♖gb3	♖c8
29	♔a1	♗xc2??

In time-trouble Black blunders; instead 29...♕xh2 would have won.

30	♖b7	h6
31	♖xc7	♖xc7
32	♖b7	1-0

Game 34

Yudasin – Fedorowicz
Novi Sad OL 1990

1	e4	c5
2	♘f3	d6
3	d4	cxd4
4	♘xd4	♘f6
5	♘c3	♘c6
6	♗c4	e6
7	♗e3	♗e7
8	♕e2	0-0
9	0-0-0	♗d7!? *(D)*

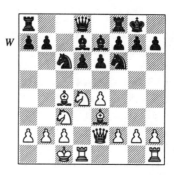

An old variation that has the benefit of avoiding the main lines. It was revived by the Americans Christiansen, Dlugy and Fedorowicz with some success in the 1980s.

10 ♗b3

This is a solid system which shelters the bishop before embarking on an attack. It is possible to adopt a more direct approach:

a) 10 f4 and now:

a1) 10...♖c8 11 ♗b3 ♕a5 12 ♘db5! d5 13 f5 dxe4 14 ♖xd7 ♘xd7 15 fxe6 ♘de5 (15...♘f6 16 exf7+ ♔h8 17 ♘d4 ±) 16 exf7+ ♘xf7 17 ♖f1 a6 18 ♕g4 ♘ce5 19 ♕e6 ±.

a2) 10...♕c8!? 11 ♘f3 ♕c7 12 ♔b1 a6 13 ♗d3 e5!? 14 f5 ♘b4 15 ♖hg1 (15 g4!) 15...d5 was equal in Wolff-Dlugy, Toronto 1989.

a3) 10...♕b8 11 f5 ♘xd4 12 ♖xd4 (12 ♗xd4!?) 12...b5? 13 fxe6 fxe6 14 e5! +– Boleslavsky.

a4) 10...♕c7 11 ♖hf1 ♖fc8 12 ♗b3 ♘xd4 13 ♗xd4 e5 14 fxe5 dxe5 15 ♘d5! ± Kremenietsky-Gorshkov, USSR 1967.

a5) 10...♘xd4 11 ♗xd4 ♗c6 12 f5 exf5 13 exf5 d5!? 14 ♗xf6 ♗xf6 15 ♘xd5 ♗xd5 16 ♖xd5 ♕c7 ±.

a6) 10...a6 11 e5! dxe5 12 ♘xc6 bxc6 13 fxe5 ♘d5 14 ♘e4 ♕a5 15 ♗g5 ♗xg5 16 ♘xg5 h6 17 ♘e4 ♖ab8 18 ♗b3 ♖xb3 (18...♘b6 19 ♕h5! c5 20 ♘f6+! gxf6 21 ♖d3 +− Timman) 19 cxb3 ♕xa2 20 ♘c5! ♘c3 21 ♕d3 ♘xd1 22 ♖xd1 ♗c8 23 ♕c3 a5 24 ♕c4 f6 25 ♘xe6 ♗xe6 26 ♕xe6+ ♔h7 27 exf6 a4 28 ♕e4+ ♔g8 29 f7+! +− Timman-Ljubojević, Novi Sad OL 1990.

b) 10 ♖hg1 and now:

b1) 10...♘xd4 11 ♗xd4 ♕a5 12 g4 ♖fc8?! 13 g5 (13 ♗b3!) 13...♘e8 14 f4 ♖xc4! 15 ♕xc4 b5 16 ♕d3 b4 17 ♘b1 e5 18 ♗e3 ♖c8 19 f5 ♗b5 ∞ Brunner-Christiansen, Novi Sad OL 1990.

b2) 10...♖c8 11 g4 (11 ♗b3 transposes to line 'a' of the following note) 11...♘xd4 12 ♗xd4 e5 13 g5 ♘g4 14 ♗xa7 ♗xg5+ 15 ♔b1 ♕a5? (15...♗e7 16 ♘d5 ♘f6 17 ♗b6 ±) 16 ♖xd6 ♕xa7 17 ♖xd7 ♘f6 18 ♖xf7! ♖xf7 19 ♗xf7+ ♔xf7 20 ♖xg5 +− Walther-Ortega, Lugano OL 1968.

10   ...   ♘xd4

The alternatives are:

a) 10...♖c8?! 11 ♖hg1 ♕a5 12 g4 ♘xd4 13 ♗xd4 e5 14 g5! ± Nikitin.

b) 10...♕b8 11 g4! ♘xd4 (or 11...♖c8 12 g5 ♘e8 13 h4 ♘a5 14 g6! is slightly better for White; Velimirović-Milić, Belgrade 1965) 12

♗xd4 b5 13 g5 ♘e8 (Espig-Kirov, Timisoara 1972) 14 ♖dg1 b4 15 ♘d1 ±.

c) 10...♕a5?! 11 ♘db5 ♘e8 12 ♗f4 e5 13 ♗e3 ♕d8 14 ♘d5 with a clear plus for White; Tukmakov-Kottnauer, Hastings 1968/69.

11   ♗xd4   ♕a5

Black has tried other paths with limited success:

a) 11...a5?! 12 a4 e5 13 ♗e3 ♗c6 14 f3 ♕d7 15 g4 ± Minev-Bobotsov, Bulgaria 1967.

b) 11...b5?! 12 e5! dxe5 13 ♗xe5 ± Simagin.

c) 11...♗c6 12 f4 (12 g4 ♕a5! 13 f4 b5 14 g5 ♘e8 15 h4 b4 = Sigurjonsson-Müller, Faeroes 1967) 12...♕a5 13 ♖hf1 b5 14 e5 dxe5 15 ♕xe5! ± Tukmakov-Minkov, USSR 1967.

12   ♖hg1!   b5?! *(D)*

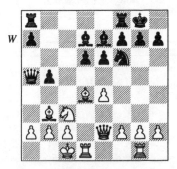

Yudasin suggests that Black should search for a different plan:

a) 12...♖fc8 13 g4 e5 14 g5! exd4 (14...♘e8 15 ♗e3 ♖xc3 16

bxc3 ±) 15 gxf6 ♗xf6 (15...dxc3 16 ♖xg7+ ♔h8 17 ♖d5 +−) 16 ♘d5 ±.

b) 12...♗c6!? 13 g4 e5 14 g5 exd4 15 gxf6 ♗xf6 (15...dxc3? 16 ♖xg7+ ♔h8 17 ♖d5! ♗xd5 18 ♖h7+ ♔h7 19 ♕h5+ ♔g8 20 ♕g5+ ♔h7 21 ♕g7#) 16 ♘d5 ♗xd5 17 ♗xd5 intending ♖d3, ♔b1, ♖h3 and ♕h5 with bright prospects.

13 e5!

White's play is consistently bold. This advance depends on the black queen's influence being temporarily cut off by ...b5 which allows 14 ♕xe5. The text is a significant improvement on the accepted continuation 13 g4 b4 14 g5 ♘e8 15 ♘d5 (15 ♘b1 ♗xg5+ 16 ♘d2 ∞) 15...exd5 16 ♗xd5 (Hennings-Navarovszky, Kecskemet 1970) 16...b3! 17 ♗xa8 (17 axb3 ♖c8 18 g6 h6! 19 gxf7+ ♖xf7 20 ♕h5 ♗e6 −+) 17...bxa2 18 b3 ♗xg5+ and ...♘f6 ∓.

| **13** | **...** | **dxe5** |
| **14** | **♕xe5** | **♖fc8** |

The rapid sharpening of the position is evident after:

a) 14...♗c6 15 ♗xe6! ♖fe8 16 ♗b3 ±.

b) 14...♕a6 15 ♘d5!? ♗d8 16 ♘c7 ±.

| **15** | **g4** | **♕c7** |

15...♗c6 would be asking for trouble after 16 g5 ♘e8 17 g6! hxg6 18 ♖xg6 +−.

| **16** | **g5** | **♘e8** |

The exchange of queens can do little to quell the might of White's

position: 16...♕xe5 17 ♗xe5 ♘d5 18 ♘xd5 +−.

17 ♘d5

White insists upon a favourable ending in which his active pieces can excel.

17	**...**	**♕xe5**
18	**♘xe7+**	**♔f8**
19	**♗xe5**	**♔xe7**
20	**♖g4!**	

Yudasin adjusts well to the changed circumstances by pinpointing the weakness at h7.

20	**...**	**♖c5**
21	**♗d4**	**♖f5**
22	**c3!**	

This simple move opens up the possibility of 23 ♗c2 ♖d5 24 ♗e4 ♖d6 25 ♗c5 winning the exchange. Now Black's impulsive decision to steer his rook into the centre rebounds on him, and he must make concessions.

| **22** | **...** | **h6** |

In answer to 22...♗c6 White can utilize the power of his bishops with 23 ♗c2 ♗f3 24 ♗xf5 ♗xd1 25 ♗e4! ♗xg4 26 ♗xa8 when Black's queenside pawns will soon vanish.

| **23** | **gxh6** | **gxh6** |
| **24** | **♖h4** | **♘d6** |

It is futile to try to hold on to the pawn: 24...h5 25 ♗c2 ♖g5 26 ♗e3 ♖e5 27 ♗e4 ♖c8 28 ♗xa7 +−.

| **25** | **♗c2** | **♖d5** |
| **26** | **♖xh6** | **♗c6** (D) |

If 26...e5 27 ♗xe5! ♖xe5 28 ♖hxd6 +−.

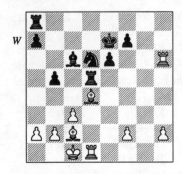

W

27	♗f6+	♔d7
28	♖xd5	♗xd5
29	♖h8!	

A quiet move of high class. White trades rooks to make room for his h-pawn to storm forward, which will tie down Black's pieces, while White's can switch their attention to the queenside.

| 29 | ... | ♖xh8 |
| 30 | ♗xh8 | ♘e4 |

The opposite-coloured bishop ending is winning after 30...♘f5 31 ♗xf5 exf5 32 b3, creating two passed pawns.

31	♗d4	a6
32	h4	♔e7
33	h5	f5
34	h6	♘g5

34...♘f6 fails to 35 ♗b3! ♗xb3 (35...♗e4 36 ♗xf6+ ♔xf6 37 ♗xe6! ♔g6 38 b4; 35...♘h7 36 ♗xd5 exd5 37 f4 +−) 36 ♗xf6+ ♔xf6 37 axb3 ♔g6 38 c4 when one pawn must queen.

| 35 | f4 | ♘h7 |
| 36 | ♗d1 | ♔f8 |

| 37 | b3 | ♔g8 |
| 38 | ♗h5 | 1-0 |

Game 35
Yudasin – Garcia Ilundain
Pamplona 1992/93

1	e4	c5
2	♘f3	d6
3	d4	cxd4
4	♘xd4	♘f6
5	♘c3	♘c6
6	♗c4	e6
7	♗e3	a6

A similar theme to the game is revealed after 7...♗e7 8 ♕e2 ♘a5 9 ♗d3 e5?! 10 ♗b5+ ♔f8 11 ♘b3 a6 12 ♗d3 ♗e6 13 0-0 ♖c8 14 ♘xa5 ♕xa5 15 ♗d2 ♕c7 16 a4 g6 17 ♗h6+ ♔g8 18 a5 ♕d8 19 ♖fd1 ♘g4 20 ♗d2 ♗g5 21 f3 ♗xd2 22 ♕xd2 ♘f6 23 ♗f1 ♖c6 24 ♘a2! ± Ehlvest-I.Ivanov, New York 1990.

| 8 | ♕e2 | ♘a5 |

Black's idea with this knight sortie is to harass White's bishop and maintain the option of keeping his king in the centre until White reveals a plan of campaign.

| 9 | ♗d3! | |

White is keen to preserve his bishop. Although optically it is less active on d3 than on b3, it provides useful support for e4, and often ends up eyeing h7.

| 9 | ... | ♗e7 (D) |

Black has tried a variety of adventurous replies:

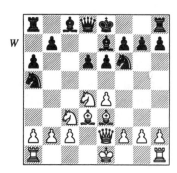

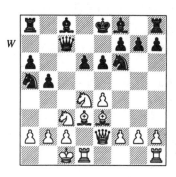

a) 9...b5 and now:

a1) 10 0-0-0 b4 11 ♘b1 ♗b7 12 ♘d2 ♗e7 13 g4 ♘c6 14 g5 ♘d7 15 ♘xc6 ♗xc6 16 f4 e5 17 ♖hg1 exf4 18 ♗xf4 ♘e5 19 ♗xe5 dxe5 20 ♗c4 ♗b5 21 ♗xb5+ axb5 22 ♕xb5+ ♕d7 23 ♕xd7+ ♔xd7 24 ♘c4+ ♔e6 25 ♖d5 f6 26 ♔b1 = Prié-Kovalev, Clichy 1991.

a2) 10 a4 b4 11 ♘b1 ♗e7 12 ♘d2 0-0 13 0-0 ♘d7!? 14 f4 ♗f6 = A.Sokolov-Aseev, USSR Ch 1989.

a3) 10 b4 ♘c4 11 ♗xc4 bxc4 12 0-0 (12 a3! ♗b7 13 f3 ± Yudasin) 12...♗b7 13 ♗g5 ♖c8 14 ♖ad1 h6 15 ♗h4 ♗e7 16 e5 ♘d5 17 ♘xd5 ♗xh4 18 ♘xe6 fxe6 19 ♕h5+ ♔d7 20 ♕f7+ ♔c6 21 b5+ axb5 22 ♘b4+ ♔c5 23 ♕xb7 ♔xb4 24 ♖b1+ ♔c3 25 ♕f3+ ♔d4 26 ♖xb5 1-0 Horvath-Jasnikowski, Balatonbereny 1985.

b) 9...♕c7 10 0-0-0 b5 *(D)* and now:

b1) 11 g4 b4 12 ♘b1 d5 13 ♘d2 dxe4 14 ♘xe4 ♗b7 15 ♘xf6+ gxf6 16 ♖he1 ♗e7 17 ♗h6 ♕b6 18 ♘f5!

♗c5 19 ♗e4 ♕b5 20 ♕f3 ♗xe4 21 ♖xe4 ♖d8 22 ♗g7 ♖xd1+ 23 ♕xd1 ♖g8 24 ♗xf6 ♘c6 25 b3 ♕b8 26 ♕d5 ♕b5 27 ♖xe6+! fxe6 28 ♕xe6+ ♔f8 29 ♘h6 ♕f1+ 30 ♔b2 1-0 Short-Cramling, Dortmund 1986.

b2) 11 ♖hg1 b4 12 ♘b1 d5 13 ♘d2 ♗b7 14 ♗g5 ♗c5 15 ♘4b3 dxe4 16 ♘xe4 ♘xe4 17 ♗xe4 ♘xb3+ 18 axb3 ♗xe4 19 ♕xe4 ∓ Wang Pin-Lerner, Beijing 1991.

b3) 11 a3 ♗e7 12 g4 ♖b8 13 ♖he1 ♘c4 14 g5 ♘d7 15 ♘f5! exf5 16 ♘d5 ♕d8 17 exf5 0-0 18 ♕h5 ♘f6 19 gxf6 ♗xf6 20 ♗xc4 bxc4 21 ♗d4 ♗xd4 22 ♖xd4 ♖e8 23 ♘f6+ gxf6 24 ♖g4+ ♔h8 25 ♖eg1 ♗xf5 26 ♕xf5 ♖b5 27 ♕xh7+! 1-0 Nunn-Pritchett, Bundesliga 1985.

10 0-0-0   0-0

If 11...b5 then 12 g4 b4 12 ♘a4!? ♗d7 13 g5! ♘g8 14 ♘xe6!? (or 14 b3) is judged unclear by Yudasin.

11 g4   b5
12 g5

White pushes his kingside pawns in an effort to seize the initiative.

12 ... ♘d7
13 f4!

This simple move has the merit of supporting g5 and controlling the e5 square. After 13 h4 the knight can leap to c4 via e5: 13...♘e5 14 f4 ♘ec4 15 ♗xc4 bxc4 (15...♘xc4? 16 ♘c6 ±) intending ...♖b8 and ...♕b6 with dynamic chances.

13 ... ♘c5

13...b4, to launch a counter-attack, is suspect due to 14 ♘a4 ♘c5 15 ♘xc5 dxc5 16 ♘b3 when White can blockade and can continue with h4, f5 and h5.

14 h4 (D)

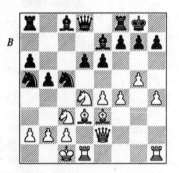

The prophylactic 14 a3 merely encourages Black to open up the b-file: 14...♖b8 15 ♖hg1! b4 16 axb4 ♖xb4 17 f5 ♘xd3+ (17...♕b6 ∞) 18 ♕xd3 (18 cxd3? ♖xd4 19 ♗xd4 ♘b3+ ∓) 18...♕c7 19 f6 ♗d8 is unclear.

14 ... b4!

14...♗b7 blocks the b-file, rendering 15 a3! more effective, followed by f5 and h5 with advantage to White.

15 ♘b1 ♕c7
16 ♘d2 ♘xd3+!

Black is conscious of the need for precise timing, as 16...♗d7 17 ♔b1 allows the capture on d3 to be met by cxd3.

17 ♕xd3 ♗d7
18 ♔b1 ♖fc8

Attempts by Black to sharpen the play with ...♗b5 fail. For example:

a) 18...♗b5? 19 ♘xb5 axb5 20 ♕xb5 b3? 21 cxb3 ±. The open lines are not sufficient compensation for the pawns.

b) 18...e5? 19 ♘f5 ♗b5 20 ♗b6! ♕b7 (20...♕xb6 21 ♘xe7+ ♔h8 22 ♕g3 followed by ♘d5 and h5 with advantage) 21 ♕f3 with a kingside attack (Yudasin).

19 ♖c1 ♗f8
20 ♕e2 e5
21 ♘4f3!

Not 21 fxe5?! (21 ♘f5?! d5!) 21...dxe5 22 ♘f5 ♗e6 with the intention of ...♘c4 and ...a5-a4 ∓.

21 ... ♘c4
22 f5 ♖ab8

A knight sacrifice to expose the king is premature: after 22...♘a3+?! 23 bxa3 bxa3 24 ♕d3 (24 c4 ♕b7+ 25 ♔c2 d5!? is simply unclear) White can continue with ♘b3, c4 and ♘fd2 ±.

23 ♘xc4 ♕xc4
24 ♕xc4 ♖xc4
25 ♘d2 ♖c7 (D)

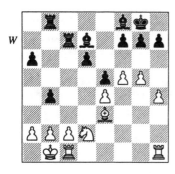

26 h5!

The ending offers White decent chances due to his imposing wave of pawns on the kingside. The key is to open lines along which his rooks can invade. Black must concentrate on fending off the initial onslaught and broaden the range of his bishops with ...d5.

26 ...   d5
27 h6   gxh6?!

This seems natural since 28 gxh6 f6! appears to solve any problems, as the rook on c7 will be able to cover g7. The alternatives are:

a) 27...d4?! 28 &f2 with the idea to undermine e5 by &g3 and ♘f3.

b) 27...g6 28 fxg6 fxg6 (alternatively, 28...hxg6!? ±) 29 exd5 &f5 30 b3 followed by ♘c4, and White is slightly better .

c) 27...dxe4 28 hxg7 and now:

c1) 28...♔xg7?! 29 ♖cf1 ♖bc8 (29...&b5? 30 ♖f2! +−) 30 ♘ex4 &c6 31 ♘f6 &xh1 32 ♖xh1 &e7! 33 ♖xh7+ ♔f8 34 ♖h8+ (34 ♘d5!? ♔g8) 34...♔g7 =.

c2) 28...&xg7 29 ♖cf1? (29 f6! ∞) 29...♖bc8! 30 ♘xe4 ♖xc2 31 ♘f6+ &xf6 32 gxf6 ♖g2! ∓ Yudasin.

28 ♖cg1!   h5

White's inspired play has given Black an assortment of problems:

a) 28...♔h8 29 g6! and &xh6 with strong pressure on the h-file.

b) 28...d4!? 29 &f2 (29 gxh6+ ♔h8 30 &g5 ♖c6 intending ...f6 ∞) 29...hxg5! 30 ♖xg5+ ♔h8 31 f6!, with the idea &g3 and ♘f3, and White has attacking chances.

29 ♖xh5   ♖bc8 *(D)*

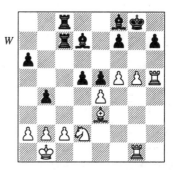

30 g6!   hxg6
31 fxg6   fxg6?

Black's only chance to stay in the fight was to blockade the g-file: 31...f6! (31...f5? 32 g7 &xg7 33 &h6 intending ♖hg5) 32 &h6! with various ideas: &xf8, exd5 or g7, with an initiative for White.

32 ♖xg6+   ♔f7

32...&g7 is met by 33 ♖g1 +−.

33 ♖g1!   d4

After 33...罩xc2 34 ᐃf3 the black pawns will fall.

34	ᐃh6	ᐃxh6
35	罩xh6	罩xc2
36	ᐃf3!	罩2c5?

Upon 36...含e7! White is still on top: 37 ᐃxe5 ᐃe6 38 ᐃg6+! 含f7 39 罩h7+ 含f6 40 e5+ 含f5 41 ᐃe7+ 含xe5 42 罩e1+! +−.

| 37 | 罩h7+ | 1-0 |

Game 36
Frolov – Bagaturov
Biel IZ 1993

1	e4	c5
2	ᐃf3	ᐃc6
3	d4	cxd4
4	ᐃxd4	ᐃf6
5	ᐃc3	d6
6	ᐃc4	e6
7	ᐃe3	a6
8	豐e2	豐c7
9	ᐃb3	ᐃe7
10	0-0-0	ᐃa5

This is one of the most fashionable lines. Black leaves his king in the centre to avoid castling kingside into White's pawn storm.

11 g4   b5

In the game Dely-Varnusz, Hungarian Ch 1967, Black put up a sluggish defence: 11...ᐃxb3+ 12 axb3 h6?! (12...b5 13 g5 transposes to the main game) 13 h4 h5 14 gxh5 罩xh5 15 ᐃg5 罩h8 16 f4 ᐃd7 17 e5 0-0-0 18 exf6 gxf6 and now 19 ᐃd5! exd5 20 豐xe7 fxg5 21 fxg5 +−.

12 g5   ᐃxb3+

Not 12...ᐃd7?! 13 ᐃxe6! ±.

13 axb3   ᐃd7 (D)

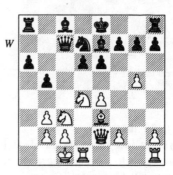

14 ᐃf5

A stunning idea that was introduced by Velimirović. White opens the central files and embarks on a violent attack. In practice it is not easy for Black to overcome his problems.

White has tried various other plans which aim to exploit Black's centralised king. Of these, 14 h4 has emerged as the main alternative. For example:

a) 14 豐h5 ᐃc5 (14...g6 15 豐h6 ᐃf8 16 豐h3 ∞) 15 b4 ᐃa4 16 ᐃxa4 (16 罩d3 豐b7 17 f3 ᐃxc3 18 罩xc3 a5 19 bxa5 b4 20 罩d3 罩xa5 21 ᐃb3 罩a8 ∓ Vogt-Tringov, Bulgaria 1973) 16...bxa4 17 罩d3 豐b7 18 罩e1!? e5 (18...豐xe4 19 ᐃd2 豐g6 20 豐f3 罩b8 21 h4 ±) 19 ᐃf5 g6 20 ᐃg7+ 含f8 21 豐h6 ᐃg4 (21...含g8 22 ᐃe8 +−) 22 ᐃf5+ 含e8 23 ᐃxd6+! ᐃxd6 24 豐g7 豐xb4 25 豐xh8+ 含d7 26

🗒xd6+! ⟡xd6 27 🗒d1+! 1-0 Thor-hallsson-Stefansson, Icelandic Ch 1993.

b) 14 b4?! 0-0 15 f4 a5! 16 ♘cxb5 ♛b7 17 ♗d2 (17 f5?! axb4 18 f6 gxf6 19 🗒hg1 ⟡h8 20 gxf6 ♘xf6 21 ♗h6 🗒g8 ∓ Kristiansen-Tukmakov, Graz 1972) 17...axb4 18 ♗xb4 (Brunner-Wolff, Maringa 1991) 18...♘c5! ∓.

c) 14 h4 b4 and now:
c1) 15 ♘a2 a5 16 ♘b5 ♛b8 17 ♛d3 🗒a6 18 ♛c4 ♘c5 19 ⟡b1 🗒b6 20 ♘xd6+ 🗒xd6 21 ♗xc5 🗒c6 22 ♗a7 ♛c7 23 ♛b5 ♗a6 24 ♛b8+ ♛xb8 25 ♗xb8 h6 26 ♗f4 ♗e2 27 🗒de1 hxg5 28 hxg5 🗒xh1 29 🗒xh1 ♗f3 30 🗒e1 e5 31 ♗d2 = de Firmian-Hellers, Reykjavik 1990.

c2) 15 ♘a4 ♘c5 16 h5 *(D)* and now:

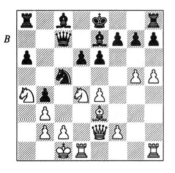

c21) 16...♘xa4 17 bxa4 ♛a5 18 g6 ♛xa4 19 ⟡b1 ♗d7 20 gxf7+ ⟡xf7 21 ♛f3+ ♗f6 22 h6 🗒g8 23 hxg7 ♛a5 24 🗒h6 ♛e5 25 🗒h5 1-0 Hartston-Mestel, British Ch 1973.

c22) 16...e5 17 ♘f5 ± Nunn-Murshed, London 1985.

c23) 16...♘xe4 17 g6 ♗f6!? (17...♗d8 18 ♗f4 ±; 17...f5 18 h6 ±; 17...♘f6 18 h6 fxg6 19 hxg7 🗒g8 20 ♗g5 ±):
c231) 18 ♗f4. Now the recommended line is 18...e5 19 ♛xe4 ♗b7, e.g. 20 ♛e2 ♗xh1 21 🗒xh1 0-0!, but a significant improvement is 20 gxf7+ ⟡xf7 (20...♛xf7 21 ♘f5!) 21 ♛f5 ♗xh1 22 ♛e6+ ⟡f8 23 ♛xf6+! gxf6 24 ♘e6+ ±; therefore the critical line is 18...♗b7 19 f3 e5 20 ♘f5 0-0 ∞.

c232) 18 gxf7+ ⟡xf7 19 🗒hg1 e5 20 ♘f3 ♗f5 21 ⟡b1 🗒ab8 22 ♘d2 ♘xd2+ 23 🗒xd2 🗒hc8 24 f4 🗒b5 25 ♛f2 exf4 26 ♗xf4 ♛c6 27 ♗g5 27 ♛xc2+! 28 🗒xc2 (28 ⟡a2 ♛xb3+! 29 ⟡xb3 ♗e6+ also wins for Black) 28...🗒xc2 29 ♛xf5 🗒xf5 30 ♗xf6 🗒cf2! −+ Emms-Hennigan, British Ch 1993.

c24) 16...♗d7 17 ⟡b1 (17 g6 ♘xb3+ 18 ♘xb3 ♗xa4 19 h6 fxg6 20 ♘d4 e5! 21 ♘e6 ♛c6 22 hxg7 🗒g8 23 🗒xh7 ♗b3 24 ♘c5 ♗f7 25 ♘d3 ♛xe4 ∓ Brunner-Van der Wiel, Lucerne 1989) 17...♘xe4?! (17...♗xa4 18 bxa4 🗒c8 19 f3!? ♘xa4 20 ♛xa6 ♘c5 21 ♛b5+ ♛d7 22 b3! 0-0?! 23 ♛xd7 ♘xd7 24 ♗d2 ± Rõtšagov-Yrjölä, USSR 1990; 17...♛b7 18 g6!? ♗f6 19 gxf7+ ⟡xf7 20 h6 g6 21 ♘xc5 dxc5 22 ♘f3 🗒hd8 23 ♗g5 ♗xg5 24 ♘xg5+ ⟡g8 25 ♛f3 🗒f8 26 ♛g3 🗒ae8 27 ♛e5! ♗c8 28 f4

♕e7 29 ♕g7+! ♕xg7 30 hxg7 1-0
Pugachev-Feher, Budapest 1992) 18
g6 f5 19 h6! hxg6 20 f3 ♘c5 21
♘xc5 dxc5 22 ♗f4 ♕b6 (Wolff-
D.Gurevich, Los Angeles 1991) and
now Wolff recommends 23 ♗c7!
♕xc7 24 ♘xe6 ♕c6 25 hxg7 ♖g8
26 ♘f8! ♕f6 27 ♖xd7 ♖xg7 28 ♖h8
♖f7 29 ♘xg6+ ♔xd7 30 ♘e5+ +−.

14 ...   exf5

Black may instead decline the
sacrifice with 14...b4 *(D)*:

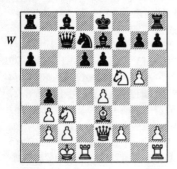

a) 15 ♘xg7+?! ♔f8 16 ♕h5
♔xg7 17 ♗d4+ ♔g8! (17...♘e5 18
f4 bxc3 {18...♗d7 19 ♖hg1 bxc3 20
fxe5 cxb2+ 21 ♗xb2 d5 22 ♕h6+
1-0 Hermlin-Voorema, USSR 1969}
19 fxe5 cxb2+ 20 ♗xb2 d5 21 exd5
± Zaichik-Korsunsky, USSR 1976)
18 ♖hg1 ♘e5 19 f4 ♘g6 20 ♗xh8
♔xh8 21 ♘e2 ♗b7 22 ♖d4 ♖c8 23
♖c4 ♕b6 24 f5 ♖xc4 25 bxc4 ♕e3+
26 ♔b1 ♗xe4! 27 fxg6 ♗xg6 28
♕g4 e5 29 ♘c1 b3 30 ♖g2 bxc2+ 31
♖xc2 ♕d2 0-1 Wahls-Rechlis, Bern
1990.

b) 15 ♘xe7 and now:

b1) 15...♔xe7 16 ♗f4!? (16 ♘a4
a5 =) 16...bxc3! (16...♘e5 17 ♘a4
intending ♗g3, f4-f5) 17 ♗xd6+
♕xd6 18 ♖xd6 cxb2+ 19 ♔xb2
♔xd6 20 ♕d2+ ♔e7 21 ♕b4+ ♔e8
22 ♕c3 ♗b7 ∞ Rechlis.

b2) 15...bxc3 16 ♘xc8 cxb2+ 17
♔xb2 ♖xc8 18 ♖d2 with an edge for
White − Boleslavsky.

15 ♘d5   ♕d8

Any other queen move is bleak
for Black:

a) 15...♕a5 16 exf5 ♗b7 17
♘xe7 ♕a1+ 18 ♔d2 ♕xb2 19 ♘c6
+−.

b) 15...♕c6 16 exf5 ♔d8? 17
♗b6+ +−.

c) 15...♕b7 16 exf5 ♘e5 17 f4
♗xf5 18 fxe5 ♗e4 (18...♖c8 19 c3
♗e4 20 ♘xe7 ±; 18...dxe5 19 ♗c5!
♗xg5+ 20 ♔b1 f6 21 ♕f3 ±
Boleslavsky) 19 exd6 ♗xd5 20
♗c5! ♗xh1 21 d7+ ♕xd7 22 ♖xd7
♔xd7 23 ♕xe7+ ♔c6 24 ♕d6+
♔b7 25 ♕d7+ ♔b8 26 ♗d6#.

16 exf5 *(D)*

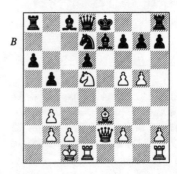

16 ...   &b7

If Black tries to castle out of trouble then White starts a stampede towards the king: 16...0-0 17 f6! gxf6 (17...&xf6 18 gxf6 ♘xf6 19 &b6 ±; 17...♘xf6 18 &b6 ±) 18 &d4 ♘e5 19 gxf6 &xf6 20 ♖hg1+ &g7 (20...&h8 21 &b6 +−) 21 &xe5 dxe5 22 ♕xe5 f6 23 ♘e7+ &f7 (23...&h8 24 ♖xd8 fxe5 25 ♖xf8+ &xf8 26 ♖g8#) 24 ♕h5+ 1-0 Velimirović-Sofrevsky, Titograd 1965.

17 f6

The only way to maintain the initiative. Other moves:

a) 17 ♖he1 &xd5 18 ♖xd5 0-0 19 f6 ♘xf6! 20 gxf6 &xf6 21 ♕d2 ♖e8! 22 ♖xd6 ♕e7 23 ♖g1 ♖ad8 = Nikitin.

b) 17 ♖hg1 &xd5 18 ♖xd5 0-0 19 f6 ♘xf6 20 gxf6 ½-½ Hindle-Hamann, Vrnjačka Banja 1967.

17 ...   gxf6 (D)

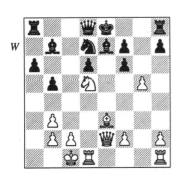

It is necessary to follow a precise move-order: 17...&xd5?! 18 fxg7

(18 ♖xd5!? gxf6 19 &d4 &f8 20 ♕h5 h6 21 ♖g1 ♘e5 22 f4 ♘g6 23 gxf6 &xf6 24 ♖xg6 &xd4 25 ♖gxd6 &e3+ 26 &b1 ♕e7 27 ♖xh6 ♖g8 28 ♖h8 ♕f6 29 ♖xg8+ &xg8 30 ♖f5 ♕e6 31 ♖g5+ &f8 32 ♕h8+ +− Koch-Kožul, Marseille 1989) 18...♖g8 19 ♖xd5 ♖xg7 20 f4 &f8 21 h4 (21 ♖e1!? ♖c8 22 &b1 ♖c6 23 &d4 f6 24 ♕h5 was slightly better for White in Tseshkovsky-Petrushin, USSR 1970) 21...♕c7 22 &d4 ♕c6 23 ♖e1 ♖e8 24 &xg7+ &xg7 24 ♖d3 ♘b6 25 ♖e3 +− Hunter-Zagorovsky, Corr 1971/72.

18 ♖he1

With a shattered kingside the time is right to profit from the e-file. On 18 gxf6 Kotov advocates 18...♘xf6! 19 ♘xf6+ &xf6 20 &g5+ &f8 21 &h6+ &g7 and Black is better.

18 ...   &xd5

In his original analysis of the line Velimirović found a forceful finale upon 18...0-0?!: 19 gxf6 &xf6 20 ♕g4+ &h8 21 ♘xf6 ♘xf6 22 &d4 ♖g8 23 ♖e8! ♖xe8 24 ♕g5 ♖e6 25 ♖g1 +−.

19 ♖xd5   ♖g8 (D)

19...0-0 is doomed after 20 gxf6 &xf6 (20...♘xf6 21 ♖g5+ &h8 22 &d4 ♖g8 23 ♕xe7 ±) 21 ♖g1+ &h8 22 ♖h5 &g7 (22...♖g8 23 ♖xh7+ +−) 23 ♖xg7 &xg7 24 ♕g4+ &h8 25 ♕f5 +−.

20 gxf6

In Hector-Fishbein, Stavanger 1991, White tried another attacking

line: 20 ♗f4 ♔f8 21 ♕d2 ♖xg5 22 ♗xg5 fxg5 23 h4 a5 24 hxg5? (24 ♖xb5!?) 24...a4 25 b4 a3 26 b3?! (or 26 bxa3 ♖xa3 27 ♕d4 ♔g8! ∓) 26...♘e5 27 f4 a2 28 ♔b2 ♘f3 29 ♕c3 ♗f6 30 gxf6 ♘xe1 31 ♖d1 ♘xc2! 0-1.

21 ...   **♘xf6**
21 ♖f5   **♖b8**

21...♘d7 22 ♗g5 ♘e5 23 ♗xe7 ♕xe7 24 f4 ♘d3+, Yurtaev-Korzubov, USSR 1983, leads to a double rook ending in which White enjoys slightly the greater freedom.

22 h4!

Whether this latest try forces Black to seek an alternative defence remains to be established, but it appears to be superior to the usual 22 ♗a7. For example: 22...♖b7 (or 22...♘d7 23 ♗xb8 ♘xb8 24 ♕f3 ♘d7! 25 ♕c6 ∞ Frolov) 23 ♗d4 ♘g4 24 ♕f3 ♕c8 25 ♕d5 ♘h6 26 ♖h5 ♖g6 27 ♗e3 (27 f4!? is another possibility) 27...♖c7?! (27...♘g8 28 ♖xh7 ±; 27...♘g4! 28 ♖xh7 ♖e6 ∓) 28 ♖xh6 ♖c2+ 29 ♔b1 ♕c6?! 30

♕d3 ♖xh6 31 ♗xh6 ♖c5 32 ♗g7 ♔d8 33 ♗d4! (33 ♕xh7 ♕f3! = B.Ivanović-Popović) 33...♖h5 (or 33...♕d5 34 ♕e3 +—; 33...♖d5 34 ♕e4 +—) 34 ♕e2 +— Popović.

22 ...   **♘e4**

Frolov points out that Black is routed after the alternatives:

a) 22...♔d7 23 ♗d4 +—.
b) 22...♘g4 23 ♗g5 ♖xg5 24 ♖xg5 ♘f6 25 ♖g7! ♔f8 26 ♖g3 +—.
c) 22...♘d7 23 ♕h5 ♘e5 24 ♕xh7 ♖g2 25 ♗d4! ±.

23 ♗f4!   **♖g6**

The open e-file produces sufficient tactics after 23...♘c5 (23...d5 24 ♕h5 +—) 24 ♖xc5 (24 ♕h5 ♖g6 25 ♕xh7 ♘d3+ 26 cxd3 ♕c8+ 27 ♔b1 ♕xf5 28 ♕h8+ +—) 24...dxc5 25 ♗xb8 ♖g6 26 f4 ♖e6 27 ♗e5 f6 28 ♕h5+ ♔f8 29 ♕h6+ ♔e8 30 ♖d1 ♕a5 31 ♔b1 +— Frolov.

24 ♕xe4   **♖e6**
25 ♕h1   **♕d7**

Black has avoided mating threats by shedding material. White can continue to make progress by targeting the pawn islands. If 25...♕a5 26 ♕c6+ ♔d8 27 ♖xe6 fxe6 28 ♖f8+ ♗xf8 29 ♗g5+ ♗e7 30 ♕xd6+ ♔c8 31 ♕xe6+ ♔b7 32 ♕e4+! ♔c8 33 ♕xe7 when White wins according to Frolov.

26 ♖h5   **♖c8**
27 ♔b1   **♖c5**
28 ♖xh7   **♖xe1+**
29 ♕xe1   **♕f5**
30 ♗xd6   **1-0**

6 ♗c4 against the Scheveningen

The desire to avoid the main lines in the Scheveningen has led to a dramatic increase in the popularity of 6 ♗c4. Black is often duped into the Sozin Attack which has already been extensively covered in this book. However, Black can continue in independent fashion with ...♘a6-c5 and ...a5. The best way to confront this system emerges from the specialist Istratescu.

Game 37

Istratescu – Suba
Romania 1992

1	e4	c5
2	♘f3	e6
3	d4	cxd4
4	♘xd4	♘f6
5	♘c3	d6
6	♗c4	♗e7

Black is waiting for White to declare his intentions before expanding on the queenside.

7	♗b3	0-0
8	♗e3	♘a6

In the event of 8...a6 the game transposes to Fischer Attack, and after 8...♘c6 to a Sozin. The difference is that now Black intends

...♘c5 and ...a7-a5-a4. The point is that unlike other lines, a tempo has been saved by avoiding ...a6.

9 f4

Alternatively, White may opt for immediately developing his queen and then advancing the g- and h-pawns. After 9 ♕f3 ♘c5 *(D)* play might continue:

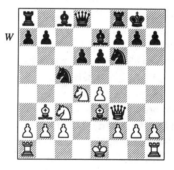

a) 10 g4 a5 11 a4 (11 g5 ♘fd7 12 ♕h5 a4 13 ♗c4 d5 14 exd5 ♘b6 15 ♗e2 ♘xd5 ½-½ Gullaksen-Maus, Gausdal 1991) 11...♘xb3 12 cxb3 ♘d7 13 0-0 ♘c5 14 ♖fd1 ♗d7 15 ♘db5 ♗xb5 16 ♘xb5 ♕b6 17 ♖ac1 ♖ac8 18 ♖c4 ♖fd8 19 ♖dc1 ♗f8 20 h4 ♖c6 21 g5 ♕a6 22 e5 ♘d3 23 ♖xc6 bxc6 24 ♕xc6 ♕xc6 25 ♖xc6 d5 26 ♗d4 ♗b4 27 ♔f1 and White

wins; Roth-Summermatter, Lenk
1991.

b) 10 0-0-0 and now:

b1) 10....♕c7 11 g4 a6 12 h4 b5
13 g5 ♘fd7 14 h5 ♗b7 15 ♕h3 b4
16 g6 ♘xb3+ 17 axb3 bxc3 18 h6
cxb2+ 19 ♔xb2 ♗xe4 20 gxh7+
♗xh7 21 hxg7 ♘f6 22 ♗g5 1-0
Sieiro Gonzalez-Santa Torres,
Sagua la Grande 1989.

b2) 10...♕a5 11 ♔b1 ♗d7 13 g4
♘xb3 13 axb3 (13 cxb3!?) 13...♖fc8
14 g5 ♘e8 15 h4 b5 16 e5?! b4 17
♘a2 ♖ab8 18 h5 ♕xe5 19 ♕g4 f5
20 gxf6 ♘xf6 21 ♕e2 ♘d5 22 ♘f3
♕f5 23 ♖hg1 ♗b5 24 ♘d4 ♗xe2 25
♘xf5 ♗xd1 26 ♘xe7+ ♘xe7 27
♖xd1 ♖c6 0-1 Brinck-Claussen–
Grotnes, Copenhagen 1991.

b3) 10...♗d7 11 g4 ♗c6 12
♘xc6 ♘xb3+ 13 axb3 bxc6 14 g5
♘d7 15 h4 d5 16 ♕h3 ♕c7 17 h5
♗c5 18 g6 ♗xe3+ 19 fxe3 ♘f6 20
♖df1 h6 21 exd5 cxd5 22 gxf7+
♕xf7 23 ♘e2 ♕d7 24 ♘f4 ± Meis-
ter-Zilbershtein, Voronezh 1988.

9 ...   ♘c5
10 ♕f3   a5 (D)

The starting point of Black's
scheme.

11 0-0-0!?

This move is a recent addition to
White's armoury. For some time the
line was in disrepute due to 11 0-0
a4 12 ♗c4 ♘fxe4 ∓ Perecz-Vadasz,
Hungarian Ch 1975. The major alternative is 11 a4. Play might continue 11...e5!? 12 ♘f5 (12 fxe5?!

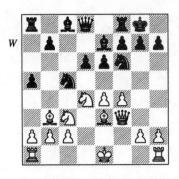

dxe5 13 ♘f5 ♗xf5 14 ♕xf5 ♘xb3
15 cxb3 ♕d3 ∓) 12...♗xf5 13 exf5
and now:

a) 13...♘xb3 14 cxb3 exf4 15
♗d4 d5 16 0-0-0 ♖c8 17 ♔b1 ♗b4
18 ♕xf4 ♗xc3 19 ♗xc3 ♖e8 =
Renet-Ghinda, Lucerne 1985.

b) 13...e4!? 14 ♕h3 (14 ♕e2!?)
14...d5 15 0-0-0 ♘xb3+ 16 cxb3
♖c8 17 ♔b1 (17 ♗d4) 17...♖xc3 18
bxc3 b5! 19 axb5 a4 20 b6? (20 b4
♕c7 ∞) 20...axb3 21 ♔b2 ♘d7 22 f6
♗xf6 23 ♔xb3 ♘xb6 24 ♗c5 ♕c7
25 ♗xf8 ♕c4+ 26 ♔b2 ♗xc3+! 27
♔c2 d4 28 ♖d3 ♕a2+ 29 ♔d1
♕b1+ 30 ♔e2 ♕c2+ 31 ♔f1 exd3
32 ♕g3 ♕e2+ 33 ♔g1 ♔xf8 34 f5
♕e3+ 0-1 Fedorov-Sakaev, USSR
1989.

11 ...   a4
12 ♗c4   a3
13 b3

The alternative 13 ♘db5 is discussed in the next game.

13 ...   ♕a5

In their analysis of the game –
upon which these notes are based –

Stoica and Istratescu investigate a trade in pieces by using the ...d5 fork. For example: 13...♘fxe4!? 14 ♘xe4 ♘xe4 15 ♕xe4 d5 16 ♕f3 dxc4 17 ♘xe6 ♗xe6 18 ♖xd8 ♖fxd8 19 bxc4! (19 f5? cxb3! 20 cxb3 ♗xb3! and wins) 19...♗f6 (19...♗xc4? 20 ♕e4 +−; 19...♖dc8 20 ♗d4 ♗xc4 21 ♕g3 ♗f8 22 f5 ♖a6 23 ♔b1 ∞; 19...♗f8!? 20 f5 ♗xc4 21 ♔b1 ♖a5 ∞) 20 ♖d1 ♖xd1+ (20...♗xc4?! 22 ♖xd8+ ♖xd8 23 ♗c5! ±) 21 ♔xd1 ♗xc4 22 ♗c5! ♗b2 23 ♕xb7 ♖d8+ 24 ♔e1 ♗xa2 25 ♕a6! ♗b1 26 ♗xa3 ♗xa3 27 ♕xa3 ♗xc2 is a draw.

14 ♘db5 ♗d7

Steady development. Instead 14...♘fxe4 (14...♘fd7 15 ♗d4 ±) 15 ♘xe4 ♘xe4 16 ♕xe4 d5 17 ♗xd5 ♕xb5 (17...exd5 18 ♕xe7 ♕xb5 19 ♗d4 ±) 18 ♗c4 ± is pleasant for White.

15 e5 ♗c6!? *(D)*

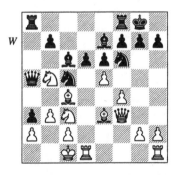

Black understandably wishes to dislodge the queen to prepare the move ...♘d5. Instead 15...dxe5 16 fxe5 ♘d5!? (16...♗c6? 17 exf6! ♗xf3 18 fxe7 ♗xd1 19 exf8♕+ ♖xf8 20 ♗xc5 ♖c8 21 ♖xd1 ♖xc5 22 b4! wins for White) 17 ♗xd5 ♗xb5 (17...exd5 18 ♘xd5) 18 ♗xc5 ♗xc5 19 ♗xb7 ♖ad8 is unclear according to Stoica and Istratescu.

16 exf6 ♗xf3

A ploy to avoid the complications rebounds: 16...♗xf6? 17 ♕g4 ♗xc3 18 ♘xc3 ♕xc3 19 ♗d4 +−.

17 fxe7 ♗xd1

After 17...♖e8 18 gxf3 ♖xe7 19 ♖xd6 White is better.

18 exf8♕+ ♖xf8
19 ♖xd1 ♖d8
20 f5!

With three pieces for the queen, the situation is slightly in favour of White, who must strive to keep his forces active. The text maintains the initiative by inviting 20...exf5?! 21 ♘d5 when the central knight has a dominant role.

20 ... d5
21 ♗e2 ♘e4

At this critical juncture, Stoica and Istratescu supply detailed analysis: 21...♖c8 22 fxe6 fxe6 23 ♗g4 ♔h8! 24 ♔b1 ♘a4!? (24...♕b4? 25 ♖d4 ♕a5 26 b4 +−; 24...♘e4?! 25 ♘xe4 dxe4 26 ♗xe6! ±; 24...♕d8 25 ♗c1! ±) 25 ♘xa4 ♕xb5 26 ♗d4 ♖f8! (26...♖c4?! is met by the accurate 27 ♖f1!, when Black has nothing better than the abject 27...♖c8, since 27...♕b4? fails to 28 c3 +−,

and 27...h5 to 28 &e2 +–) 27 ♘c3
♕a6! 28 &f3 ♕d6 with an unclear
position.

22	♘xe4	dxe4
23	♖xd8+	♕xd8
24	fxe6	fxe6
25	g3!	

It is important to make sure that
the queen has no entry squares into
White's position, otherwise it will
exploit the momentary lack of harmony: 25 ♘xa3? ♕h4 26 &d2 (26
♘c4 b5 and ...♕e1+ –+) 26...♕xh2
27 g4? ♕d6 –+.

25	...	♕f6
26	♘d4	&h8
27	&d2?!	

A more precise way of regroup-
ing is 27 c3! intending &d2 and
♘c2 ±. Now Black finds a manoeuvre to increase the power of his
queen.

27	...	♕d8!
28	&c3	

If 28 &c1 to avoid the threat ...e5,
then 28...♕a5 29 &d2 ♕c5 and the
prospect of ...♕c3 gives Black the
advantage.

28...♕b6 29 &d2 ♕d6 30 &c3
♕c5+ 31 &d2 e5!?

31...♕d6 would have secured a
draw but Black wishes to prolong
the battle.

32 ♘b5 ♕b4+ 33 c3 ♕xb3! 34
axb3 a2 35 ♘a3 a1♕ 36 ♘c2 ♕h1
37 g4!

White has constructed a fortress
that Black should not be able to

break down. 37 h4 ♕h2 38 g4 ♕xh4
39 c4 ♕d8+ 40 &c3 ♕a5+ 41 b4
♕a4 is less clear.

The game now drifts towards a
draw.

37...♕xh2 38 c4 ♕h4 39 b4
♕d8+ 40 &c3 h6 41 c5 g6 42
&b2!? &h7 43 b5 ♕a5 44 b6 ♕a4
45 &c3 &g7 46 &b2 h5 47 gxh5
gxh5 48 &xh5 ♕b5+ 49 &c1 ♕f1+
50 &b2 ♕b5+ 51 &c1 ♕f1+ ½-½

Game 38
Istratescu – Zetocha
Bucharest 1992

1 e4 c5 2 ♘f3 d6 3 d4 cxd4 4 ♘xd4
♘f6 5 ♘c3 e6 6 &c4 &e7 7 &e3
0-0 8 &b3 ♘a6 9 f4 ♘c5 10 ♕f3 a5
11 0-0-0 a4 12 &c4 a3
    13 ♘db5!? (D)

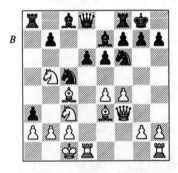

White allows his king position to
be punctured, but in return seizes
control of d6 to promote his own
counterattack. It also worth noting
that the black pawn on b2 actually

provides some shelter for the white king.

13	...	axb2+
14	♔b1	♕a5

The prospect of e5 with a pin prompts this decision to divert the queen, in order to put pressure on c3. White does not fear 14...♘a4!? 15 e5 ♘xc3+ 16 ♘xc3 ♕c7 17 exf6 ♗xf6 18 ♗d4 e5 (18...♕xc4?! 19 ♗xf6 gxf6 20 ♕g3+ ♔h8 21 ♕h4 ♕xc3 22 ♖d3! +−) 19 fxe5 dxe5 20 ♗b3 exd4 21 ♘d5 ♕d6 22 ♘xf6+ gxf6 (22...♕xf6 23 ♕xf6 gxf6 24 ♖xd4 ±) 23 ♖he1 ∞ (Istratescu and Stoica).

15	e5	dxe5
16	fxe5	♘fd7
17	♕g3	♘b6?! *(D)*

With White engaged in kingside manoeuvres, Black gambles on quickly transferring the pieces to the other flank in an effort to create a breakthrough. It would be more prudent to take evasive action before embarking on a counter-attack. Istratescu-Stohl, Budapest 1993, saw Black try the cautious 17...♔h8. White continued: 18 ♖hf1?! (18 ♗g5! f6 19 exf6 ♘xf6 20 ♗xf6 ♗xf6 21 ♕d6 ♗d7! 22 ♕xc5 ♖fc8 =) 18...♘b6 19 ♗xc5 (19 ♗g5 ♗xg5 20 ♕xg5 ♗d7! {20...♘xc4 21 ♖xf7! ♖g8 22 ♖xg7 ♖xg7 23 ♖d8+ ♕xd8 24 ♕xd8+ ♖g8 25 ♕f6+ ♖g7 26 ♕f8+ ♖g8 27 ♕xc5 ±} 21 ♘d6 ♘xc4 22 ♘xf7+ ♖xf7 23 ♖xf7 ♘a3+ 24 ♔xb2 ♘c4+ −+)

19...♗xc5 20 ♗b3 ♗d7 21 ♘d6 ♗xd6 22 ♖xd6 ♗c6 (22...♗a4? 23 ♖xb6 ±; 22...♘a4! 23 ♘xa4 ♗xa4 ∓) 23 ♖d4 ♘d7 24 ♖e1 ♘c5 26 ♖h4 ½-½ (analysis by Stohl).

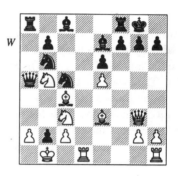

18	♗h6!	g6
19	♗xf8	♗xf8

The game concluded:

20 ♕f4 ♘xc4 21 ♕xc4 ♗d7 22 ♖hf1 ♗c6 23 ♘d6

This cuts out the bishop and forces Black into trying to justify his material investment; otherwise White can simply double rooks on the f-file.

23...♗xd6 24 exd6 ♘e4 25 ♘xe4 ♗xe4 26 a4!

The key move. It is extremely difficult for Black to make progress as the passed d-pawn is a serious distraction and any endgame is bleak. If 26...♕xa4 27 ♕xa4 ♖xa4 28 d7 and White wins.

26...♗d5 27 ♕b5 ♕xb5 28 axb5 ♗c4 29 ♖fe1 ♗xb5 30 ♔xb2 ♗c6 31 g4 ♔f8 32 c4 ♖a5? 33 d7 1-0.

7 Benko Variation

It was Benko who popularized 6...♕b6 by playing it against Cardoso in the 1958 Portorož Interzonal. The idea is that by hitting b2 and d4 the usual strategy of ♗b3 is thwarted. The drawback is that that White can gain time by attacking the exposed black queen. In the 1960s and 1970s it attracted the attention of Larsen and Stein who contributed much to the understanding of the position. In recent times, Timman has taken up the gauntlet in an effort to avoid the complications of the main lines.

Game 39
Galdunts – Serper
Kherson 1991

1	e4	c5
2	♘f3	♘c6
3	d4	cxd4
4	♘xd4	♘f6
5	♘c3	d6
6	♗c4	♕b6 *(D)*
7	♘b3	

This is considered the critical reply. For the other important option, 7 ♘de2, see Game 41, Ljubojević-Benko.

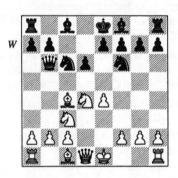

There are some minor alternatives:

a) The gambit 7 ♗e3?! is flawed after 7...♕xb2 8 ♘db5 ♕b4! 9 ♗d3 ♕a5 10 ♗d2 ♕d8 11 ♘d5 ♘xd5 12 exd5 ♘e5 13 ♗e2 (13 0-0 a6 14 ♘d4 g6 ∓ Boleslavsky) 13...a6 14 ♘d4 ♕c7 15 0-0 g6 ∓ Nikitin.

b) 7 ♘db5 and now:

b1) 7...g6? 8 ♗e3 ♕a5 9 ♗d2 ♕d8 10 ♘d5 ♘xd5 11 exd5 ± Boleslavsky.

b2) 7...a6 8 ♗e3 ♕a5 9 ♘d4 and now:

b21) 9...♘xe4? 10 ♕f3 ♘e5 (10...f5!? 11 ♘xc6 bxc6 12 0-0-0 d5 13 ♘xd5! cxd5 14 ♗xd5 ♖b8 15 ♗c6+ ♔f7 16 ♗xe4 +−) 11 ♕xe4 ♘xc4 12 ♘b3 ♕c7 13 ♘d5 ♕c6 14 ♘d4 ♕d7 15 0-0-0 +− Boleslavsky.

b22) 9...♘g4 10 ♘xc6 bxc6 11
♗d2 g6 (11...♘xf2?! 12 ♗xf7+
♔xf7 13 0-0; 11...♕c5 12 ♕e2 ♘e5
13 ♗b3 a5 14 ♗e3 ♕b4 15 a3 ♕b8
16 f4 ♘d7 17 0-0-0 e6 18 ♖fe1 ♗e7
19 e5! d5 20 f5 ± Boleslavsky) 12
♗e2!? ♘e5 13 f4 ♘d7 14 ♘d5 ♕d8
15 ♗c3 e5 16 ♘e3 ♘c5 17 ♗f3 f6
18 fxe5 fxe5 19 0-0 ♗e6 20 ♕e2
♗e7 21 ♗g4 ♗f7 22 ♘c4 0-0 23
♗a5 ♕b8 24 b4 ♘a4 25 ♕d3 ♕a7+
26 ♔h1 ♕d4 ∞ Koch-Grønn, Manila
OL 1992.

b23) 9...e6!? 10 0-0 ♗e7 11 f4
0-0 12 ♗b3 ♗d7 13 ♕f3 ♖ae8 14
♘de2 h6 (14...♔h8 15 g4 g5 16 e5
dxe5 17 fxg5 e4 18 ♕h3 ♘d5 19
♘xd5 exd5 21 ♖ad1! ± Velimirović-
Kožul, Yugoslav Ch 1991) 15 ♖ad1
♗c8 16 g4 ♘h7 (Korneev-Dok-
hoian, Berlin 1992) 17 ♕f2!? ♕d8
18 ♗b6 ♗h4 ∞.

b3) 7...♗g4 8 f3 (8 ♘d5!? ♘xd5
9 ♕xg4 ♘db4! ∞) 8...♗d7 9 ♕e2 a6
10 ♗e3 ♕a5 11 ♘d4 b5 12 ♗b3 e6
13 a3 ♘xd4 (13...♗e7 14 0-0 {14
0-0-0 0-0 15 g4 ∞ Velimirović}
14...♕c7 15 ♘xc6 ♗xc6 16 ♖ad1
0-0 17 ♗d4 ♕b7 Sax-Csom, Hun-
garian Ch 1976) 14 ♗xd4 b4 15
♘b1 bxa3+ 16 ♘d2 ± Velimirović.

c) 7 ♘xc6 bxc6 8 0-0 *(D)* and
now:

c1) 8...g6 9 ♗b3 ♗g7 10 ♗f4
♘d7 (10...0-0?! 11 e5 dxe5 12 ♗xe5
± Prié-Mirallès, Chanac 1989) 11
♗g5 a5 12 ♕f3 ♘e5 13 ♕g3 ♗a6
14 ♖fe1 ♕c7 15 ♖ad1 ♘d7?! 16 e5!

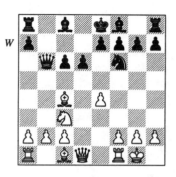

dxe5 17 ♕f3 f6 18 ♗e3 ♗b7 19
♕g4 f5 20 ♕c4 0-0-0 21 ♘a4 ♔b8
22 ♕c3 ♗f6 23 ♖xd7! ♖xd7 24
♗b6 ♕d6 25 ♘c5 ♕d2 26 ♘xd7+
♕xd7 27 ♕xa5 ± Prié-Tukmakov,
Aix-les-Bains 1991.

c2) 8...e6 9 ♕e2 (9 b3 ♗e7 10
♗b2 0-0 11 ♕e2 e5 12 ♔h1 ♕c7 13
♖ae1 ♘d7 14 ♘a4 ♗b7 15 ♗d3 ±
Karpov-Stein, USSR Ch 1971)
9...♘d7 10 b3 ♗e7 11 ♘a4 ♕c7 12
♗b2 0-0 13 f4 d5 (13...♗f6?! 14
♗xf6 ♘xf6 15 e5 ±) 14 ♗d3 g6 15
c4 ♗f6 (Prié-Mirallès, French Ch
1989) 16 ♖ac1 ♗xb2 17 ♕xb2 ♘b6
18 ♘c5 ♕e7 19 cxd5 exd5 20 exd5
cxd5 21 f5 ♘c4 22 bxc4 ♕xc5+ 23
♔h1 ♗d7 ± Prié.

c3) 8...♘d7?! 9 ♗b3 e6 10 ♗e3
♕a5 11 f4 d5 12 f5 ♗c5 13 ♗xc5
♕xc5+ 14 ♔h1 ♗a6! 15 fxe6 fxe6
16 ♖f3 ♘e5 17 ♖h3 0-0-0 ± Molner-
Lorincz, Hungary 1972.

c4) 8...e5 9 ♕d3 (9 b3!?) 9...♗e7
10 a4 a5 11 ♗e3 ♕c7 12 h3 0-0 13
f4 ♘d7 = Marjan-Deze, Novi Sad
1976.

7 ...   e6
8 0-0

The direct 8 ♗f4, putting pressure on d6, is a reasonable choice. After 8...♘e5 9 ♗e2 *(D)* play may continue:

a) 9...a6 10 ♗g3 h5! (10...♛c7 11 f4 ♘c4 12 e5! dxe5 13 fxe5 ♘xe5 14 ♛d4 ♘fd7 15 0-0-0 is good for White) 11 h3 ♛c7 12 f4 ♘c4 = Ivanchuk-Kramnik, Linares 1993.

b) 9...♗e7 10 ♗e3 ♛c7 11 f4 ♘c6 12 ♗f3 a6 13 0-0 0-0 14 a4 b6 15 g4 ♖b8 16 g5 ♘d7 17 ♗g2 ♖e8 18 ♖f3 ♘c5 19 ♖h3 g6 20 ♛g4 ♘b4 21 ♛h4 h5 22 ♗f3 ♗f8 23 ♗xh5! gxh5 24 ♛xh5 ♗g7 25 ♗d4 (threatening 26 ♛h8+ ♗xh8 27 ♖xh8#) 25...e5 26 f5 ♘xe4 (26...exd4 27 ♛h7+ ♔f8 28 f6 +–) 27 ♛h7+ ♔f8 28 ♘xe4 ♗xf5 29 ♛xf5 exd4 30 ♘f6! ♛xc2 31 ♘xd4 ♛xb2 32 ♖d1 ♖e5 33 ♘d7+ ♔e7 34 ♘xe5 ♗xe5 35 ♛e4 1-0 Kasparov-Anand, Linares 1994.

It is also possible for White to confront Black's ambitions on the queenside, e.g. 8 ♗e3 ♛c7 9 ♛e2 a6 10 ♗d3 b5 11 f4 ♗e7 12 a4?! (12 0-0!? ♗b7 13 ♖ae1 ♘b4 14 a3 ♘xd3 15 cxd3 ♖c8?! 16 ♘d4 ♛d7 17 ♘d1 ♗d8 18 ♘f2 0-0 19 g4 with an edge for White in Zaitsev-Ungureanu, Moscow-Bucharest 1969) 12...b4 13 ♘b1 e5 14 f5 ♗b7 15 ♘1d2 ♘b8! 16 g4 d5 17 g5 dxe4 18 ♗c4 ♘d5 19 f6 gxf6 20 gxf6 ♗f8 21 0-0-0 ♘d7? (20...♘xe3!) 22 ♘xe4! ♘7b6 23 ♗xb6 ♘xb6 24 ♘a5 ♘xc4 25 ♘xc4 ♗h6+ 26 ♔b1 ♔f8 27 ♖hg1 b3 28 cxb3 1-0 J.Polgar-Fedorowicz, Amsterdam 1990.

8 ...   ♗e7

Black may instead concentrate on developing his queenside:

a) 8...♗d7 9 ♗g5 ♘e5 10 ♗e2 ♖c8!? (10...♗e7 11 ♔h1 0-0?! 12 f4 intending 13 e5 ±) 11 ♗xf6 gxf6 12 ♔h1 h5 13 f4 ♘c4 14 ♗xc4 ♖xc4 15 ♛d3 ♖c7?! 16 f5 ♗e7 17 ♖ab1! ♔d8 18 fxe6 fxe6 19 ♘d4 a6 20 b4! ♖g8 21 b5 ♛a5 22 ♖b3 ♖g5 23 bxa6 bxa6 24 ♘ce2! e5 25 ♖b8+ ♖c8 26 ♖xc8+ ♔xc8 27 ♘b3 ♛b6 28 c4 ± Wolff-Shamkovich, New York 1992.

b) 8...a6 9 ♗g5 ♘e5 10 ♗e2 ♗e7 11 ♔h1 h5 12 a4 ♗d7 13 a5 ♛c7 14 f4 ♘g6 15 ♗f3 h4 16 ♛e2 ± Brunner-Lobron, Berne 1990.

9 ♗g5

The point of the text is to have the option of ♗xf6 when recapture by the bishop will result in d6 falling. 9 ♗e3 is examined in the next game.

9 ...   ♘e5 (D)

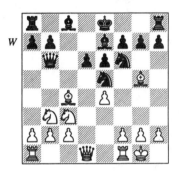

Black drives back White's 'Sozin' bishop, and simultaneously defends d6. Black has also tested the validity of White's threat:

a) 9...♗d7 10 ♔h1 (10 ♗xf6!?) 10...h6 11 ♗xf6 gxf6 (Tseitlin-Stein, USSR 1971) 12 ♕h5 ±.

b) 9...a6 10 ♗xf6 gxf6 11 ♕h5 and now:

b1) 11...♘e5 12 ♗e2 0-0 13 ♔h1 ♔h8 14 a4 (14 f4!?) 14...♗d7 15 a5 ♕c7 16 ♘d2! ♘g6 17 ♘c4 ±.

b2) 11...♗d7 12 ♔h1 0-0-0 (12...♘e5 13 ♗e2 0-0-0 14 a4 ♔b8 15 f4 ♘g6 16 ♖ad1 ± Kupreichik-Kovacs, Stary Smokovec 1975) 13 f4 ♖df8 14 a4 ♕c7 15 a5 ♘b4 16 ♕e2 ∞ Sveshnikov-Vaiser, Volgodonsk 1983.

b3) 11...♘d4!? 12 ♖fd1 ♘xb3 (12...♘xc2?! 13 ♖ac1 ♘b4 14 ♘d4 ±) 13 axb3 ♖b8 (13...♗d7? 14 ♗b5! ±) 14 ♕h6 ♕c5 15 ♕g7 ♖f8 16

♕xh7 b5 17 ♗d3 ♗b7 18 ♘e2 (18 ♕h6!?) 18...♔d7 19 ♕h6 ♖g8 20 b4 ♕b6 21 ♕f4 ♖g5?! 22 ♘g3 ♖bg8 23 ♗e2 ♗d8 24 ♖a3 ± Nunn-Martinović, Amsterdam 1985.

10   ♗e2   0-0
11   ♔h1   a6
12   f4   ♘g6 (D)

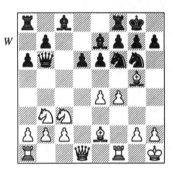

13   f5!?

This is a logical choice as otherwise 13...h6, forcing the exchange of the bishop, is likely. In the game Neverov-Lukin, Blagoveshchensk 1988, White gave the game another character by using an idea of Sveshnikov's: 13 ♗h5!? ♕c7 (13...h6?! 14 ♗xg6 hxg5 15 ♗xf7+ ♖xf7 16 fxg5 ♗d7 17 e5! dxe5 18 gxf6 ♗xf6 19 ♘e4 ♗c6 20 ♕g4; 16...♘d7 17 ♖xf7 ♔xf7 18 ♕h5+ ♔g8 19 ♖f1 ♕d8! 20 e5!? ♗xg5 21 ♘e4 ♗h6 22 ♘xd6 ± Lukin and Sakaev) 14 ♗xg6 hxg6 15 ♕e1 b5 16 e5 b4! 17 exf6 gxf6 and now White should have continued 18 ♘d5!? exd5 19 ♗h6 ♖e8 20 f5! ♗xf5 (20...g5 21

♗xg5 fxg5 22 f6 ±) 21 ♖xf5 ♗f8 22
♗e3 gxf5 (22...♕xc2?! 23 ♖f3 ±) 23
♕g3+ (23 ♘d4!?) 23...♔h7 24
♕h3+ ♔g8 25 ♕g3+ =.

13 ...   ♘e5
14 ♕d2   ♕c7
15 ♖ad1   ♔h8?!

Black underestimates the danger
by omitting 15...♖d8!?. The idea of
the text is to prepare for ...♖g8 in
anticipation of White exchanging on
f6. Note that 15...♘c4? 16 ♗xc4
♕xc4 17 ♗xf6 ♗xf6 18 ♕xd6 ± is
also unsatisfactory.

16 ♗xf6   gxf6
17 ♘d4

White declares his intention to
put pressure on e6 and shift attention
to the kingside.

17 ...   ♗d7

Galdunts points out that after
17...♖g8 White maintains the advantage. For example: 18 ♗h5 (18 ♕h6
♕d8 19 ♗h5 ♖g5 20 ♘f3 ♘xf3! 22
♖xf3 ♕g8 23 ♘a4 ∞) 18...♕d8
(18...♖g5? 19 ♗xf7! ♘xf7 20 fxe6
♘e5 21 ♘d5 ♕d8 22 ♘f5 ♘c6 23
♘fxe7 ♘xe7 24 ♘xf6 ♖g7 25 ♕xd6
♕xd6 26 ♖xd6 ♘c6 27 ♘d5 +−) 19
♘ce2 intending ♘f4 ±.

18 ♗h5   ♕c8
19 ♘ce2   ♖g8
20 ♘f4

An important and common manoeuvre, fighting to restrict Black to
the defence of e6. Now a future ...e5
would give White d5 as a powerful
knight outpost.

20 ...   ♘c4
21 ♕c1   ♖g7 (D)

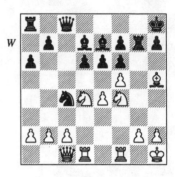

22 ♗xf7!

A superb move which devastates
Black's position. Galdunts has seen
that Black's counterplay, involving
forking White's knights, will fail to
direct measures on the kingside.

22 ...   e5
23 ♘g6+!   hxg6
24 fxg6   ♖xf7

In answer to 24...♖h7 White wins
with 25 ♘f5! ♗xf5 26 ♖xf5 ♖h4 27
g3 ♖h3 28 ♔g2.

25 ♕h6+   ♔g8
26 gxf7+   ♔xf7
27 ♕h7+   ♔f8
28 ♖xf6+!

The last defence is broken down
to ensure access to the king.

28...♗xf6 29 ♖f1 ♕d8 30 ♕g6
exd4 31 ♖xf6+ ♕xf6 32 ♕xf6+
♔g8 33 ♕xd4

Black has a rook and two pieces
for the queen but it is insufficient.
With an exposed king and the white

army of extra pawns ready to romp towards the eighth rank, there is no respite.

33...♘e5 34 ♕xd6 ♖e8 35 ♕d5+ ♔f8 36 ♕xb7 ♗c8 37 ♕c7 ♘f7 38 h3 ♗e6 39 ♕b6 ♗c8 40 c4 ♔g7 41 ♕c6 ♖d8 42 b4 1-0

Game 40
Yudasin – Ye Rongguang
Moscow 1992
---

1 e4 c5 2 ♘f3 d6 3 d4 cxd4 4 ♘xd4 ♘f6 5 ♘c3 ♘c6 6 ♗c4 ♕b6 7 ♘b3 e6 8 0-0 ♗e7
9 ♗e3
A popular continuation that nudges the queen while developing another piece.

9 ...   ♕c7
10 f4   0-0
It is feasible to delay castling in order to try to defuse the might of the attack: 10...a6 11 ♗d3 b5 12 ♕f3 ♗b7 13 ♕h3 ♖b8 14 ♔h1 b4 15 ♘e2 e5 16 ♖ae1! ♗c8 17 ♕f3 0-0 (17...♗g4 18 ♕f2 ♗d7 19 h3 intending f5 and g4) 18 f5! d5 19 exd5 e4 20 ♗xe4 ♘e5 21 ♗f4! ♘xf3 (21...♗d6! 22 ♗xe5 ♗xe5 23 ♘ed4 ♗xh2 24 g4! ±) 22 ♗xc7 ♘xe1 23 ♗xb8 ♘xe4 24 ♖xe1 ♗xf5 25 ♘ed4! ± Yudasin-Garcia Ilundain, Leon 1992.

11 ♗d3   a6 (D)
A familiar theme in this variation. Black intends to disrupt White's ambitions on the kingside by creating

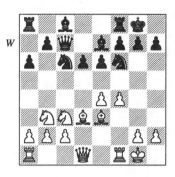

counterplay on the other flank. The intended ...b5 will gain space and increase the pressure on e4 with the threat ...b4. On 11...♖d8!? 12 ♕f3 a6 14 ♘a4 ♘d7 14 ♕f2 b5 15 ♘b6 ♖b8 16 ♘xc8 ♖dxc8 17 c3 ♘b6 chances are equal; Hartston-Dorfman, New Delhi 1982.

12 ♕f3
It is possible to conduct the attack with a slightly different approach:
a) 12 ♖f3 ♘g4 13 ♖h3 ♘xe3 14 ♕h5! h6 15 ♖xe3 ♘b4 16 ♖g3 ♔h8 17 e5 ♘xd3 18 cxd3 dxe5 19 fxe5 f5 20 d4 b6 21 ♖f1 ♖a7 22 ♘e2 ♗d8 23 ♖e1 ♕b8 24 ♘f4 ♖g8 25 ♖ee3 ♖c7 26 ♖g6 ♖e7 27 ♖h3 ♕a7 28 ♕g5 ♖ge8 29 ♖gxh6+! gxh6 30 ♘g6+ 1-0 Bukvić-Jovanović, Belgrade 1989.
b) 12 g4 b5 13 g5 ♘e8 (13...♘d7 14 ♕h5 g6 15 ♕h4 ♖e8 16 ♖f3! ± Schoneberg-Malich, East German Ch 1968) 14 ♕h5 g6 15 ♕h6 f5 16 exf5 gxf5 17 ♘d4 ♘d8 18 ♖ae1 ♘g7 19 ♖f3 ♘f7 20 ♕h4 ♘h8 21 ♖h3 h5 22 ♗e2 ♘g6 23 ♕f2 b4 24

♘d1 e5 25 ♗h5 ♘xh5 26 ♖xh5
exd4 27 ♗xd4 ♗b7 28 ♖h6 ♔f7 29
♕e2 ♗e4 30 ♕h5 ♖g8 31 ♖xg6
♖xg6 32 ♕h7+ ♔e8 33 ♕xg6+ ♔d7
34 ♘f2 ♕c4 35 ♘xe4 ♕xd4+ 36
♘f2 ♕xf4 37 ♕e6+ ♔c6 38 ♕xe7
♖g8 39 ♕e3 ♖xg5+ 40 ♔h1 1-0
Fischer-Saidy, USA Ch 1966.

12	...	b5
13	♖ad1	♗b7
14	♕h3	

A standard attacking feature
which targets h7 and can be backed
up by e5 or g4.

| 14 | ... | ♘b4 |
| 15 | g4 | ♖fe8 |

If Black tries to break out in the
centre with 15...d5 then the pawn
avalanche is not hindered after 16 e5
♘e4 17 ♗d4! intending 18 f5 with
excellent prospects.

| 16 | g5 | ♘d7 |
| 17 | f5!? | |

Better than 17 a3 ♘xd3 18 cxd3
♘c5 when White has merely en-
couraged Black's best response.

17	...	exf5
18	exf5	♘xd3
19	cxd3	♗d8

Black must proceed in precise
fashion: 19...♗f8 (19...b4 20 ♘e4 ±)
20 ♖f4! intending ♖h4 ±.

| 20 | ♘d4 | ♘e5?! |

It is tempting to occupy e5 but it
is more astute to keep the e-file
open: 20...b4! 21 ♘ce2 ♘c5 22 f6
♕d7 23 ♕g3 g6 24 h4 ±.

21 f6! (D)

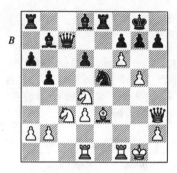

| 21 | ... | gxf6 |

White sacrifices a pawn to give
his knight an excellent post on f5
and to shatter Black's pawn structure. In his analysis of the game –
upon which these notes are based –
Yudasin reveals the plethora of
problems that Black can face:

a) 21...♘g4 22 ♕xg4 ♖xe3 23
♘f5 ±.

b) 21...♗c8 22 ♘f5 with the idea
♘d5 ±.

c) 21...♕d7 22 ♘f5 ♕c6 23 fxg7
♘f3+ (23...♕h1+ 24 ♔f2 ♕f3+ 25
♕xf3 ♗xf3 26 ♖d2 ±) 24 ♔f2 ♖xe3
25 ♘xe3 ♗xg5 (25...♘xg5 26 ♕g3)
26 ♘e4 ±.

| 22 | ♘f5 | ♔h8 |
| 23 | ♘e4 | ♖g8 |

Not 23...♘xd3? 24 ♘exd6 ♖xe3
25 ♕h6 +–.

| 24 | ♘fxd6! | ♗d5 |
| 25 | ♘xf6 | |

The knights have managed to invade Black's camp. Now White
must be careful not to allow his exposed king to become a liability.

25 ...   ♗xf6
26 ♖xf6   ♖g6
27 ♖c1   ♕d8!

If 27...♕e7 (27...♖xf6 28 ♖xc7
♘f3+ 29 ♔f2 ♘xg5+ 30 ♕f5
♖xf5+ 31 ♘xf5 ±) 28 ♖xg6! fxg6
(28...♘xg6 29 ♖c8+) 29 ♖c8+ ♖xc8
30 ♕xc8+ ♔g7 (30...♔g8 31 ♕c5;
31 ♕c3 +—) 31 ♘e8+ ♔f7 32 ♘f6
+—.

28 ♕g3   ♕xf6

The complications favour White:
28...♖xf6 (28...♘f3+ 29 ♕xf3! ♗xf3
30 ♘xf7+ is winning for White) 29
♕xe5 ♕xd6 30 ♗d4 ♕xe5 31 ♗xe5
♗xa2 32 ♗xf6+ ♔g8 33 d4 h6 34
gxh6 ±.

29 gxf6   ♖xg3+
30 hxg3   ♘xd3 *(D)*

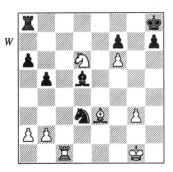

31 ♖d1!   ♖d8

31...♗c4 is crushed: 32 ♖xd3
♗xd3 33 ♘xf7+ ♔g8 34 ♘h6+
♔h8 (34...♔f8 35 ♗c5+ ♔e8 36 f7+
+—) 35 ♗d4 ♖d8 36 f7+ +—.

32 ♗f4   ♗c4
33 ♖xd3   1-0

Game 41
Ljubojević – Benko
New York 1985

1 e4 c5 2 ♘f3 d6 3 d4 cxd4 4 ♘xd4
♘f6 5 ♘c3 ♘c6 6 ♗c4 ♕b6

7 ♘de2   e6
8 0-0   ♗e7

Black proceeds to develop his
kingside in order to whisk the king
to safety. In Kasparov-Timman, Linares 1992, Black chose to delay
castling after 8...a6 9 ♗b3 ♗e7 10
♗g5 ♕c7 11 ♘g3 (11 ♕d2!?) 11...b5
12 ♔h1?! (12 ♕d2!?) 12...h5! 13
♗xf6 gxf6 14 ♘xh5 ♗b7 15 ♘g3
0-0-0 16 a4 b4 17 ♘ce2 ♔b8 18
♖c1? (18 c4 ♘e5 ∓ Timman)
18...♕a5? (18...d5! 19 exd5 f5! —+
Kasparov) 19 c3 ♖h4?! 20 ♘g1!
♘e5 21 ♕d2 d5 22 exd5 ♘c4 23
♕e2 ♗xd5 24 ♖fd1 ♖c8 25 ♘f3
♖f4 26 ♖d4 ♗d6! 27 ♖c2 bxc3 28
bxc3 (28 ♖xc3 ±) 28...f5 29 ♕d1
1/2-1/2.

9 ♗b3

The desire to maintain an influence on the a2-g8 diagonal has
prompted 9 a3 which seeks to avoid
exchanges after a possible ...♘a5.
The drawback is that the attack is a
little slower. For example: 9...0-0 10
♗a2 ♘e5 11 ♔h1!? ♘ed7 (11...♕a6
12 f4 ♘c4 13 ♕d3 ±; 11...♗d7?! 12
f4 ♘eg4 13 ♕d4 ±) 12 ♘g3 ♕c6 13
f4 ♘c5 14 e5 dxe5 15 fxe5 ♘fe4
(A.Sokolov-Ruban, St. Petersburg
1993) 16 ♘cxe4 ♘xe4 17 ♘h5 f5

18 exf6 ♘xf6 19 ♘g3 with an edge for White – Ruban.

9 ... 0-0 (D)

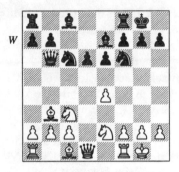

10 ♕d3!?

White employs a relatively new system to wrest the initiative. The alternatives are:

a) 10 ♔h1 ♘a5 11 ♗g5 ♕c5 12 f4 b5 13 ♘g3 b4? (13...♗b7! 14 ♘h5 ♔h8 15 a3 ♖ae8! ∓ Scholl-Langeweg, Amsterdam 1971) 14 e5! dxe5 15 ♗xf6 gxf6 16 ♘ce4 ♕d4 17 ♕h5! ♘xb3 18 ♕h6 exf4 19 ♘h5 f5 20 ♖ad1! ♕e5 21 ♘ef6+ ♗xf6 22 ♘xf6+ ♕xf6 23 ♕xf6 ♘c5 24 ♕g5+ ♔h8 25 ♕e7! ♗a6 26 ♕xc5 ♗xf1 27 ♖xf1 1-0 Fischer-Benko, USA 1959.

b) 10 ♘g3 ♘a5! 11 ♔h1 a6 12 ♗g5 ♕c7 13 f4 b5 14 ♕e2 (Donchev-Züger, Lucerne OL 1982) 14...♘xb3 intending ...♗b7 ∞.

c) 10 ♗g5 ♘a5 11 ♘g3 ♕c5 12 ♕d2 b5 13 ♖ad1 b4 (13...♘xb3?! 14 cxb3 ♗b7 15 ♖c1 ♕b6 16 ♘h5! ♔h8 17 ♗xf6 gxf6 18 ♕h6 is good for

White; Ljubojević-Ree, Amsterdam 1975) 14 ♘a4 ♕b5 ∞ Minić.

d) 10 ♗e3 ♕c7 11 h3 a6 12 g4 b5 13 ♘g3 ♘a5 14 f4 ♘c4 = Marović-Nagy, Romania 1970.

10 ... ♘a5

Bronstein-Gulko, USSR 1975, went 10...a6 11 ♕g3 ♔h8 12 ♗g5 ♕c5 13 ♗e3 ♕a5 14 f4 b5 15 a3 and White had a promising position.

11 ♗e3!?

In previous games the emphasis had been on creating an attack after 11 ♕g3 ♔h8. The text aims for a more positional response intending to restrict Black's activity and to put pressure on d6. White hopes to provoke ...e5, which gives the vital square d5 to White's pieces and leaves the d-pawn backward.

11 ... ♕c7

Although 11...♕d8 rules out the queen being hounded by White's knight, it means the king's rook is unable to lend support to the d-pawn after 12 ♖ad1 a6 13 ♗f4 ±.

12 ♘b5 ♕b8
13 ♗f4 ♖d8
14 ♖ad1 ♘e8

If 14...e5 then 15 ♗xe5 wins.

15 e5 d5

Now 15...dxe5 would at least allow Black to relieve the immediate pressure: 16 ♕xd8 ♗xd8 17 ♖xd8 ♔f8 18 ♘d6 ♕xd6 19 ♖xd6 ♘xd6 20 ♗xe5 ±.

16 c3 ♘xb3
17 axb3 b6

18   ♘bd4 *(D)*

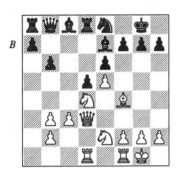

White has succeeded in forcing Black into a defensive posture which can be prolonged now that the queenside is relatively closed. White will focus his attention on the king-side where his greater mobility can be used to launch an attack.

18	...	**♕c7**
19	**♖fe1**	**a5**
20	**♕h3**	**♗d7**
21	**♖d3**	**b5**

Black can do little but sit and watch as White regroups his attacking forces. His only hope is somehow to create a diversion.

22	**♕g4**	**♖dc8**
23	**♖h3**	**g6**
24	**♗g5**	**♕d8**
25	**♕h4!**	

White has settled on a plan of campaign. His bishop has played its role in shielding the h4 square, and the queen now penetrates Black's camp with a double attack on e7 and h7.

25	...	**♗xg5**
26	**♕xh7+**	**♔f8**
27	**♖f3**	**♘f6**
28	**exf6**	**♗xf6**
29	**♘f4**	

Single-mindedly pursuing the king by threatening the devastating 30 ♘xg6+.

29	...	**♖a6 *(D)***

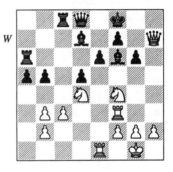

This sets up the resource 30 ♘xg6+ fxg6 31 ♕xg6 e5! which defends f6.

30   ♖e5!

A marvellous move that brings the game to an abrupt halt. With ...e5 no longer an option White can go on the rampage.

30	...	**♔e7**
31	**♘xd5+**	**♔d6**
32	**♘xf6**	**♔xe5**
33	**♕xf7**	**♗e8**
34	**♖e3+**	**1-0**

8 ♗c4 against the Dragon

The Fischer-Sozin Attack has a striking similarity to a popular system against the Dragon. The primary idea is to avoid the complications inherent in the main lines, while maintaining an initiative. White castles kingside followed by rapid development and by and large aims for a positional edge.

This system is particularly popular in England, where it has attracted the attention of Adams, Hebden, Short and Watson.

Game 42
Emms – Hodgson
British Ch 1993

1	e4	c5
2	♘f3	d6
3	d4	cxd4
4	♘xd4	♘f6
5	♘c3	g6
6	♗c4 (D)	

It is also possible to employ the move-order 6 h3 and 7 ♗c4.

6 ... ♘bd7!?

This is slightly unusual in tournament practice, although it is based on a sound commitment to exert pressure on e4 via ...♘c5.

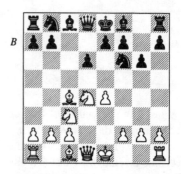

7 0-0

Castling short is a natural reaction. However, Black was hoping to inspire complications by luring White into the ultra-aggressive Yugoslav Attack. A plausible continuation: 7 f3 ♗g7 8 ♗e3 a6 9 ♕d2 ♕c7 (9...♘c5!?; 9...b5!?) 10 ♗b3 b5 11 0-0-0 ♗b7 12 ♗h6 ♗xh6 13 ♕xh6 ♘e5 14 f4 ♘c4 15 e5 dxe5 16 ♘f3 exf4 17 ♗xc4 bxc4 18 ♖he1! ± Torre-Fubler, Adelaide 1975.

7	...	♗g7
8	♖e1	0-0
9	♗g5 (D)	

White develops naturally, putting his bishop on a useful square. His plan is a simple one: to centralize his rooks and then play ♘d5 at a suitable moment. A similar strategy is

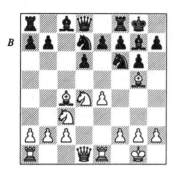

employed in the next game, Kve-inys-Szalanczy.

9 ...   a6
10 ♕d2   ♖e8

A useful move which has the primary purpose of avoiding the exchange of dark-squared bishops as 11 ♗h6 ♗h8 is now possible. Not 10...b5? 11 ♗d5! ♘xd5 12 ♘xd5 followed by 13 ♘c6 and White is winning.

11 ♖ad1?!

Hereabouts, White's initiative runs out of steam. It would be more effective to prevent Black's dynamic thrust ...b5 with 11 a4!, maintaining a slight advantage.

11 ...   b5
12 ♗b3

Of course, 12 ♗d5 ♘xd5 13 ♘xd5 is ineffective because e7 is already defended, so Black can play 13...♗b7! with bright prospects as his bishop-pair will dominate the position.

12 ...   ♗b7!
13 ♗h6   ♗h8

14 a4!?

The dramatic 14 ♘e6 fails to deliver upon 14...♕b6 (14...fxe6?? 15 ♗xe6#) 15 ♘g5 ♘e5 which cancels out the pressure on f7.

14 ...   ♘c5
15 axb5   axb5
16 ♘dxb5   ♘cxe4? *(D)*

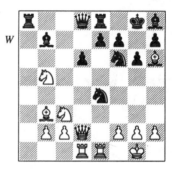

If the position is assessed solely by material balance, then it is equal. In reality, White has excellent chances due to his commanding bishop bearing down on f7 which offers tactical possibilities against Black's weakest point.

Moreover, Black will have difficulty staging a defence to a direct attack as f8 is covered, while ...e6 merely shifts attention to d6. It was better to play more energetically with 16...♘xb3! 17 cxb3 ♕b6 when the pair of bishops and sound pawn structure offer compensation for the pawn. However, White should have equal chances as a passed b-pawn is always a worry.

17 ♘xe4   **♘xe4**

17...♗xe4? is refuted with great force: 18 ♖xe4! ♘xe4 19 ♕d5 e6 20 ♕xe4 ♗xb2 21 c3! ± (Emms).

18 ♕f4!

The start of a clever queen manoeuvre designed to exploit the frailty of f7. This will provoke concessions.

18 ...   **♘f6**
19 ♕c4   **d5**
20 ♕c7! *(D)*

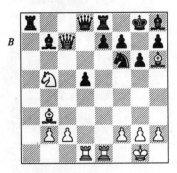

A cunning square for the queen. White has reached the climax of the game by forcing a situation where the hidden agenda is to capture the key defensive pawn on e7. After 20...♗a6 21 ♕xd8 ♖exd8 22 ♘c7 ♖a7 23 ♖xe7 White has a clear advantage due to the extra pawn and the pressure against the isolated d-pawn.

20 ...   **♖b8**
21 ♕xd8   **♖bxd8!?**
22 ♘c7   **e6**
23 ♘xe8   **♘xe8**

Black has chosen to sacrifice the exchange in the correct assumption that it is the best way to continue the struggle. The hope is that the central pawns can be pushed forward supported by the minor pieces. However, this ruse should be easily contained in such an open position by the prospect of a rook using the a-file to infiltrate the opposition's camp.

24 c3   **♘d6**
25 ♗f4   **♗f6**
26 ♖a1   **g5**
27 ♗e5   **♔g7**
28 ♗xf6+   **♔xf6**
29 ♗c2   **h5**

The pawns rush forward but to no avail. Only if White ignores the kingside and allows ...g4, ...h4 and ...e5-e4 will Black show signs of genuine counter-play.

30 ♗d3   **g4**
31 f4!

At a stroke White breaks up Black's kingside pawn structure and opens a file for his rooks.

31 ...   **gxf3**
32 gxf3   **♘c4**
33 ♗xc4!   **dxc4**
34 ♖ad1   **♗d5**
35 ♔f2   **♖b8**
36 ♖d2

It would appear that Black has made some progress by preventing the passed b-pawn from advancing. In fact, the overall picture remains unchanged. The bishop on d5 is very restricted in its movements while h5 is an obvious target.

36...♖b5 37 ♖g1 ♗c6 38 h4 ♖f5 39 ♖g3 ♗d5 40 ♖d4 ♔e5 41 ♖g5 ♖xg5 42 f4+

Immense precision by Emms.

42...♔f5 43 fxg5 f6 44 gxf6 ♔xf6 45 ♔e3 1-0

Game 43
Kveinys – Szalanczy
Budapest 1992

1 e4 c5 2 ♘f3 d6 3 d4 cxd4 4 ♘xd4 ♘f6 5 ♘c3 g6

6 ♗c4   ♗g7

The natural-looking 6...♘c6? is a serious error. After 7 ♘xc6! bxc6 8 e5 play might proceed:

a) 8...dxe5? 9 ♗xf7+ +–.

b) 8...♘d7? 9 exd6 exd6 10 0-0 and ♖e1+ ±.

c) 8...♘h5?! 9 ♕f3! e6 (9...d5 10 ♘xd5!) and now:

c1) 10 exd6 ♕xd6 11 0-0 ♗b7 12 ♖d1 ♕c5 13 ♕d3 ♕e7 (13...♘f6 14 ♘e4!) 14 ♗g5! f6 15 ♗e3 ♔f7 16 ♕d7 1-0 Bilek-Bactiar, Beverwijk 1966.

c2) 10 g4 ♘g7 11 ♘e4 ♕a5+ (11...d5 12 ♘f6+ ♔e7 13 ♕a3+) 12 ♗d2 ♕xe5 13 ♗c3 +– (Fischer).

d) 8...♘g4!? and now:

d1) 9 exd6 ♕xd6 10 ♕xd6 exd6 11 ♗f4 ♗e6 12 ♗b3 (12 ♗a6 ♖b8 13 h3 ♖b4 14 ♗d2 = Makarychev; 12 ♗xe6 fxe6 13 ♘e4 e5 14 ♗g5 ♗e7 =) 12...d5 13 h3 ♘f6 14 ♗e5

♗e7 15 0-0-0 0-0 16 ♖he1 ♘d7 17 ♗f4 ♘c5 18 ♘e2 a5 19 ♘d4 ♖fc8 20 c3 ♗f6 21 ♗c2 ♗d7 22 ♗e5 ♔g7 23 ♗xf6+ ♔xf6 = F.Silva-Sosonko, Lucerne 1982.

d2) 9 ♗f4! ♗h6 (9...♕b6 10 ♕f3 ♗f5 11 exd6 exd6 12 0-0 0-0-0 13 ♖fe1 d5 14 h3 ± Lipnitsky; 9...d5 10 ♘xd5 ♗g7 11 ♘c3 ±) 10 ♗xh6 ♘xh6 11 ♕d2 ♘f5 12 exd6 ♘xd6 (12...♕xd6 13 0-0-0 ±; 12...exd6 13 0-0-0 0-0 14 g4! ♘e7 15 ♕xd6 ♕xd6 16 ♖xd6 ♗xg4 17 ♖e1! ± Makarychev) 13 0-0-0 ♕c7 14 ♕f4 0-0 15 ♘e4 ± Suetin-Makarychev, Moscow Ch 1983.

7 h3

A precautionary measure to fend off a future ...♘g4. There is no intention to play the reckless g4?!.

7 ...   ♘c6

Black can also seek to expand immediately on the queenside. After 7...0-0 8 ♗b3, 8...a6 is considered in Game 44, whilst 8...♘c6 is the subject of Game 45. The reason why, after 7...0-0, White's bishop does best to drop back to b3 is discussed in the note to White's 8th move in Game 44, where the drastic consequences of 8 ♗e3 ♘c6 9 0-0 ♘xe4 are revealed.

8 0-0   0-0

9 ♖e1

White has a straightforward plan of development. The text has a dual purpose by reinforcing e4 and indicating that ♘d5 is likely because

...①xd5, exd5 would give play on
the e-file.

    9   ...   **♗d7**
   10 ♗g5 *(D)*

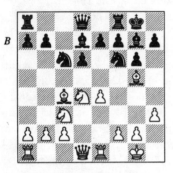

Now White's approach is becom-
ing clearer; his intention is to follow
up with ②d5 which threatens to
double Black's pawns after exchanges on f6, while the preventive
...e6 would result in d6 being weak.

  10   ...   **Ic8**
  11 ♗b3   **♕a5**
  12 ②d5!

A natural progression of White's
strategy, which had to be finely calculated in view of the possibility of
Black's bishop swooping down to
b2.

  12   ...   ②xd5
If 12...②xd4 then 13 ♗xf6! ±.

  13 ②xc6   **bxc6**
  14 exd5   **cxd5**
  15 ♗xe7   **Ife8**
  16 c3
White blunts the scope of Black's
dark-squared bishop and plans

gradually to increase the pressure on
d5. However, Kveinys feels that 16
♗xd5! is preferable, e.g. 16...♗xb2
(16...♗e6 17 Ixe6 fxe6 18 ♗xe6+
♔h8 19 ♗xc8 Ixe7 ±) 17 ♕f3 ♗e6
18 Ixe6 ♗xa1 19 Ie5!! Ixe7
(19...♗xe5 20 ♕xf7+ ♔h8 21 ♗f6+
+−) 20 Ixe7 ±.

  16   ...   **♗e5**
  17 ♗g5   **♗c6**
  18 ♗e3   **Ic7**
  19 Ie2

A precise way to make progress.
If 19 ♕d2 and Iad1 then Black can
line up on the b-file to deter ♗xd5.

  19   ...   **♕b5**
  20 Id2   **a5**
Black actively strives for counterplay by aiming to force the bishop to
move.

  21 Ib1   **Ib8**
  22 ♗xd5   **♗xc3** *(D)*

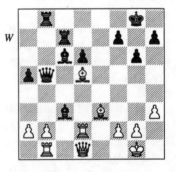

    23 Id3!
White avoids multiple exchanges
and thus obliges Black to misplace
his bishop in order to block the b-

file. 23 ♗xc6 ♖xc6 24 ♖xd6 ♖xd6 25 ♕xd6 ♗e5 ± is less convincing.

23 ... ♗b4

Instead 23...♗e5 fails to 24 ♖b3 +−.

24	a3	♗xd5
25	♖xd5	♗c5
26	b4	♕b7

It would be unwise to try to simplify with 26...axb4? 27 ♖xb4! +−.

27	♗h6	♖e7
28	♕f3	♖e6
29	♕c3	

White is using the peril of the c5-bishop to conjure up an attack. Black is obliged to maintain the pin while the bishop's influence on c5 is limited.

29	...	f6
30	♖dd1	axb4
31	axb4	♕e4

The queen keeps a focus on b1 when faced with the alternative 31...♗a7 32 ♕b3 ♖be8 33 ♖xd6.

32	♖e1	♕f5

Not 32...♗xf2+ 33 ♔xf2 ♕h4+ 34 ♕g3 +−.

33	♖b2	♗d4
34	♕b3	♖e8?

The pin on the e6-rook should be broken immediately with 34...d5 35 ♖xe6 ♕xe6 36 ♖d2 ♕e5 37 ♕a4, but White is in any case better due to his passed pawn.

35 g4! ♕f3 36 ♕xf3 ♖xe1+ 37 ♔g2 ♗xb2 38 ♕b3+

This is the motivation behind 35 g4. Black is lost.

38...♖8e6 39 ♕xb2 ♔f7 40 b5 g5 41 b6 ♔g6 42 b7 1-0

Game 44
Pekarek – Ernst
Dortmund 1992

1 e4 c5 2 ♘f3 d6 3 d4 cxd4 4 ♘xd4 ♘f6 5 ♘c3 g6 6 ♗c4 ♗g7

7	h3	0-0
8	♗b3	

It is imperative to avoid an old main line with 8 ♗e3 ♘c6 9 0-0 (9 ♗b3 is considered in the next game) that has come under close scrutiny from the Latvian/Polish Grandmaster Wojtkiewicz who discovered an important improvement. This explains the popularity of the move-order in the game. For example: 9...♘xe4 10 ♗xf7+ and now:

a) 10...♖xf7 11 11 ♘xe4 h6 12 c3 ♗d7 (12...♔h7 13 ♕b3 d5 ± Kupreichik-Pigusov, Moscow 1989) 13 ♖e1 ♕a5 14 ♕b3 ♕a6 15 a4 ♘a5 16 ♕a2 ♘c4 17 ♘d2 ♖c8 18 ♘xc4 ♕xc4 19 ♕xc4 ♖xc4 20 a5 a6 21 ♘c2 ♖a4 22 ♗b6 ♖xa1 23 ♖xa1 = Jansa-Watson, Oslo 1991.

b) 10...♔xf7! (Wojtkiewicz) 11 ♘xe4 ♘xd4 12 ♗xd4 e5 13 ♗e3 d5 14 ♘g3 (14 ♗g5 ♕d7 15 ♘c3 h6 16 ♗h4 d4 17 ♘e4 ∓ Jansa-Hellers, Herning 1991) 14...♔g8 15 c3 ♗e6 16 ♘e2 g5!? 17 ♕d2 h6 18 h4! gxh4 19 ♗xh6 ♕f6 20 ♗g5 ♕g6 21 ♗xh4 ♖f5 22 f4 ♕g4 23 ♗g5?! (23 ♗e7!? ∓) 23...♖af8 24 ♖f2 d4 25

cxd4 exf4 26 ♗xf4 ♗c4 27 ♗e3
♖xf2 28 ♗xf2 ♗xe2 0-1 Adams-
Shirov, Biel 1992.

8 ... a6

Black wishes to expand on the
queenside which will put pressure
on e4 via ...b5 and ...♗b7. Upon
8...♘bd7 White can continue to develop in similar fashion to the main
game: 9 0-0 ♘c5 10 ♖e1 a6 (10...a5
11 a4 ♘xb3 12 ♘xb3 b6 13 ♘d4
♗b7 14 f3 {Kholmov-Makropoulos,
Herkulesfurdo 1984} 14...e5 15
♘db5 d5 =) 11 ♗g5!? (11 f4 e6 12
e5 dxe5 13 fxe5 ♘fd7 14 ♗f4 b5 15
♕d2 ♗b7 16 ♖ad1 ± Bradvarević-
Velimirović, Yugoslavia 1966) 11...h6
12 ♗h4 e6 13 ♕f3 g5 (13...♕e7 14
♖ad1 ♖e8 15 e5! ± Popović-Chibur-
danidze, Subotica 1986) 14 ♗g3
♘fd7 15 ♖ad1 ♘e5 16 ♕h5 ♕f6 17
♘de2 a5 (Am.Rodriguez-Ricardi,
Havana 1988) 18 ♖xd6! ± W.Wat-
son.

9 0-0 b5

With the more subdued 9...b6
Black intends to absorb some pressure before trying to counter-attack:
a) 10 ♗g5 ♗b7 11 ♖e1 ♘bd7 12
♘d5 e6 13 ♘xf6+ ♘xf6 14 ♕d3
♕c7 15 c3 ♕c5 16 ♗h4 with an
equal position; Short-W.Watson,
Lugano 1986.
b) 10 ♘d5 e6?! (10...♗b7) 11
♘xf6+ ♗xf6 12 ♗h6 ♖e8 13 ♗f4
with an edge for White; Popović-
Renet, Clichy 1986/87.

10 ♖e1 (D)

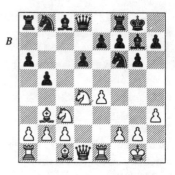

One of the most reliable continuations, by which White supports e4.
He has two other moves at his disposal:
a) 10 a4 ♗b7 11 ♗g5 and now:
a1) 11...♘xe4? 12 ♘xe4 ♗xe4
13 ♖e1 ± (Miles).
a2) 11...b4 12 ♘d5 ♘bd7 13 a5
♖c8 14 ♖e1 ♘c5 15 ♗xf6 exf6 16
♘xb4 ♘xb3! 17 cxb3 ♖e8 18 ♕d2
f5 19 exf5 ♖xe1+ 20 ♖xe1 with an
edge for White; Ljubojević-Miles,
Amsterdam 1978.
b) 10 ♘d5 ♗b7 11 ♘xf6+ ♗xf6
12 ♗h6 ♖e8 (12...♗g7 13 ♕d2 e5
14 ♗xg7 ♔xg7 ± Kindermann-
Kir.Georgiev, Lugano 1986) 13 ♖e1
♘c6 (13...♘d7 14 c3 ♘c5 15 ♗d5
♕d7 = Jansa-Sax, Warsaw 1987;
13...♖c8 14 c3 ♘c6 15 ♘xc6 ♗xc6
16 ♕f3 a5 17 a3 ± Jansa-Pekarek,
Namestovo 1987) 14 ♘xc6 ♗xc6
15 ♕f3 e6 16 c3 ♗g5 17 ♗xg5
♕xg5 18 ♖ad1 ♖ed8 19 ♕e3! ±
Jansa-Petursson, Gausdal 1988.

10 ... ♗b7
11 a4

White takes steps to undermine Black's queenside pawns. There is another way forward: 11 ♗g5!? ♘bd7 12 ♘d5 ♖e8 13 c3 ♘xd5 14 ♗xd5 ♕c7 15 a4 bxa4 16 ♖xa4 ♘c5 ± Klundt-W.Watson, Kecskemet 1988.

11 ...   bxa4
12 ♗xa4

Not 12 ♖xa4?! ♘bd7 13 ♗d5 ♘xd5 14 exd5 ♘b6 15 ♖b4 ♕c7 ∓ Nicholson-Watson, British Ch 1986.

12 ...   ♕c7
13 ♗g5   ♘bd7

Nicholson-Hodgson, British Ch 1986, went 13...e6 14 ♕d2 ♘bd7 15 ♗xd7 ♘xd7 16 ♗h6 (=) ♗xh6 17 ♕xh6 ♘c5 18 ♖e3?! e5 19 ♘f5?! f6 20 ♘g3 ♘e6 ∓.

14 ♗xd7   ♕xd7
15 ♘b3   ♖ac8
16 ♕d3

The situation has become somewhat clearer, with fair prospects for both sides. White can try to improve the position of his pieces by playing ♘d5 while bearing in mind the weakness of a6. Black has a certain amount of play against e4 and along the c-file, with ...♖xc3 possible in some cases.

16 ...   ♕e6
17 ♖ad1

Ernst points out that it would be foolhardy to snatch the a-pawn: 17 ♘a5? ♗a8 18 ♕xa6 ♘xe4 19 ♘xe4 ♗xe4 20 f3 ♕f5 21 ♗xe7 ♗d4+ 22 ♔h1 ♗xf3 −+.

17 ...   ♘d7?

The beginning of a faulty manoeuvre. The knight unmasks the dark-squared bishop and aims to emerge on c5, but it would be more prudent to seek an ending after 17...♕c4 with equal chances.

18 ♘d5!   ♖fe8
19 c3

White has a superior position. He has good play against the e-pawn which ties Black's rook to its defence, while ♘d4 is a serious threat. Black must try to release the pressure against e7 without having to compromise his pawn structure with ...f6.

19 ...   ♘c5
20 ♘xc5   ♖xc5
21 b4   ♖cc8
22 c4 *(D)*

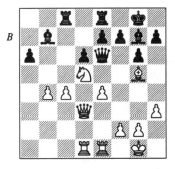

22 ...   ♗xd5

Black can no longer tolerate White's strong knight. Instead, passive defence was doomed since White could turn the screw with moves such as f4 and f5 or e5, harassing the black queen.

23 exd5   ♕d7

Possible now that White's knight has disappeared.

24 ♖e4!

This feint to double on the e-file is also designed to facilitate c5 and ♖ec4.

24	...	♕b7
25	♗d2	♕c7
26	♖c1	♗b2
27	♖c2	♗e5
28	♖e1	e6?
29	♖xe5!	

White smashes through Black's defences. His connected passed pawns will be a formidable force.

29	...	dxe5
30	d6	♕d7
31	c5	♖c6
32	♗g5?	

White is beginning to drift. He could have terminated the battle immediately with the forceful 32 ♖a2 ♖a8 33 ♕e4.

32	...	f5
33	♖a2	e4
34	♕d4	♖b8
35	♗d2	♕g7
36	♕c4	♕e5
37	♖xa6 *(D)*	

37 ...   ♕xd6!

The start of an inspired sequence to rescue the draw.

38	♗f4	♕xf4
39	♖xc6	♖xb4!
40	♕xb4	

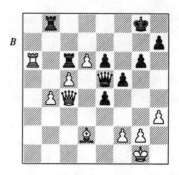

B

If 40 ♕xe6+ then 40...♔g7 41 ♕e7+ ♔h6 42 ♕f8+ ♔g5! = (Ernst).

40	...	♕c1+
41	♔h2	♕f4+
42	♔g1	½-½

Game 45

Popović – Sinanović
Yugoslav Ch 1991

1	e4	c5
2	♘f3	d6
3	d4	cxd4
4	♘xd4	♘f6
5	♘c3	g6
6	♗c4	♗g7
7	h3	0-0
8	♗e3	♘c6
9	♗b3	♗d7
10	0-0 *(D)*	
10	...	♘a5

Black has a wide range of alternatives:

a) 10...♘xd4 11 ♗xd4 ♗c6 12 ♕d3 and now:

a1) 12...b5?! 13 ♖fe1 ♕d7 (13...a6 14 ♖ad1 ♖c8 15 ♘d5 ♗xd5

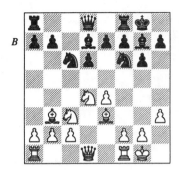

16 exd5 ♘d7 17 ♗xg7 ♔xg7 18
♕d4+ ♔g8 19 ♖e3 ± Ermenkov-
Spiridonov, Varna 1986) 14 ♘d5!
♘xd5 15 exd5 ♗b7 16 ♗xg7 ♔xg7
17 ♖e3 f6 18 ♖ae1 ♖f7 19 ♕e2 ♔f8
20 ♖e6 ± Sigurjonsson-Miles, Hastings 1974/75.
  a2) 12...♘d7 13 ♗xg7 ♔xg7 14
♖fe1 ♕a5 15 ♘d5 ♖fe8 16 c3 ♖c8
17 ♕g3 ♗xd5 ± Byrne-Rachels,
New York 1987.
  a3) 12...♕a5 13 ♖ad1 ♘d7 14
♘d5 ♖fe8 15 ♗xg7 ♔xg7 16 f4
♖ad8 17 ♔h1 ♕c5 18 ♕g3 ±
Messa-Garcia, Dubai OL 1986.
  b) 10...a6 11 f4 and now:
  b1) 11...b5!? 12 a3 ♖c8 13 ♕f3
♘a5 14 ♖ad1 ♘c4!? (14...♘xb3 15
cxb3 ♕c7 16 g4! ♕b7 17 e5 ♕xf3
18 ♘xf3 ♘e8 19 ♘d5! ± Chis-
tiakov-Taimanov, USSR 1951) 15
♗c1 ♕c7 16 ♔h1 e5! 17 ♘de2 ♗c6
18 f5 h6 19 ♗xc4 bxc4 20 ♘d5
♗xd5 21 exd5 e4 22 ♕e3 g5 23 h4
g4 24 ♕g3 ♖fe8 25 ♗e3 h5 26 ♘f4
♖e5 27 ♗d4 ♖ce8 (Hector-Tivi-
akov, Haninge 1992) 28 ♗xe5!? ∞.

  b2) 11...♕c7 12 g4 ♘xd4 13
♗xd4 e5 14 fxe5 dxe5 15 ♗e3 ♗c6
16 ♕f3 h6 17 ♖ad1 ± Watson-Find-
lay, British Ch 1986.
  c) 10...♖c8!? 11 ♖e1 and now:
  c1) 11...a6 12 f4 b5 13 a3 e6?! 14
♕d2 ♕c7 15 ♖ad1 ♖fd8 16 ♕f2
♕b7 17 f5! ♘xd4 18 ♗xd4 ± Sigur-
jonsson-Karlsson, Denmark 1982.
  c2) 11...♘a5 12 ♕d3 a6 13 f4
♕c7 14 ♖ad1 b5 15 ♔h1 ♘c4 16
♗c1 ♕c5 17 a4 ♖fe8 18 axb5 axb5
19 ♘f3 ± Gobet-Striković, Geneva
1986.
  c3) 11...♘e5 12 f4 (12 ♕e2?!
♖xc3! 13 bxc3 ♘xe4 14 f4!? ♘xc3
15 ♕f1 ♘c6 16 ♕d3 ♕a5 17 ♘xc6
♗xc6 18 ♗d4 ♗xd4+ 19 ♕xd4 e6
20 ♖xe6? ♘b5! 21 ♕e3 fxe6 22
♕xe6+ ♔h8 23 ♖d1 ♕b6+ 0-1 Mit-
kov-Tiviakov, Mamaia 1991)
12...♘c4 13 ♗xc4 ♖xc4 14 ♕d3
♕c8?! (14...♖c8! 15 ♖ad1 a6!? =
Tiviakov) 15 e5! ♘h5 16 ♘d5 ♖e8
17 exd6 exd6 18 ♗f2 ± Ljubojević-
S.Garcia, Ljubljana 1975.
  d) 10...♕a5 transposes to Game
47, Short-Wagman.
  11 ♖e1   ♖c8
  12 ♕d3!
  White has no desire to allow the
knight to hop into c4.
  12 ...   a6
  13 ♘d5   ♘xb3
  In the game Watson-Larsen,
Esbjerg 1988, Black chose to trade
knights, and withstood White's pressure on the e-file: 13...♘xd5 14

exd5 罝e8 15 c3 ♕c7 16 ♗g5 ♘xb3
(16...♔f8 17 罝e4!) 17 axb3 ♕c5! 18
♘f3 e5 19 dxe6 罝xe6 20 ♗e3 ♕b5
21 c4 ♕b4 22 ♘d4 ♗xd4 23 ♕xd4
罝ce8 24 罝ed1 ♕xb3 25 c5 d5 26
罝d3 ♕c2 27 罝d2 ♕f5 28 ♕xd5 =.

14 axb3 ♗c6?!

Popović suggests it would be an
improvement to hang on to the
bishop with 14...e6 although White
would still be slightly better.

15 ♘xc6! 罝xc6
16 c3 (D)

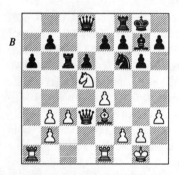

With this move White rules any
possibility of ...♗xb2, and maintains
a safe advantage due to his greater
freedom and chances to open lines
for his rooks. Black must manoeuvre carefully and seek equality with
a well-timed ...e6.

16 ... ♘d7
17 ♗g5 罝e8
18 ♕e3!

A cunning move. White inciden-
tally threatens a decisive invasion on
a7, while building up his forces on

the kingside. Black finds it hard to
generate counterplay while he is being kept busy on both flanks.

18 ... ♘c5
19 b4 ♘e6
20 ♗h6

White logically wishes to exchange Black's most active piece.

20 ... ♘c7

20...♗h8 21 f4 leaves Black under pressure.

21 罝ad1 ♗xh6
22 ♕xh6 e6

After 22...♘xd5? 23 exd5 罝c4 24
b3! 罝xc3 25 罝d4 the rook sweeps
across to h4 with decisive effect.

23 ♘e3 ♕e7
24 罝d3?!

A more precise measure is 24
♘g4 to prevent ...♕f8. Then, since
24...♔h8? fails to 25 e5! dxe5 26
罝d7 ♕xd7 27 ♘f6 +−, Black should
opt for 24...罝d8 intending ...♘e8
when White still has work to do.

24 ... ♕f8
25 ♕h4 ♕e7
26 ♕g3 罝c8 (D)

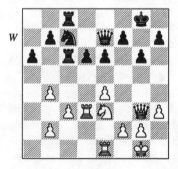

27 ♖ed1

As the immediate attack has been beaten off, White must tie Black down by attacking d6 and avoid an ending where it would be difficult to break through the fortress.

27...♘e8 28 ♕f4 ♕f6 29 ♕g3 ♖6c7 30 ♘g4

The knight is bound for f3 where its flexibility is increased as the outposts d4 and g5 would be available.

30...♕g7 31 ♕e3 h5 32 ♘h2 ♖c4 33 ♘f3 ♖4c7 34 ♘g5 ♕f6 35 f4

White must play actively since Black is content to adopt a no-risk policy by shuffling his army around the board. Now 36 e5 is the threat.

35...e5 36 fxe5 dxe5 37 ♖f1 ♕c6 38 ♖d5

Forcing a concession.

38...f6 39 ♘f3 ♔h7 40 ♖fd1 ♕e6? 41 ♖xe5!

At the end of a time-scramble, White finds a tactical trick to speed up the winning process. If 41...fxe5, then 42 ♘g5+ picks up the queen.

41...♕a2 42 ♖ed5 ♕xb2 43 ♖d7+ ♘g7 44 e5!

A smart move that enables the knight and queen to join the affray despite c3 falling off.

44...♖xd7 45 ♖xd7 ♖xc3 46 ♖xg7+ ♔xg7 47 exf6+ ♔xf6 48 ♕e5+ ♔f7 49 ♘g5+ ♔g8

If instead 49...♔f8 50 ♕f6+ ♔e8 51 ♕e6+ ♔d8 52 ♘f7+ ♔c7 53 ♕d6+ ♔c8 54 ♕d8#.

50 ♕e8+ ♔g7 51 ♕e7+ ♔h6 52 ♘f7+ ♔g7 53 ♘e5+ ♔h6 54 ♕f8+ ♔g5 55 h4+ 1-0

9 ♗c4 against the Accelerated Dragon

1	e4	c5
2	♘f3	♘c6
3	d4	cxd4
4	♘xd4	g6

This is the Accelerated Dragon. White can now choose to play the Maroczy Bind, 5 c4, but instead, in line with the main theme of this book, we shall investigate plans with the move ♗c4.

5	♘c3	♗g7
6	♗e3	♘f6
7	♗c4	0-0
8	♗b3	a5!?

Black decides to try to take advantage of White's move-order which has neglected an early h3. Other paths:

a) 8...d6 9 h3 ♗d7 10 0-0 transposes to Game 45, Popović-Sinanović.

b) 8...♘a5? 9 e5 ♘xb3 (9...♘e8 10 ♗xf7+! ♔xf7 11 ♘e6 +– Fischer-Reshevsky, USA Ch 1958/59) 10 exf6 ♘xa1 11 fxg7 ♘xc2+ 12 ♕xc2 ♔xg7 13 f4 ± Bastrikov-Shamkovich, USSR 1958.

c) 8...a6?! 9 f3 b5 10 ♕d2 ♘a5 11 e5 ♘xb3 12 ♘xb3 ♘e8 13 ♗h6 ♕c7 14 ♗xg7 ♘xg7 15 0-0-0 ± Zwaig-Bleiman, Barcelona 1965.

d) 8...d5?! 9 exd5 ♘a5 10 h3 b6 11 ♘c6 ♘xc6 12 dxc6 ♕c7 13 ♕f3 ♗a6 14 0-0-0 ♖ac8 15 ♗a4 ± Zhidkov-Kondratiev, USSR 1964.

e) 8...e6!? 9 ♘xc6 dxc6 10 e5 ♘d5! (10...♕xd1+ 11 ♖xd1 ♘g4 12 ♗c5 ♖e8 13 f4 Gufeld) 11 ♕d4 ♘xe3 12 ♕xe3 ±.

f) 8...♘g4 9 ♕xg4 ♘xd4 10 ♕d1 ♘xb3 11 axb3 b6 12 ♗d4 f6 13 ♕d3 ♗b7 14 0-0-0 ♗c6 15 h4 ♕c7 16 h5 ♗h6+ 17 ♔b1 ± Tukmakov-Faibisovich, USSR 1962.

g) 8...♕a5 9 f3 e6 10 ♕d2 d5 11 exd5 exd5 12 0-0-0 ± (Korchnoi).

9	a4 *(D)*	

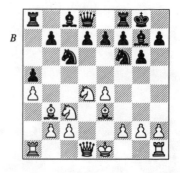

It is also possible to deter ...♘g4 with 9 f3 d5 10 exd5 (10 ♗xd5 ♘xd5 11 exd5 ♘b4 12 ♘de2 e6 {12...♗f5 13 ♖c1 b5 = de Firmian-Forintos, Reykjavik 1982} 13 a3 ♘xd5 14 ♘xd5 exd5 15 ♗d4 ♗h6 16 0-0 ♖a6 17 ♔h1 ♖e8 18 ♗f2 a4 19 ♖e1 = Hector-Rom.Hernandez) 10...♘b4 11 ♘de2 a4 12 ♘xa4 ♘fxd5 13 ♗f2 ♗f5 (13...♖xa4 14 ♗xa4 ♕a5 15 0-0 ♖d8 16 a3 ± Sax-Haik, Smederevska Palanka 1982) 14 0-0 b5 15 ♘ac3 ♘xc3 16 ♘xc3 ♕xd1 17 ♖fxd1 ♗xc2 18 ♗xc2 ♘xc2 19 ♖ac1 = Matulović-Ristoja, Helsinki 1981. Also possible: 9 a3 ♘g4 10 ♕xg4 ♘xd4 11 ♕d1 ♘xb3 12 cxb3 d6 13 ♗d4 ♗e6 14 ♗xg7 ♔xg7 15 ♕d4+ ♔g8 16 b4 axb4 17 ♕xb4 ± Barlov-Abramović, Palma de Mallorca 1989.

9 ...   ♘g4

A simplifying measure that has the benefit of nullifying White's attacking ambitions.

10 ♕xg4   ♘xd4
11 ♕d1

The aggressive 11 ♕h4 is feasible: 11...♘xb3 12 cxb3 ♖a6 13 0-0 ♖e6 (13...d6 14 ♘d5 ♖e8 15 ♖ac1 ♖c6 16 ♗g5 f6 17 ♗e3 ± Ilijin-Kaidanov, Bled 1989) 14 ♖fe1 (14 ♖ad1 ♗f6 15 ♕g3 ♗xc3!? 16 bxc3 ♖xe4 gave White insufficient compensation for the pawn in Watson-Shabalov, Oslo 1991) b6 15 ♗h6 ♗b7 16 ♗xg7 ♔xg7 17 ♖e3 ♖e5 18 f4 ♖c5 19 ♖d1 gave White an edge

in Hebden-Kristensen, Hastings 1990.

11 ♗xd4 was tried in Ivanović-Cebalo, Yugoslav Ch 1983: after 11...♗xd4 12 ♕g3 d6 13 0-0-0 ♗xc3 14 ♕xc3 ♗e6 the position was balanced.

11 ...   ♘xb3
12 cxb3   d6
13 0-0   ♗e6
14 ♖a3!?

White is assuming that the rook will have a temporary job in securing the pawn. The plan is ♗d4, exchange the bishops and then b3-b4. Other possibilities:

a) 14 ♘d5 ♗xb2 15 ♖b1 ♗g7 16 ♗b6 ♕d7 17 ♖c1 ♗xd5 18 ♕xd5 e6 ½-½ Prasad-Hernandez, Calicut 1988.

b) 14 f4 ♕d7 15 ♖f2 ♖ac8 16 ♘b5 f5 17 exf5 ♖xf5 18 ♗b6? ♖cf8 19 g3 g5 20 fxg5 ♕c6 21 ♕e2 ♕xb6 22 ♕xe6+ ♔h8 and Black wins; J.Szabo-Neamtu, Romania 1969.

14 ...   ♖a6
15 ♕d2   f5

This is a radical attempt to change the nature of the position. Black wants to open the f-file and undermine White's control of d5.

16 exf5   ♖xf5
17 ♖e1   ♗f7
18 ♗g5   ♕b6 *(D)*

Black's forces are impressively coordinated; in particular his pair of bishops exert great influence over the queenside. Nevertheless, White

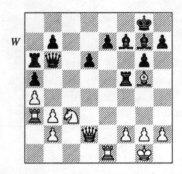

is still in the game, with e7 an attractive target.

Black would also enjoy slightly the better chances after 18...d5!? 19 ♗xe7 (19 ♖xe7 ♖xg5 20 ♕xg5 ♗f6 −+) 19...♕d7! (19...♕b6 20 ♘b5! ♗h6 21 ♕e2 ♗f4 22 ♗h4 ∞) intending ...♖e6.

19 ♖xe7

Not 19 ♗xe7? ♖xf2 20 ♕xf2 ♗d4 −+.

19 ...   d5

A trick to gain material is faulty: 19...♗xc3 20 bxc3 ♕c5 21 b4!.

20 ♘b5   ♗f8?

It is very tempting to skewer White's rooks, but Shabalov points out that a more refined approach is required: 20...h6! 21 ♗e3 d4 22 ♗xd4 ♗xd4 23 ♘xd4 ♖d5 24 ♖e4 ♕f6 25 ♖a1 ♖ad6 26 ♖ad1 g5 ∓.

21 ♖c7   ♗b4

The upshot is that 21...♗xa3 22 bxa3 would leave the dark squares around the black king vulnerable to an attack based on ♗h6, ♕c3 and ♖c8+.

22 ♕e3

A cool, calculated move that seeks an ending where White can eventually force a strong passed pawn, notwithstanding a material loss. Instead a king hunt with 22 ♖c8+ ♔g7 23 ♗h6+ ♔f6 24 ♕c2 g5 is ineffective.

22 ...	**♕xe3**
23 ♗xe3	**♗xa3**
24 bxa3	**d4!**

Black surrenders this pawn to activate his bishop. Now White has to be careful in view of the threat of back rank mate, e.g. 25 ♗xd4 ♖c6 or 25 ♘xd4 ♖d5 26 h3 ♖ad6.

25 ♖c8+	**♔g7**
26 ♗xd4+	**♔h6** *(D)*

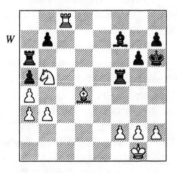

27 ♗e3+

Shabalov suggests 27 ♖c7 as a troublesome move in time-trouble: 27...♗xb3 (27...g5!) 28 ♗e3+ g5 29 h4 ♗xa4 30 ♘d4 ♖d5 31 hxg5+ ♔g6 32 ♘f3 ±.

27 ...	**♔g7**
28 ♖c7	**♖d5**

29 h3

A necessary precaution, since 29 ♗d4+? ♖xd4! 30 ♘xd4 ♖d6 loses.

29 ...   ♖a8
30 ♖xb7   ♖d3
31 b4   axb4
32 axb4   ♖xa4

The situation has clarified. White has a passed pawn that is well supported by his knight and bishop, but Black should be able to put enough obstacles in its path to hold the draw.

33 ♗d4+ ♔f8 34 ♖b8+ ♔e7 35 ♗c5+ ♔f6 36 ♘d6 ♖a6 37 ♘xf7 ♔xf7 38 ♖b7+ ♔g8 39 b5 ♖a1+ 40 ♔h2 ♖b1 41 b6 ♖d5 42 ♗e3 ♖f5 43 g4 ♖f7 44 ♖a7 ♖f6

Black's defends in robust style, refusing the exchange on a7 since after 44...♖xa7 45 bxa7 ♖a1, 46 ♔g3 with the plan ♔f4-e4, ♗d4, f2-f3-f4-f5-f6 and bringing the king to b7, secures victory (Shabalov).

45 ♖a6 ♖b5 46 ♔g3 ♔f7 47 ♖a7+ ♔g8 48 ♖b7 h5 49 ♔g2 ♖b3 50 ♔g3 hxg4 51 hxg4 ♖b5 52 ♔h4 ♖e6 53 ♗d4 ♖d6 54 ♖b8+ ♔f7 55 ♗e3 ♖e6 56 ♔g3 ♔e7 57 ♔f3 ♔d7 58 ♖b7+ ♔e8 59 ♔f4 ♔f8 60 ♖c7 ♖f6+ 61 ♔g3 ♖bxb6 62 ♗xb6 ♖xb6 63 ♔f4 ♖b5 64 f3 ½-½.

Game 47

Short – Wagman

Lugano 1986

1 e4 c5 2 ♘f3 ♘c6 3 d4 cxd4 4 ♘xd4 g6 5 ♗e3 ♘f6 6 ♘c3 ♗g7

7 ♗c4   ♕a5

A relatively unusual continuation.

8 0-0   0-0

Black is struggling for equality with other moves:

a) 8...♕b4 9 ♗b3 ♘xe4? 10 ♘xc6 bxc6 11 a3 ♘xc3 12 ♕f3 +-.

b) 8...d6 can be met by 9 ♗b5 ♗d7 10 ♘b3 ♕d8 11 ♗e2 0-0 with a pleasant form of Classical Dragon, or 9 h3 0-0 10 ♗b3, transposing to our main game.

c) 8...♘g4 9 ♘b3 (9 ♕xg4 ♘xd4 10 ♕h4! ♘xc2 11 ♘d5 ± Boleslavsky) 9...♕h5 10 ♗f4 ♗e5 11 ♗xe5 ♘cxe5 12 h3 ♘xc4 13 hxg4 ♕e5 14 f4 ♕d6 15 ♘d5 ♘b6 16 ♕d4 0-0 17 c4 ♘xd5 18 cxd5 b6 19 e5 ± *ECO*.

9 ♗b3 *(D)*

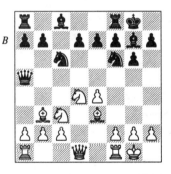

This is in the same style as previous games but there is a major alternative that was very popular in the 1960/70s. After 9 ♘b3 ♕c7 (9...♕d8?! 10 f4 d6 11 h3 {11 ♗e2 leaves White a clear tempo up on the main line Classical Dragon} ♗d7 12 ♕f3 ♕c8 13 ♗d3 ♗e6 14 ♖ae1 ♘b4 15 f5 ♗c4 16 ♕e2 ♘xd3 17 cxd3 ♗a6 18 ♖f2 ♕d7 19 ♕d2 b6 20 d4 gxf5 21 exf5 ♔h8 22 ♗g5 ± Safranska-Oney, Katerini 1992) 10 f4 d6 11 ♗e2 play might proceed:

a) 11...b6 and now:

a1) 12 g4 ♗b7 13 g5 ♘d7 14 ♘d5 ♕d8 15 ♖b1 ♘c5 16 ♗f3 e6 17 ♘c3 ♕e7 18 ♕d2 ♖fd8 19 ♖bd1 (19 ♖be1 ♖ac8 20 h4 ♘a5 21 ♘xa5 bxa5 22 ♕g2 ♗c6 23 ♗xc5 ♗xc3 24 bxc3 dxc5 = Moller-Baumbach, Corr 1986) 19...♘a5!? 20 ♘xa5 bxa5 21 ♕g2 = Zagorovsky-Baumbach, Corr 1986.

a2) 12 ♗f3 ♗b7 (12...♗a6 13 ♖f2 ♖ab8 14 ♘d5 ♘xd5 15 exd5 ♘a5 16 ♗d4 ± Jansa-Toran, Siegen OL 1970) 13 ♕d2 ♘a5 14 ♘xa5 bxa5 15 ♖ad1 ♗c6?! (15...♖fd8 Silman) 16 e5 dxe5 17 ♗xc6 ♕xc6 18 fxe5 ♘g4 19 ♘d5 ± Lutzkat-Baumbach, Corr 1986.

b) 11...♖d8 12 ♗f3 e5?! (12...♗e6 13 ♖f2 ♗c4 14 ♘d5 ♗xd5 15 exd5 ♘a5 16 ♗d4 ♘e8 17 c3 ♘xb3 18 axb3 ± Ostojić-Musil, Yugoslavia 1968; 12...♗d7 13 ♕e2 ♘a5 14 ♘xa5 ♕xa5 15 ♗f2 ♗c6 16 ♖ab1 ♖ac8 17 b4 ♕c7 18 ♖b3 b6 19 ♖d1 e6 20 ♗h4 ♖d7 21 ♖d2 ♘e8 22 ♘b5 ♕b8 23 c4 ♗xb5 24 cxb5 ♖dc7 = Apicella-Ivkov, Cannes 1989) 13 f5 d5 14 ♘b5 ♕b8 15 fxg6 dxe4 (15...hxg6 16 exd5 e4? {16...♗f5!? Silman} 17 dxc6 ♖xd1

18 c7 ±) 16 gxf7+ ♔h8 17 ♕c1 exf3 18 ♗h6 e4 19 ♕g5 +− Kosenkov-Dubinin, Corr 1977.

c) 11...a5 12 a4 ♘b4 13 ♖f2! and now:

c1) 13...♗e6 14 ♘d4 ♗c4 15 ♗f3 ♖fd8 16 ♖d2 ♕b8 (16...♕c8 17 ♘db5 ♘d7 18 ♖b1! ± Boleslavsky) 17 b3 ♗a6 18 ♘db5 ♗xb5 19 ♘xb5 ± Jansa-Petersen, Kapfenberg 1970.

c2) 13...e5 14 ♗f3 ♗d7 15 ♖d2 ♖fd8 16 ♔h1! ♗c6 17 ♕g1 ♘d7 18 f5 ± Fischer-Olafsson, Bled 1961.

c3) 13...♗d7 14 ♗f3 ♗c6 15 ♖d2! ♘d7 16 ♘d4 ♘c5 17 ♘cb5 ♕c8 18 c3 ♘ba6 19 ♕c2 ♕e8 20 b3 f5?! 21 exf5 ♗xf3 22 gxf3! gxf5 23 ♖g2 ♔h8 24 ♘xf5 ♗f6 25 ♘h6 ± Heemsoth-Baumbach, Corr 1981.

10	...	d6
10	h3	♗d7

Steadily developing. Other moves achieve very little:

a) 10...♘xd4 11 ♗xd4 ♗e6 12 f4 a6 13 ♕f3 ♕h5 14 ♕f2 ♖ac8 15 ♖ae1 ♗c4 16 e5 dxe5 17 ♖xe5 ± Tal-Stefanov, Kislovodsk 1966.

b) 10...♘h5 11 ♘de2 ♗e6 12 g4 ♘f6 (Ciocaltea-Bilek, Bucharest 1968) 13 ♘f4 ±.

11 f4

White strikes out with the most aggressive continuation. Other tries:

a) 11 ♘d5!? ♘xe4 12 ♘xc6 bxc6 13 ♘xe7+ ♔h8 14 ♗d4 ♘d2 15 ♗xg7+ ♔xg7 16 ♖e1 ♘xb3 17 axb3 ♕c5 18 ♕d2 ± Bachler-Szpisjak, Corr 1991.

b) 11 ♖e1 and now:

b1) 11...♖fc8? 12 f4 ♕h5 13 ♘f3 ♖d8 14 ♕e2 e6 15 ♖ad1 with an edge for White; Pietzsch-Damjanović, Sarajevo 1966.

b2) 11...♕h5 12 ♕d2 b5?! 13 ♘xc6 ♗xc6 14 ♘d5 ♖fe8 15 ♘xe7+! ♖xe7 16 ♕xd6 ♖ae8 17 ♕xc6 ♘xe4 18 ♖ad1 ♗xb2 19 ♗xa7 ♗c3 20 f3! ♗xe1 21 ♖xe1 ♖d8 22 ♗c5 ♖ee8 23 fxe4 ♖c8 24 ♗xf7+ ♔xf7 25 ♕d7+ 1-0 Mariasin-Kapengut, Minsk 1983.

b3) 11...♘xd4 12 ♗xd4 ♗c6 13 ♘d5! ♗xd5 14 exd5 ♖fe8 15 c3 ♖ac8 16 ♕f3 ♘d7 17 ♗xg7 ♔xg7 18 ♖e3 ♘f6 19 ♖d1 ♖c7 20 ♖d4 ± Liu-Muco, Lucerne 1982.

b4) 11...♖fe8 12 ♕e2 ♘xd4 (12...♖ad8?! 13 ♖ad1 ♘xd4 14 ♗xd4 ♗c6 15 ♕f3 b5 16 ♘d5 ♗xd5 17 exd5 ♖c8 18 ♖e3 ♘d7 19 ♗xg7 ♔xg7 20 ♕e2 ♘e5 21 c3 ± Popović-Renet, Dubai OL 1986; 12...♕h5! = Ree-Sosonko, Wijk aan Zee 1986) 13 ♗xd4 ♗e6 14 ♖ad1 ♖ac8 15 ♕e3 b6 16 ♘d5 ♗xd5 17 exd5 ♘d7 18 ♗xg7 ♔xg7 19 ♖d4 ♕c5 20 ♖e4 ± Vogt-Roizman, USSR 1969.

b5) 11...♖ac8 12 ♕d2 ♖fe8 13 ♖ad1 a6 14 ♘f3! b5 15 ♗h6 ♗h8!? (15...♘d8 16 ♘d4 ♖c5 17 a3 ♗xh6 18 ♕xh6 ♖h5 19 ♕f4 ♘e6 20 ♗xe6 ♗xe6 21 g4! ♖xh3 22 f3 ± Tal-Hansen, Reykjavik 1986) 16 ♘g5 ♘e5 17 f4! ♘c4 18 e5 ♘h5?! (18...b4 19 ♘ce4 ♘xe4 20 ♖xe4 ♗e6! 21 ♗xc4

♗xc4 22 b3 ± Jansa) 19 ♕f2 ♘g7 20 g4 b4 21 ♘d5 ♘e6 22 f5! ♘xg5 23 ♗xg5 ♘xe5 24 ♘xe7+ ♖xe7 25 ♗xe7 ♗c6 26 ♖e3 ♕b6 27 ♗xd6 ♗f3 28 ♗xe5 ♗xd1 29 ♗xh8 ♔xh8 30 ♖e8+ 1-0 Jansa-Watson, Gausdal 1988.

11 ... e5?! (D)

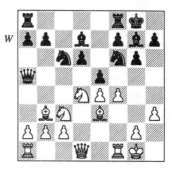

This suspect idea allows White to control d5 and establish a menacing pawn on f5. There are three other possibilities:

a) 11...♘xd4 12 ♗xd4 ♗c6 13 ♕d3 ♖ad8 (13...♘d7 14 ♗xg7 ♔xg7 15 ♔h1 ♘c5 16 ♕d4+ f6 17 ♗d5 ± Zhidkov-Pavlenko, Kharkov 1967) 14 ♖ad1 b5 15 a3 (15 ♘d5 ♗xd5 16 exd5 ± Short) 15...b4 16 axb4 ♕xb4 17 e5 dxe5 18 fxe5 ♘d5 19 ♘e4 ♘f4? (19...a5!?) 20 ♖xf4 ♗xe5 21 ♗xe5 ♖xd3 22 ♖xd3 ♕e1+ 23 ♖f1 ♕a5 24 ♗c3 +– Short-Hellers, Wijk aan Zee 1986.

b) 11...♕h5 and now:

b1) 12 ♘f3 b5 13 a3 a5 14 ♘d5 a4 15 ♗a2 ♘xd5 16 exd5 ♘a5 17

&d4 ♕h6 18 &xg7 ♕xg7 19 c3 ♖ac8 20 ♕e2 ♖fe8 21 ♘d4 ♘c4 with equality; Wang-Levitan, Manila OL 1992.

b2) 12 ♕d3 a5 13 a4 ♘b4 14 ♕d2 ♖ac8 15 f5 ♖xc3!? 16 bxc3 ♘xe4 17 ♕e1 ♘a6 18 ♘e2 ♘ac5 18 fxg6 ♘xb3 20 gxf7+ ♖xf7 21 cxb3 ♖xf1+ 22 ♕xf1 ± Klovan-Kapengut, USSR 1969.

c) 11...♖ac8 and now:

c1) 12 ♕f3 ♕h5 13 ♕f2 ♘a5 14 ♘de2 ♘c4 15 &d4 ♕a5 16 &xf6 &xf6 ½-½ Watson-Barczay, Kecskemet 1987.

c2) 12 ♘f3 ♖cd8?! (12...♖fd8 13 ♕e1 &e8 14 f5! b5 15 fxg6 hxg6 16 ♕h4 ♘e5 17 ♘g5 ♘c4 18 ♘d5 ♘xe3 19 ♘xe7+! ♔f8 20 ♘xg6+ fxg6 21 ♖xf6+ ♔e7 22 ♖f2 b4 23 ♘e6+ g5 24 ♕h7 ♕e5 25 ♘xg7 1-0 Zaitsev-Zdroj, Polanica 1970; 12...♕h5 13 ♕e1 b5 14 a3 a5 15 ♖d1 a4 16 &a2 b4 17 ♘d5 ± Klundt-Kapengut, Ybbs 1968) 13 ♕e1 &c8 14 ♖d1 e6 15 ♕h4 ♘e8 16 f5! exf5 17 ♖d5 ♕c7 18 &g5 &e6 19 exf5 &xc3 20 fxe6 fxe6 21 bxc3 exd5 22 &xd5+ ♔h8 23 &xc6 1-0 Kurajica-Kuijpers, Beverwijk 1970.

12 ♘xc6   &xc6
13 f5   &xe4?!

This allows a forced continuation that is to the detriment of Black's game. Another idea is 13...b5 14 a3 when White is better.

14 ♘xe4   ♘xe4
15 fxg6   hxg6 *(D)*

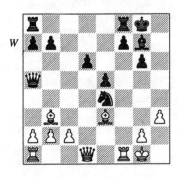

16 ♖xf7!

A startling blow. Black's kingside is ripped apart by tactical means.

16 ...   ♖xf7
17 &xf7+   ♔xf7
18 ♕f3+   &f6

18...♘f6 is met by 19 ♕xb7+ and White wins.

19 ♕xe4   d5
20 ♕g4   ♖e8
21 ♖f1   ♔g7
22 ♖xf6!   1-0

In view of 22...♔xf6 23 &g5+ ♔f7 24 ♕d7+ +–.

10 The Pseudo-Dragon

This name is applied to the move 6...♗d7 in the Sozin Attack when Black's plan is to play ...g6 and enter certain lines of the Dragon. White must handle the opening carefully since Black is not yet committed to a fianchetto and may find a favourable transposition to a line with ...e6.

Black's scheme came to prominence in the game Vidmar-Bernstein, San Sebastian 1911 and later Euwe included it in his repertoire. It had a renewed bout of interest in the 1950s amongst the Soviets, with Averbakh as one of the leading practitioners. The relative success of other side-lines such as the Benko variation have reduced it to the level of a surprise weapon.

Game 48
Fischer – Gligorić
Bled Ct 1959

1	e4	c5
2	♘f3	♘c6
3	d4	cxd4
4	♘xd4	♘f6
5	♘c3	d6
6	♗c4	♗d7 (D)

7 ♗b3

This is consistent with other lines in the book as it is not yet clear whether Black will continue with ...e6 or ...g6. Early castling is fine but it rules out the possibility of opposite-side castling. White has tried the following:

a) 7 0-0 g6 8 ♘xc6!? (8 h3 ♗g7 9 ♗e3 0-0 10 ♗b3 transposes to the main game Popović-Sinanović) 8...bxc6 (8...♗xc6 9 ♕e2 ♗g7 10 ♖d1 ♘d7 11 ♗e3 0-0 12 ♗b3 ♕c7 13 ♗d4 ♘c5 14 ♗xg7 ♔xg7 15 ♘d5 ♗xd5 16 exd5 = Vidmar-Bernstein, San Sebastian 1911; 9 ♘d5 ♗g7 10 ♗g5 ♗xd5 11 exd5 0-0 12 ♕e2 ± Euwe) 9 f4 ♗g4 (9...♕c7 10 e5! dxe5 11 fxe5 ♕xe5 12 ♗xf7+!

±) 10 ♕d3 ♗g7 11 h3 (11 e5 ♘d7 12 exd6 ♘b6 13 ♗a6 0-0 ∞ Nunn-Balashov, Toluca IZ 1982) 11...♗c8 12 e5 ♘d7 13 exd6 ♘b6 14 dxe7 ♕xe7 15 ♗b3 0-0 16 ♗e3 ± Chandler-Kupreichik, Minsk 1982.

b) 7 ♗g5 *(D)* and now:

b1) 7...♘xe4? 8 ♘xe4 ♕a5+ 9 c3! ♕e5 10 ♕e2 d5 11 ♗xd5 ♕xd5 12 0-0-0! ♕xa2 13 ♘d6+ ♔d8 14 ♘xc6+ bxc6 15 ♘b7+ ♔c8 16 ♖xd7 ♔xd7 17 ♖d1+ ♔c8 18 ♕e4 ♕a1+ 19 ♔c2 ♕xd1+ 20 ♔xd1 ♔xb7 21 ♕b4+ ♔c8 22 ♕c4 +− Nimzowitsch–Duz-Khotimirsky, Karlsbad 1911.

b2) 7...♕a5 8 ♗xf6 gxf6 9 ♘b3 ♕g5 10 0-0 ♖g8 11 g3 h5 12 ♘d5 ♖c8 13 f4 ♕g7 14 ♕d2 h4 15 ♖f3 ♕h6 16 ♗f1 ± Geller-Averbakh, Zurich Ct 1953.

b3) 7...e6 8 0-0 a6 9 ♘xc6?! ♗xc6 10 ♕e2 ♗e7 11 ♖ad1 b5 12 ♗d3 ♕c7 and 13...♖d8 = Lasker.

c) 7 ♗e3 ♘g4 (7...g6 transposes to main lines of the Dragon) 8 ♘xc6

(8 ♗g5!?) 8...bxc6 9 0-0 ♘xe3 10 fxe3 e6 11 ♕f3 ♕f6! 12 ♕xf6 gxf6 13 ♖xf6 ♗g7 14 ♖f2 ♖b8 15 ♖af1 ♖f8 ∓ Espig-Liberzon, Zinnowitz 1967.

7 ...   g6

Black declares his intention to enter the Dragon. The alternatives are worth noting:

a) 7...e6 8 ♗e3 transposes to the note to Black's 7th move in the main game Golubev-Kožul.

b) 7...♖c8 8 0-0! g6 9 ♘xc6 ♗xc6 10 ♗g5 ♗g7 11 ♘d5 ± Nunn-Robatsch, Cleveland 1979.

c) 7...♘xd4?! 8 ♕xd4 g6 9 ♗g5 ♗g7 10 0-0-0 0-0 11 ♕d2 ± Rohrl-Auer, Austria 1972.

d) 7...a6 (Taimanov) 8 0-0 g6 (8...e6 9 ♗e3 ♗e7 10 f4 transposes to the note after Black's 8th move in the main game Velimirović-Popović) 9 h3 ♗g7 10 ♗e3 0-0 11 f4 ♖c8 12 ♘f3 ♘a5 with an edge for White − Nikitin.

8 f3

It is also feasible to play 8 h3 and transpose to the illustrative game Popović-Sinanović.

After the text, Black can opt for a Yugoslav Attack with 8...♗g7 9 ♗e3 ♗g7 10 ♕d2.

8 ...   ♘a5

Black prefers a less common path, envisaging swift play on the c-file with ...♖c8 and ...♘c4.

9 ♗g5   ♗g7
10 ♕d2   h6

A device to avoid the routine attack arising from 10...0-0 11 ♗h6 intending h4-h5 which would give White bright prospects.

11 ♗e3   ♖c8
12 0-0-0   ♘c4
13 ♕e2!? (D)

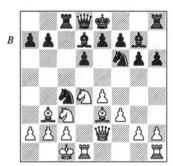

The usual continuation before this game was 13 ♗xc4 ♖xc4 14 g4 with roughly equal chances. Fischer prefers to concede the dark-squared bishop and still instigate an attack.

13 ...   ♘xe3

If 13...♕c7 then 14 ♘db5! when White wins.

14 ♕xe3   0-0

In the game Fischer-Merini, Mar del Plata 1960, Black deferred castling, but 14...♕b6 (threatening ...e5) 15 ♕d2 ♕c5 16 f4 h5?! (16...b5!?) 17 ♘f3 ♗h6 18 e5! gave White the better game.

Fischer – upon whose analysis these notes are based – has suggested an improvement: 14...♕a5 15 f4 (15 ♔b1 ♕c5 16 ♕d3 a6 is equal;

15 g4?! ♕g5! ∓) 15...0-0 16 h3 e6 with equality as the two bishops are compensation for Black's weak d-pawn.

15 g4   ♕a5
16 h4   e6

It is futile to try to stop the pawn roller with 16...h5 in view of 17 g5 ♘e8 18 f4! intending f5.

17 ♘de2!

A necessary finesse in view of 17 g5 hxg5 18 hxg5 ♘h5 19 f4 ♕c5 when Black retains some play by threatening ...e5.

17 ...   ♖c6
18 g5   hxg5

18...♘h5 19 gxh6 ♗f6 20 f4 gives White a clear advantage.

19 hxg5   ♘h5
20 f4   ♖fc8
21 ♔b1

21 f5 exf5 22 ♘d5 allows Black a neat trick: 22...♕xa2!.

21 ...   ♕b6
22 ♕f3   ♖c5
23 ♕d3!

The logical 23 f5 fails to impress: 23...exf5 24 ♖xh5 (24 ♘d5 ♕d8 25 exf5 ♗xf5 26 ♖xh5? ♖xc2! wins for Black) 24...gxh5 25 ♘f4 ♖xc3 26 bxc3 ♖xc3 27 ♕xh5 ♖xb3+ 27 cxb3 ♕e3 when the weak dark squares around White's king are a cause for concern.

23 ...   ♗xc3

Black has difficulty defending the d-pawn and instead finds a way to win a pawn. White is on top after the alternatives:

a) 23...♖8c6 24 ♘a4 +–.

b) 23...♖4c6 24 f5! exf5 25 ♖xh5! gxh5 26 exf5 +–.

c) 23...♗f8 24 f5! exf5 25 ♘d5 ♕d8 (25...fxe4 26 ♕xe4 ♗f5 27 ♕xf5 +–) 26 ♖xh5 gxh5 (26...♖xd5 27 ♗xd5 gxh5 28 exf5 +–) 27 ♘f6+ ♔g7 28 ♕h3 +– Fischer.

24 ♘xc3   ♘xf4
25 ♕f3   ♘h5 *(D)*

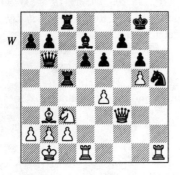

Upon 25...e5, 26 ♘e2! highlights the weakness of f7.

26 ♖xh5!

A glorious finale which breaks down the last barrier surrounding the black king. We now see why Fischer was happy to shed his f-pawn; he saw that his queen and rook could use the h-file.

26 ...   gxh5
27 ♕xh5   ♗e8

If the king goes for a stroll it is soon caught: 27...♔f8 28 ♕h8+ ♔e7 29 ♕f6+ ♔e8 30 ♖h1 ♗b5 31 ♗xe6 fxe6 32 ♕xe6+ ♔d8 (or 32...♔f8 33 ♖h8+ ♔g7 34 ♕f6#) 33 ♖h8+ ♔c7 34 ♖xc8#.

28 ♕h6   ♖xc3
29 bxc3

Not 29 ♖h1 ♕d4 when Black can struggle on.

29 ...   ♖xc3

Bronstein demonstrates that the attack continues in earnest upon the superior 29...♕e3 30 ♖h1 ♕xc3 31 g6 ♕g7 32 ♕h2 +–.

30 g6!   fxg6
31 ♖h1   ♕d4
32 ♕h7+   1-0

Index of Variations